Insider's Guide to
PowerPC™ Computing

Jerry L. Young

Publisher: David P. Ewing

Associate Publishing: Michael Miller

Publishing Director: Joseph B. Wikert

Managing Editor: Michael Cunningham

Marketing Manager: Ray Robinson

Dedication

For my father and my son

Credits

Publishing Manager
Brad R. Koch

Acquisitions Editor
Angela J. Lee

Product Director
Steven M. Schafer

Production Editor
Thomas F. Hayes

Copy Editors
Lorna Gentry
Patrick Kanouse
Jeanne Lemen
Susan Ross Moore
Linda Seifert

Technical Editors
Clara Serrano
Michael T. Vaden

Acquisitions Coordinator
Patricia J. Brooks

Editorial Assistant
Michelle Williams

Book Designer
Amy Peppler-Adams

Cover Designer
Dan Armstrong

Production Team
Meshell Dinn, Teresa Forrester,
Joelynn Gifford, Bob LaRoche,
Tim Montgomery, Marc Shecter,
Dennis Sheehan, Rebecca Tapley,
Sue VandeWalle, Mary Beth
Wakefield

Composed in *Stone Serif* and *MCPdigital* by Que Corporation

About the Author

Jerry Young has degrees in Electrical Engineering (BS E.E.) and Music Theory (M.Mus) and Composition (B.Mus) from the University of Texas at Austin. He is a part of Motorola's RISC Applications Engineering and was primary contributor to the PowerPC 601 RISC Microprocessor User's Manual. He has been a free-lance writer since the 1970s and has published articles on a variety of subjects in newspapers and magazines. He has been a columnist for the Austin American-Statesman since 1984. He is an avid gardener, collector of mahonias, and is least well known for his musical compositions, such as Ur-Bugle, TARTR, Ur-Vogel, and Why Do You Not Sneeze?

He is a member of the I.E.E.E. and for some reason is included in Who's Who in the Southwest and Who's Who in America.

He currently resides in Austin, Texas, with his wife Helen and his son Jules.

Acknowledgments

Most of all, I want to thank Helen for her encouragement and endless patience at having to be a single mother off and on for the past several months, and to my son, Jules, to whom I owe a few dozen weekends.

I would like to acknowledge the many folks at Motorola, IBM, and at the Somerset Design Center for their assistance. I wish especially to express my deep appreciation to Clara Serrano for her always helpful advice and support.

I also would like to thank Mike Vaden, Brad Suessmith, Tom Cihak, and Bob Bailey for their useful comments and suggestions. Special thanks to Mike Vaden and Terry Potter for their patient explanations of 601 instruction timing, and to the folks in Motorola RISC Applications for their consistent patience and good humor, especially Vanessa Glover, Christina Leicht, Douglas McQuaid, Mary Thomas, and Peter Van Overen. What a great team to be on.

Also, I must express my gratitude to Phil Brownfield, Phil Pompa, Rob King, and Les Crudele for their efforts in making this book possible, and Brad Koch, Angela Lee, and the editors at Que for all the extra time and boundless patience. Special thanks has been earned by the copy editors for letting me use the passive voice.

Trademark Acknowledgments

All terms mentioned in this book that are known to be trademarks or service marks have been appropriately capitalized. Que cannot attest to the accuracy of this information. Use of a term in this book should not be regarded as affecting the validity of any trademark or service mark. Trademarks indicated below were derived from various sources.

Contents at a Glance

Contents

7 Introducing the PowerPC Processor Family   87

8 Apple's PowerPC Systems   109

9 The RS/6000 POWER Connection   121

18 The PowerPC 603 RISC Processor

Index

Introduction

In October of 1991, when Apple, IBM, and Motorola announced an alliance to jointly develop a series of high-performance microprocessors, two computer terms suddenly gained broader circulation—RISC (reduced instruction set computing) and processor architecture, which refers to the underlying criteria and specifications that determine the design of a processor.

This book examines the PowerPC revolution from the perspective of the PowerPC Architecture. It is intended for the computer user and for the computer professional who are looking for a guide to PowerPC Architecture, PowerPC microprocessors, and the systems based on this technology poised to guide the next generation of personal computers well into the 21st century.

Who Needs This Book?

This book is intended for a broad range of readers—from the non-professional computer user who wants to understand the terminology and concepts assoicated with the new technology, to the more experienaced user and computer professional who wants a closer look at the PowerPC Architecture, microprocessors, and computers based on those processors.

The book is in two parts:

The first part (Chapters 1-8) of the book provides general information for a broad range of readers, including the following:

- Computer users who want a clearer understanding of what architecture is, and what the advantages are of RISC architecture in general, and of PowerPC Architecture in particular.

- Computer buyers who now have another option when it comes time to purchase a new computer.

- Computer users and professionals who want a better understanding of the basic relationships between an architecture, the processors designed for that architecture, and the systems based on the processors.

- Current PC and Macintosh users who want to know how the advantages of RISC processors will be realized in upcoming computer systems.

- Corporate users and system administrators who want to better understand hardware, operating system, and application software issues related to PowerPC-based systems.

- Students of computer science who want a historical overview of RISC architecture and an in-depth look at the PowerPC Architecture.

The second part (Chapters 9-18) of the book provides a technical overview of the PowerPC Architecture and the first two PowerPC processors. This part is intended for the following:

- Computer professionals and hobbyists who want to understand the more technical aspects of the PowerPC Architecture.

- Computer professionals and hobbyists who want to know more about the inner workings of the first two PowerPC processors, the PowerPC 601 and the PowerPC 603.

- Software programmers who want to learn about the programming model, instruction set, exception model, and memory management facility defined by the PowerPC Architecture.

- Curious readers who want to understand how the high-performance RISC design philosophy provides fast instruction processing in the 601 processor. Although a thorough understanding of instruction timing is primarily of interest to compiler writers and other special-purpose programmers who would be dealing directly with the PowerPC assembly code, this chapter is presented in such a way that readers who are inexperienced with this level of programming can come away with an understanding of the performance advantages of RISC processors.

What Kind of Information Will You Find?

The first part of the book describes the features and advantages of the PowerPC Architecture and provides a historical overview of the development of RISC architecture, tracing it from its earliest experimental designs, through IBM's POWER architecture, the PowerPC Architecture jointly developed by IBM, Motorola, and Apple. This part looks at the basic tenets of RISC design and how those tenets guided the creation of the PowerPC Architecture.

The second part of the book takes a more detailed look at the architectural definition itself, featuring a complete listing and description of the registers, instructions, and exceptions defined by the architecture, as well as functional descriptions of the memory management and cache models. This part concludes with technical overviews of the two parts that have already been released, and culminates with a close-up look at how instructions are processed in the 601 processor.

What Aspects of the PowerPC Architecture Are Covered?

This book discusses the PowerPC Architecture and describes the different resources used for 32- and 64-bit implementations. This book takes an in-depth look at the 601 and 603 microprocessors, including details of the implementation that are not defined by the PowerPC architectures. The book also emphasizes the flexibility of the PowerPC Architecture, how that is realized in the first two PowerPC processors and the first personal computers based on PowerPC microprocessors.

A Word from the Author

The users of personal computers have enjoyed an almost exponential growth in virtually every aspect of personal computer design—except for one.

While a computer's architecture may seem far removed from the day-to-day relationship one has with the computers in one's life, it has become the critical factor that contributes to the high cost of the incremental improvements to existing architectures. The first decade of personal computing was one of surprises that bordered on miracles at every turn. Remarkable things continue to happen, but each advancement in multimedia, or semiconductor process technology, or advanced communications, tests the seams of the existing architectures.

The PowerPC Architecture provides personal computer manufacturers with an opportunity to resume the fast pace that it has lost in the past few years, and has already begun to offer users a whole new set of high-performance toys and tools.

Chapter 1

Introduction to PowerPC Concepts

Throughout most of this century, flight was the field of technology used to measure scientific progress. But at about the same time that the first spacecraft escaped our solar system, our fascination had shifted. Now, the increasing power and shrinking size of the computer has become the measuring stick for technological advances. In just over 20 years, the personal computer has become a necessary part of everyday life.

As forward-looking as the earliest PC (personal computer) designers seemed in the early 1970s, they could not have foreseen the broad acceptance and popularity of those mysterious machines that now occupy the desktops, kitchen tables, store counters, workbenches, and game rooms around the world. And it has been that immense popularity that has driven those advances.

A Short History of Computers

In its short history, virtually every aspect of personal computing has advanced exponentially. Prices continue to shrink as performance continues to advance—and the pace of technology shows no apparent signs of slowing down, especially as more options continue to open into more and more applications and environments.

Although microprocessor design has participated in many of these advances, the fundamental architecture—at the mercy of which all software and hardware are designed—was defined long before words like modem, boot, hacker,

This chapter touches on the following:

- The basic concepts of computer architecture, especially RISC architecture

- A brief overview of the role that computer architecture has played in personal computing

- Informal definitions of some of the basic terms used in this book

and backwards-compatibility became part of our vocabulary. That architecture was designed for the technology of its time, and it continues to drive the vast majority of our personal computers today, requiring a compatibility with processors that have gone the way of eight-track tapes, disco, and shag carpeting.

Today's personal computers are still being driven by an architecture of the 1970s, but not because the field of computer architecture has not kept pace with technology. In the early 1980s a new approach to microprocessor design, called reduced instruction-set computing (or RISC), quickly evolved and began to dominate new processor design—providing the speed, efficiency, and precision needed by high-powered (and expensive) workstations, a market in which RISC architecture has dominated. Perhaps the most resounding testimonial to the importance of RISC architecture is that in the past five years, all new processor designs have adopted RISC techniques. The only complex instruction-set computing (or CISC) processor design efforts has been remodeling, mainly done to accommodate wider buses and to integrate floating-point arithmetic (math coprocessors).

> **Note**
>
> As personal computing becomes more closely integrated with television and other forms of electronic communication, greater demands are placed on microprocessors. The question is no longer whether personal computers will shift to a RISC design, but when.

But notions of computer architecture are still fairly exotic and obscure, even in a world where youngsters and TV commercial announcers use jargon like Super VGA, baud-rate, and flash ROMs. Nevertheless, the processor, and what goes on inside it, remain essentially a mystery, a hermetically sealed black box over which the consumer has little choice.

Terms and Definitions

Although there is a microprocessor chip in every personal computer, most users seldom come face to face with the inner workings of a microprocessor or with the architectural specifications that govern a processor's design.

So to understand the significance of the changes taking place, it is useful to know some of the special language used to describe what goes on within microprocessors, especially RISC microprocessors.

Architecture

The term architecture is used to refer to a broad assortment of things in the computer industry. In the context of microprocessor architecture, it refers to the specifications upon which the design of a processor or family of processors is based. The architecture consists of the instruction set (most important), the programming model (that includes the register set and memory conventions), the exception model, and other specifications that characterize a set of compatible processors.

The instruction-set portion of the architecture is often referred to as the instruction-set architecture, or ISA. An ISA specifies such things as the functionality of instructions, instruction formats, and addressing modes.

Reduced Instruction Set Computing

Reduced instruction set computing (RISC) consists of instructions that reduce operations into their simplest tasks so that most instructions take roughly the same amount of time to execute (that time is typically short). The instruction machine codings are typically of a fixed length, and instructions use simple addressing modes. This makes it easier for the processor to decode instructions, which in turn speeds up instruction execution and simplifies the processor design.

The most common characteristic among RISC processors is that arithmetic instructions read source operands from and write their results to registers rather than system memory; memory is accessed by a set of explicit load/store instructions. For this reason, RISC architecture is sometimes called register-to-register architecture, or load/store architecture. RISC architectures do not necessarily have smaller instruction sets.

But a simple definition of RISC says nothing about the advantages that come from implementing an instruction set that meets the criteria described above. Discussing those advantages requires introducing a few terms that have become so intimately tied with RISC processors that they have been confused with the definition of RISC—terms like pipelining, superscalar, and parallel execution. These and other techniques take advantage of the regularity of the RISC instruction set, so most RISC architectures implement pipelining, parallel processing, and superscalar dispatch, as do some CISC processors.

Pipelining

A technique found in several contexts, such as bus pipelining and instruction pipelining. At its simplest, pipelining refers to the ability to begin a second task before the first one ends.

Instruction pipelining schemes resolve instruction processing tasks into simple stages—typically fetch, decode, dispatch, execute, and write back. An instruction passes from one stage to the next, leaving room for the subsequent instruction to occupy a stage as it moves stage-by-stage through the pipeline. This is analogous to an assembly line, where a different job is performed at each station. When the work is complete at one stage, the product is passed to the next one.

Many of the advantages to such an arrangement are clear. Resources are not forced to remain idle while an instruction is begin processed. While it may take three, four, or many more cycles for a single instruction to complete processing, once the pipeline is full, one instruction may complete execution on every clock cycle.

Superscalar

A superscalar processor is one in which there are multiple execution units such that more than one instruction can be dispatched and executed at a time. The term superscalar evolved out of the distinction that is made between scalar computers (conventional computers which are designed for calculating single values, or scalars) and vector computers (high-powered computers designed to calculate vectors for scientific and engineering calculations).

Execution unit

A unit that executes instructions. The most common examples are the integer (or fixed-point) unit, the branch processing unit, and the floating-point unit.

Floating point unit

An execution unit that performs floating-point arithmetic. Floating-point arithmetic can perform mathematical calculations using very precise values and is used for scientific, engineering, and graphics calculations. An on-chip math coprocessor. This is frequently abbreviated as FPU.

Integer unit

An execution unit that performs integer arithmetic. Integer arithmetic performs mathematical operations on integer values (or more specifically, fixed-point values) and do not require the same high degree of precision required for floating-point operations. This is frequently abbreviated as IU.

Instruction parallelism

Instruction parallelism is the ability to execute instructions simultaneously and is a characteristic of a superscalar processor. For example, if an implementation has an integer unit implemented in parallel with a floating-point unit, instructions can be dispatched to each of these units at the same time, and both instructions can be executed simultaneously. The advantages of instruction parallelism lie in that more instructions can execute within a given time. The advantages of parallel execution are obvious to anyone who has ever been stuck in a check-out line at the grocery store when only one cashier is on duty.

Latency

The time required to perform a particular task or series of tasks, such as instruction execution or a memory access.

Throughput

Throughput is the number of instructions that complete execution and record their results in a given time. For superscalar, pipelined processors, the throughput provides a better measure of a processor's execution performance than does latency.

Orthogonality

Orthogonality is the lack of duplication of functionality within the instruction set. Typically, a RISC instruction set is orthogonal in that instructions perform very basic tasks that are not duplicated by other instructions.

Reservation station

A buffer provided at the front-end of an execution unit where dispatched instructions can be queued when they cannot enter the execution unit's pipeline—typically because the stage is busy or because more than one instruction has been dispatched to the same unit in the same clock.

Implementation

In this book, the noun implementation refers to a chip, typically a microprocessor design based on the PowerPC Architecture. An embedded controller also would be considered an implementation.

Summary

This section has provided a brief look at what processor architecture is and the role that it plays in personal computer design. It also has presented a few of the most general concepts related to RISC architecture to help provide a context for topics discussed in this book.

The next chapter discusses various approaches to architecture design, focusing on the characteristics and techniques of RISC architecture and the advantages that the RISC architecture can bring to the personal computer industry.

Chapter 2

What Is RISC Architecture and Why Do We Need It?

If you have ever driven in Boston, you can easily understand the need for RISC architecture. In Boston, the streets are narrow, they twist and turn as if to bypass imaginary objects, and it is difficult to find your way around. Likewise, the microprocessors in most of today's personal computers suffer from the similar bottlenecks that come from outgrowing their original design.

The reasons for Boston's problems are apparent. In the 18th century it seemed reasonable to Boston's famous reasonable men to put streets and sidewalks where people were already going, so horse trails and foot paths became Boston's current streets and roads. There was less traffic, it was slower, and vehicles were smaller, so the narrow streets, blind corners, hairpin turns, and curious traffic circles posed few problems.

Boston's street builders could not have predicted the growth of technology or of the population. Now millions of cars, trucks, and buses try to negotiate those same narrow winding streets where great American thinkers walked and rode. Boston remains a city of great minds, great music, great museums, and great fish, but it also has provided a great counter-example for subsequent city planners.

In this chapter, you learn the following:

- The basic characteristics of RISC and CISC architectures

- Basic concepts associated with RISC processing and how they offer performance gains

- Examples of optimization techniques, such as pipelining and instruction parallelism

Microprocessor design has suffered from many of the same problems as Boston's city planning (Harvard architecture aside)—congested traffic competes for narrow data paths that technology has hopelessly outgrown, and complicated tricks are often necessary to help it do so. And users continue to pay the toll for the sake of maintaining backwards compatibility.

CISC versus RISC Processing

In CISC (complex instruction-set computing) architectures, more complicated instructions have been tacked on to meet special needs, just as new streets were added as the city's needs changed. The city grew to incorporate smaller towns and boundaries became blurred, just as the chips expanded to accommodate on-chip floating-point units (FPUs), caches, and memory management units.

RISC (reduced instruction-set computing) architecture takes a different approach to microprocessor design—borrowing a lesson from the assembly line, the innovation that drove the industrial revolution. Before the assembly line, essentially one person had to master all of the manufacturing steps. The number of objects that could be made was limited by the number of people who knew how to perform all the steps. This was great for job security, but it was tough to produce goods in quantity, and the work stopped entirely if the craftsman got sick.

With assembly lines, the work required to manufacture an item is broken down into simpler steps, each taking about the same length of time to complete. People are trained to do the work required at only one of the stages. They pick up the item from the person at the previous stage, perform their tasks (at which they would become extremely proficient), and then pass the item on to the person at the next stage. This way, it is possible for ten less-experienced workers on an assembly line to produce more goods in one day than ten experienced craftsmen could. In addition, critical paths can be identified, and performance can be optimized.

In processor design, the assembly line is replaced with pipeline. In a fully optimized RISC processor, the work at each stage can be performed in the same amount of time (one clock cycle).

Table 2.1 shows a simple pipeline example consisting of four stages—fetch, decode/dispatch, execute, and write back.example

Clock Cycle	Fetch	Decode/Dispatch	Execute	Write Back
Table 2.1 A simple pipeline example				
1	Inst 1			
2	Inst 2	Inst 1		
3	Inst 3	Inst 2	Inst 1	
4	Inst 4	Inst 3	Inst 2	Inst 1
5	Inst 5	Inst 4	Inst 3	Inst 2

As shown in table 2.1, the first instruction (Inst 1) is fetched from memory in the first clock cycle.

In clock cycle 2, Inst 1 has moved to the decode/dispatch stage where the processor looks at each bit in the instruction encoding to determine what subsequent actions are required and then issues the instruction to the execution unit. Because Inst 1 has vacated the fetch stage, Inst 2 can be fetched.

In clock cycle 3, Inst 1 is executed (execution can consist of an arithmetic or logical operation, a load or store operation, or another task). Inst 2 is decoded and Inst 3 is fetched.

In clock cycle 4, Inst 1 writes back its results and has completed processing and each of the subsequent instructions move forward by one stage. At this point, the entire pipeline is full, and although it takes four clock cycles for each instruction to be processed, from this point on (at least in this ideal model) one instruction can execute per clock cycle.

This number of cycles that can be executed per clock cycle is called *throughput*, and it provides a much better measure of the efficiency of a pipelined processor than does *instruction latency*, which tells how many clock cycles an instruction takes to execute.

In a pipelined execution unit, latency corresponds to the number of stages; but, in general terms, it doesn't matter how many stages are in a pipeline. After the pipeline has filled, and assuming that there is nothing to interrupt the instruction flow, the pipeline can have a throughput of one instruction per clock cycle. So, in a pipelined model, latency is mostly a factor of how long it takes to fill the pipeline.

Throughput
The number of cycles that can be executed per clock cycle.

Instruction latency
The amount of time it takes an instruction to complete execution.

Pipelining
The ability to begin a second task before the first one ends. Instruction pipelining reduces instruction processing into simple stages (typically fetch, decode, dispatch, execute, and write back). As an instruction passes through the pipeline, it vacates one stage and moves to the next.

Instruction throughput
The ratio that tells how many instructions can be executed in a given time, usually expressed in instructions per internal processor clock cycle.

It should be reiterated that many CISC processors also use *pipelining*, sometimes extensively, but RISC processors are designed to take the greatest advantage of this technique.

But pipelining is only half of the punch line. You also can have several pipelines working in parallel. By isolating tasks that are not dependent on one another, a chip designer (or an assembly-line designer) can set up another pipeline to work in parallel and results can be brought together at a later stage. While one pipeline can handle floating-point arithmetic, another can handle integer arithmetic, another can handle load and store instructions, and so on. It should be noted that there must be a mechanism that ensures that instructions write back in an orderly manner (although that order does not have to be strict). As the number of instruction pipelines increases, the mechanism for maintaining order becomes more complex.

Or, if there is so much demand for results from one pipeline that it can't keep up with the other pipelines (that is, it becomes the critical path) the designer can set up another one just like it to produce results twice as fast. Many processors duplicate the integer unit, so two integer instructions can execute at the same time.

> **Note**
>
> The ability to execute multiple instructions at the same time is called instruction parallelism, and a processor that implements multiple pipelines is called superscalar.

If instructions are designed and handled properly, and if the hardware that executes those instructions takes advantage of the consistency of the instructions, it is easy to see that a superscalar, pipelined machine can optimally execute more than one instruction per clock cycle. As with pipelining, CISC processors can also take advantage of instruction parallelism, but because of the complex nature of CISC instruction sets, such implementations are more complicated, and cause the chip to be much larger. As you will see, RISC architectures are designed to take advantage of pipelining and instruction parallelism, which explains how the PowerPC chips can offer greater performance with smaller chips and with lower power consumption.

> **Note**
>
> RISC architectures were first developed in the mid-1970s. The earliest example was a processor project that was intended to serve as a very fast telephone switching system. The instruction set consisted of very simple instructions that transferred data between memory and a set of registers in the processor. Although this project was never completed, the basic concepts were further explored both by IBM and by several academic institutions. In the early 1980s, commercial RISC processors began to emerge primarily for use in powerful workstation computers and special-purpose systems.

Price versus Performance

The design goals of all processors, computers, and peripheral devices is price vs. performance—the best performance for the lowest possible price. CISC processors sought to achieve greater performance by adding *microcode* to execute ever more complicated assembly language instructions.

Microcode
Refers to the micro-instructions required to execute an instruction in a CISC processor.

This approach to greater performance assumes that an assembly language (the elemental language distinct to each processor or architecture) is more efficient if it offers instructions that closely resemble those of higher-level languages (such as C). That performance could be improved by closing that so-called "semantic gap" between the assembly language and higher-level languages. However, as instructions become more complicated, the microcode on the chip required to decode and execute the instruction also becomes more complicated.

So CISC instruction sets often include gadget instructions that are powerful at doing seldom-needed tasks. For example, the VAX has an assembly language instruction that can solve polynomials. Some scientific applications require such operations, but most applications don't.

Instructions that require longer sequences of micro-instructions also take longer to execute. This makes it more difficult to fully enjoy the advantages of pipelining and instruction parallelism. In a pipeline, all subsequent instructions, regardless of how much work they need to do, have to wait for this slow instruction ahead of it.

Grocery stores deal with this same problem by setting up express lanes. By analogy, processors can implement a type of instruction parallelism that sends slower instructions to one pipeline and faster ones to another. But, because dependencies can exist among instructions, these faster instructions may still have to wait for the complicated, time-consuming instruction to complete.

Transistors have become cheaper over the past 30 years, and manufacturing processing is constantly making them smaller and faster. Memory, power requirements, transistor limits, and most other physical limitations pose fewer restrictions on chip designers than they did a quarter of a century ago. So the choice becomes using these cheaper, smaller transistors to add more complicated instructions, or stepping back and reconsidering the overall design knowing that memory and logic is now less expensive and easier to integrate.

We can't start Boston all over, but processor architecture is another story. The small gains that can be achieved at increasingly greater cost—both in terms of cost to the consumer and the size and power requirements of the chip— make the reasons for starting over with a RISC design grow louder and more convincing.

The major drawback to starting from scratch is the huge investment in software written for existing processors, but RISC processors have such greater performance that they can run older software in emulation comparable to the systems for which the software was written.

Cache
A memory resource from which a processor can read or write instructions and/ or data without necessarily having to access external memory.

So instead of spending transistors on complex instructions—which may be seldom used—RISC processors spend them on chip logic that maximizes pipelining, which makes it easier to implement parallel, superscalar designs. This hardware optimizes throughput, and the benefits can be shared by many instructions. More resources on the chip are working simultaneously. Fetching, dispatch, execution, and feed-forwarding mechanisms are more complex, and on-chip memory resources, such as *caches*, TLBs, and registers, take up more space. However, this hardware is put to work a greater percentage of the time than if the same transistors were spent on individual, complex instructions.

RISC Design Basics

To achieve high throughput, RISC design adheres to several basic, interrelated principles:

- Uniform length instructions with consistent encodings.

- Primarily simple instructions. Complex tasks generally require multiple instructions which can typically be pipelined and executed in parallel.

- A register-to-register (or load/store) architecture with primitive addressing modes.

- Large register files that allow individual registers to be accessed independently.

The benefits of these criteria are described in the following sections.

Uniform Length Instructions

Having all the instructions the same size allows a simpler design for instruction fetch, decode and dispatch, which allows greater flexibility for pipelining and address calculation.

If all instructions are a word (32-bits) long, for example, the fetcher can expect instructions on predictable 32-bit boundaries. If instructions are buffered in an instruction queue (as they are in the *PowerPC 601 processor*, the first PowerPC processor), instruction accesses to the cache can be easily indexed by the number of instructions fetched.

Likewise, the instruction queue in the 601 is eight words (instructions) long, which is the same size as a cache block. When a block of instructions is loaded from memory, there can be no instructions that fall into two cache blocks.

Having uniform length instruction also makes it simpler to identify and handle branch instructions earlier. By pulling out branch instructions early, the direction can be predicted (and the branch instruction can be replaced in the instruction stream by the predicted target instruction, meaning one fewer instruction has to execute), and the prediction can be proven correct or incorrect (resolved) early. Some processors (such as the 601 and 603) even begin speculatively executing instructions from a target stream before the branch is resolved. There are many techniques available for lessening the time required to handle branch instructions, all made easier by having uniform length instructions.

Simpler Instruction Tasks

Breaking complex operations into simpler instructions isolates instructions from contention stalls and data dependencies. For example, if a load or store

PowerPC 601 processor
The first PowerPC processor, which became available in mid-1993, used in the first generation of IBM and Apple PowerPC-based systems.

Integer unit (IU)

Performs integer, or more precisely, fixed-point calculations. Integer operations do not require the degree of precision required for floating-point arithmetic.

encounters a delay while accessing the cache or system memory, the *integer unit (IU)* or *floating-point (FPU)* is not forced to remain idle. Instead, it can begin executing the next instruction. This makes it easier to pipeline instructions.

Simpler instructions that have a predictable latency can achieve a throughput that approaches one instruction per clock cycle. Most instructions implemented in the 601 integer unit require one cycle to execute and can have a throughput of one instruction per cycle. Likewise, although there are three stages in the FPU, once the pipeline is full, the FPU can achieve a throughput of one instruction per clock cycle and a double precision throughput of one instruction every two clock cycles.

Floating-point unit (FPU)

Executes floating-point calculations, those arithmetic calculations that require a high-degree of precision.

Register-to-Register Architecture

Register-to-register operations make it easier to pipeline operations because most instructions can be designed to execute in a single cycle.

Arithmetic instructions use a register file for source and destination operands, instead of accessing memory directly (either a cache or system memory). A separate set of load and store instructions are used to transfer source and result data from memory. By making these tasks independent from one another, the ALU is free to begin calculating while a store instruction writes the previous results to memory.

Likewise, advances in compiler technology allow compiles to be designed to take advantage of instruction independence. This allows a programmer who uses a high-level language to enjoy the benefits of improved performance without having to come to terms with all of its intricacies.

Typically, these two simpler instructions can be implemented to take one cycle each, which simplifies pipelining.

Feed forwarding

A technique for reducing instruction latency caused by data dependencies.

Additional paths (called *feed forwarding* paths) can be created to allow result data to be made available to a subsequent dependent instruction before that data is written back to a register file. This eliminates pipeline stalls.

Large Register Files

By providing large register files, multiple instructions can be executing simultaneously and in parallel with limited contention for register resources. Moreover, additional schemes can be implemented, such as rename registers and feed forwarding, that reduce the latency due to data dependencies or register contention.

Having spacious register resources emphasizes reuse rather than destruction of operand data. Most RISC arithmetic instructions have a three-operand instruction syntax—two source operands and one destination operand. The destination register is typically not one of the source registers, which prevents data destruction and encourages reuse of data.

Chapter 5, "The Genesis of the PowerPC RISC Architecture," provides an overview of the history of RISC architecture and shows how the principles of RISC design have evolved since the first experiments with RISC processors in 1975.

Breadth of Implementation

In the early days, the processors designed for personal computers had to respect the limitations of the technology of the day—power requirements, size, transitor density, memory cost, and the speed of peripheral devices. While there were advanced techniques implemented in architectures for mainframes and supercomputers, these were not practical for the size, cost, and power restrictions of microprocessors.

Because of all the restrictions placed on processor design, it seemed beyond belief that personal computers would ever threaten the domain of mainframe computers. That has been proven wrong.

However, powerful centralized mainframe computers still play a critical role in technology. Even though PCs have replaced terminals and gateways, which were previously dedicated, single-purpose devices, the mainframe architectures and operating systems present an unbreachable gap for current microprocessor architectures intended for more modest roles.

> **Note**
>
> Existing microprocessor architectures tend to favor certain types of implementations. Many of the first generation of RISC chips are intended for use with high-end scientific and graphics workstations and minicomputers, while recent generations of CISC chips remain best suited to desktop systems, servers, and lower-end workstations.

Now it is reasonable for both large mainframe implementations, workstations, desktop, and portable computers to share the same architecture, and the PowerPC Architecture is deliberately designed to provide a common foundation for a wide range of purposes—from battery-powered, hand-held devices to multiprocessor systems that will compete with mainframe computers.

The first four PowerPC processors illustrate the wide range of implementations for which the PowerPC Architecture is suited. These four processors are described as follows:

■ The 601 processor is aimed at desktop and workstation systems. It also can be used in multiprocessor systems that rival the computing power of mainframe systems. It implements 32-bit addressing. The PowerPC 601 processor is shown in Figure 2.1.

Figure 2.1
The PowerPC 601 processor.

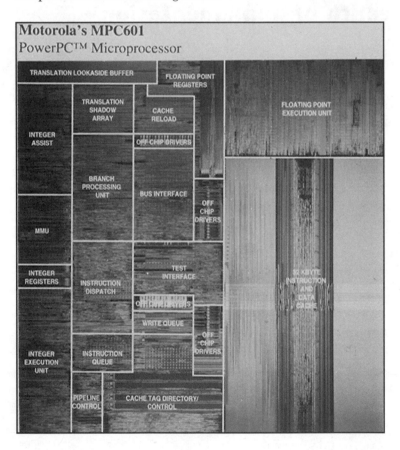

■ The 603 processor, which also implements 32-bit addressing, is designed for low-power systems, such as conventional notebook and hand-held computers, as well as many other battery-powered devices.

The fact that the PowerPC RISC architecture requires much less complexity makes it especially suitable for implementations where space, heat dissipation, and power consumption are critical concerns. The PowerPC 603 processor is shown in Figure 2.2.

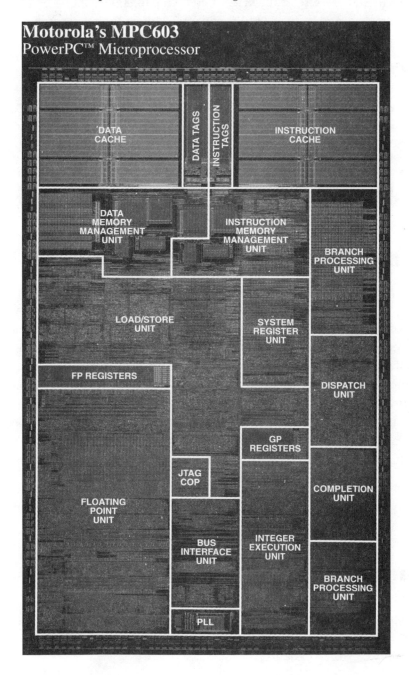

Figure 2.2
The PowerPC 603 processor.

- The 604 processor, due for release this year, also is intended for the desktop market and also implements 32-bit addressing but has a substantially different design from the 601, for even faster performance.

- The 620 processor is the first PowerPC chip to implement 64-bit addressing, and is aimed at high-end workstations and microcomputer implementations.

> **Note**
>
> Chapter 7, "Introducing the PowerPC Processor Family," provides an overview of each of the PowerPC processors. Even though each chip has a substantially different design (which attests to the great versatility of the architecture), all four processors support the same software and operating systems. Chapter 4, "Operating Systems and the PowerPC Architecture," has additional information about operating system support.

What All of This Means to the User

So far, we have reviewed issues concerning the inside of a microprocessor and we have introduced a few concepts and defined some of the jargon used with RISC. To the user it's impossible to measure how important these particular concepts are in a world of PCI buses, object-oriented operating systems, EISA interfaces, and voice-recognition systems. The proof will reside in how computer-makers take advantage of all this speed. And from all indications, those are expected to do more than make faster high-end computers for business applications. Instead, IBM, Apple, and others are building systems that will let your computer operate faster, and it will make it possible for you to do things at your computer that you may have never thought about doing.

It won't be anything like trying to fight with thousands of other Boston drivers competing to get through the narrow Callahan Tunnel to get to Logan International Airport.

Summary

This chapter reviewed some of the basic concepts and philosophies of RISC architecture, starting with the problems inherent in the current CISC designs and the ways in which those problems are avoided by implementing simple, fixed-length instructions and by allowing computational instructions to access on chip registers, rather than physical memory, for source data and for recording results.

The next chapter takes a brief look at the alliance between IBM, Apple, and Motorola that has spawned the new RISC-based PowerPC Architecture, and new families of high-performance computer systems.

Chapter 3

The PowerPC Alliance

In October 1991, IBM, Apple, and Motorola announced plans to jointly design a new architecture that would form the basis of the next generation of IBM and Macintosh personal computing systems. At a combined investment of over one billion dollars, the three companies created the Somerset Design Center in Austin, Texas.

Alliance Goals

For IBM and Macintosh, the ability to mix PowerPC systems is a major source of attraction. The PowerPC alliance provides greater opportunities for compatibility and more efficient mixed network environments. One product of this collaboration is an IBM-certified Apple Token Ring card. The relationship also has spawned other joint efforts:

- Kaleida Labs is a new company funded by IBM and Apple to create common standards for the fast-growing multimedia products.

- Taligent is a new company, also jointly funded by Apple and IBM, that is developing an object-oriented operating system due for completion in the mid-1990s.

- PowerOpen is a jointly funded effort aimed toward developing a new version of the UNIX operating system, combining features from IBM's AIX and Apple's A/UX operating systems. This open-system platform will allow users to have access to Macintosh and AIX-based applications.

This chapter reviews the following events in the first two years of the PowerPC Alliance:

- Announcements of the PowerPC processors

- Announcements of the PowerPC-based systems

- Key events for the PowerOpen Association

- Announcements of various hardware and software adapters

The History of the PowerPC Alliance

The following is a chronological listing of the events surrounding the PowerPC Alliance:

- October, 1991. Apple, IBM, and Motorola jointly announced the formation of an unprecedented alliance. With that announcement, details were first presented about the development of the PowerPC Architecture and of the PowerOpen Environment.

- January, 1992. Bull HN Information Systems, Inc., announces adoption of the PowerPC Architecture for their server and workstation systems.

- April, 1992. CETIA, a subsidiary of Thomson-CSF, announces an agreement with IBM to develop products based on PowerPC Architecture.

- May, 1992. Motorola, IBM, and Apple dedicate the Somerset Design Center in Austin, Texas.

- October, 1992. Motorola, IBM, and Apple unveil the first PowerPC processor—the PowerPC 601 saw "first silicon."

- November, 1992. Harris Corporation announces an agreement with IBM to develop real-time workstations based on PowerPC Architecture.

- December, 1992. Tadpole Technology PLC announces an agreement with IBM to produce notebook computers based on PowerPC Architecture.

- January, 1993. Thomson-CSF CETIA announces PowerPC VME systems and Lynx real-time software.

- March, 1993. Apple, Bull, Harris, Motorola, Tadpole Technology, and Thomson-CSF announce the formal founding of the PowerOpen Association with the goal of providing an open system and compatibility.

- April, 1993. SunSoft announces plans to support Solaris on PowerPC-based systems.

- April, 1993. Motorola announces general sampling of the PowerPC 601.

- May, 1993. Motorola and IBM announce the availability of PowerPC 601 tools catalog.

- May, 1993. Ford announces that their next generation of Power Train Electronic Controller (PTEC) will be based on PowerPC Architecture.

- June, 1993. Kaleida Labs, Scientific-Atlanta, and Motorola announce plans for interactive multimedia devices developed using PowerPC processors.

- September, 1993. IBM announced the first PowerPC-based systems in their RISC System/6000 series. The POWERstation 25T, POWERstation 25W, POWERstation 25S, and the POWERstation/POWERserver 250.

- October, 1993. Announcement of an 80 MHz 601.

- October, 1993. Joint announcement that the PowerPC 603 had reached first silicon.

- October, 1993. CETIA, a subsidiary of Thomson-CSF, introduces a family of VME single-board computers and workstations, based on the PowerPC 601 processor.

- October, 1993. Bull announces their first PowerPC-based system—the Bull DPX/20 Model 150. The system, which uses the PowerPC 601, is made available in three configurations—the 150, a compact desktop server; the 150S, a desk-side server; and the 155W, a single-user workstation.

- October, 1993. Motorola's RISC Microprocessor Division announces five software development packages for optimizing performance of the PowerPC 603—the first tool set designed specifically for the 603. These include C and FORTRAN compilers, an architectural simulator, a 603 timing simulator, and a source-level debugger.

- October, 1993. Apple announced commitments from seven additional software developers—Artwork Systems, N.V., Canto Software, Inc., Fractal Design Corp., Graphisoft, Great Plains Software, ITEDO Software GmbH, and Wolfram Research, Inc. These were in addition to Adobe Systems Inc., ACIUS Inc., Aldus Corporation, Claris Corporation, Deneba Software, Frame Technology, Insignia Solutions, Microsoft Corporation, Quark, Inc., Specular International, and WordPerfect Corporation. At the same time, they announced plans to ship upgrade products simultaneously with the first PowerPC systems. This announcement included upgrade options for the Apple Workgroup Server Series.

■ November, 1993. Microsoft and Motorola announce that a port to Windows NT is being jointly developed with IBM's Power Personal Systems Division. The port to Windows NT, which conforms to the PowerPC Reference Platform, operates in little-endian mode and is the first operating system to take advantage of PowerPC's bi-endian feature.

■ November, 1993. IBM announced the PowerPC Reference Platform, a non-proprietary standard specified by the IBM Power Personal Systems Division. Operating systems ported to the PowerPC Reference Platform, or PReP, include AIX, Workplace OS, Windows NT, Solaris and Taligent, through which support will be provided for OS/2, AIX, DOS, Windows, Win32, UNIX and Taligent, and will support Macintosh applications under PowerOpen.

■ November, 1993. A broad group of computer subsystem manufacturers announced support for the PowerPC Reference Platform—including Austek Microsystems, Cirrus Logic, Matrox, National Semiconductor, NCR, S3, and SMC Weitek.

■ November, 1993. Motorola's Semiconductor Products Sector, Kaleida Labs, and Scientific-Atlanta announced plans to use Malibu—a multiplayer display accelerator chip, designed by Kaleida and produced by Motorola. The chip provides functionality for enhanced 2- and 3-dimensional graphics and animation and for displaying high-resolution text. The chip will be used in a set-top design by Scientific-Atlanta to provide interactive, multimedia services to home subscribers through broad-band television networks.

■ February, 1994. Insignia Solutions and Apple announce an agreement to include SoftWindows™ in selected configurations of PowerPC-based Macintoshes.

Summary

This chapter presented a quick look in the eventful first three years for the PowerPC alliance, showing the eager acceptance among a broad spectrum of hardware and software developers.

Because the PowerPC Architecture is suitable for a wide range of applications, from low-powered portables to high-end workstations and servers, it offers a suitable platform for a wide variety of operating systems. The next chapter examines the relationships between PowerPC-based systems and the variety of operating system options the architecture can support.

Chapter 4

Operating Systems and the PowerPC Architecture

The personal computer began life as a specialized tool. To use it, you had to learn a new language—DOS. Although learning DOS was simple enough, especially considering the rewards available to those who learned it, the early masters of DOS were considered to be computer specialists. Owning a PC in the 1970s was much like owning a car 60 years before—you had to be your own mechanic.

Providing a friendlier interface would have been expensive and would have stretched the limitations of memory resources. The market was small and specialized, and the operating system and all the applications were expected to fit comfortably in 640KB of memory, which seemed generous when compared to many other early personal computers.

But as the personal computer escaped the cold confines of the business and scientific world, many potential computer customers were intimidated. Then came Apple's Macintosh—and although it was based on a different processor with a different architecture than IBM's PC, it was the interface that sold the computer because it made the other resources available to them. The operating system was given such a low profile that it was one of the few aspects of the Macintosh that was not given an imaginative name—it was simply called "The System."

Battle lines were drawn, and arguments were passionate between PC diehards and Macintosh devotees.

This chapter emphasizes the following:

■ A general overview of the relationship between an architecture and operating systems

■ IBM's operating system and software support

■ Apple's operating system and software support

■ Emulation versus native software

■ The PowerOpen Association and the PowerOpen Environment

Which Operating System Is Best?

The answer to that question is, resoundingly, the one that is best for you. Each has advantages and disadvantages. Apart from the intuitively designed graphical interface the Macintosh provided, it provided something more important, an alternative that broke down the barriers for many millions of users, something from which all of us have benefited directly or indirectly.

As the range of personal computing has broadened in all directions, the cast of operating systems and user interfaces has grown and become more specialized. UNIX and AIX are more useful in high-end systems, and the market demand for a graphical interface has also brought us Windows and OS/2.

And as processors become more powerful and memory becomes less expensive, the choice of operating systems gets more complicated. The PowerPC 603 processor, which is roughly the size of a fingernail, can run software that only a few years back would only have been possible on high-end workstations.

Amidst the confusion, a squadron of provocatively named new products— Windows NT, Taligent, Chicago, OSF/Motif—is poised to enter the fray.

Clearly, a new architecture would have very little appeal if users had to completely pitch all of their software, shake all of the warm, familiar keyboard commands out of their fingers, and be forced into having to interpret baffling new icons. Or if you only speak DOS and you are faced with an inscrutable blinking prompt that doesn't flinch when you type DIR.

Of course, a microprocessor design is typically intimately tied to the operating system—an operating system depends on the instructions and resources provided by a processor. If that operating system is to run on another processor, the operating system has to be fooled into thinking those resources are present.

Emulation of an operating system designed for another processor typically yields a combination of poor performance and huge memory demands. It's a little like the dancing dog—it is not so much that he dances well, it is enough of a feat that he can dance at all. However, the performance can be greatly offset if the processor that is doing the emulation is intrinsically more powerful.

Software that can take advantage of the PowerPC Architecture (that is, native software) can perform better than software that can't, but the overall performance advantage provided by the PowerPC Architecture allows it to support non-native operating systems and applications with efficiency comparable to the processors for which they were designed.

With the PowerPC Architecture comes the ability to offer both more choices to the users and greater interoperability. To UNIX users, the PowerOpen Association offers the possibility of a clean start. So files, applications, and other resources can be shared—without customization—among users who are accessing those resources through the interface of their choice.

Apple and Operating Systems

The most important fact for the Macintosh user is that System 7 will be the operating system for the first generation of the PowerPC-based Macintosh, so PowerPC-based Macintosh users will be able to use the same operating system (with the same familiar graphical interface) that has been shipping with 680x0 Macintosh systems. On its first three Power Macintosh systems, Apple is installing a ROM-based emulation chip (called the 68LC040) that supports emulation of the existing 680x0-based software.

Apple is revising portions of System 7 to make more native calls to the PowerPC processor, so the new Power Macintosh systems will both take better advantage of the PowerPC processor design and provide additional benefits for applications running on current systems. For instance, the Macintosh Toolbox procedures, such as QuickDraw, will take better advantage of the RISC design.

Some PowerPC-based Macintoshes will also support PowerOpen, which can provide access to the UNIX operating system and the ability to run MS-DOS, A/UX, AIX, or System 7 applications. It is anticipated that this will be the preferred solution for client/server and multiple-user installations.

To support DOS and Windows, Apple is working closely with Insignia Solutions to develop a native PowerPC version of SoftPC, which they call SoftWindows.

System 7 Pro is being updated for the PowerPC. Other capabilities developed as stand-alone system software extensions such as AppleScript and

QuickDraw GX will be available on both 680x0-based and PowerPC-based Macintosh systems.

PowerPC-based Macintoshes will also support AOCE (Apple Open Collaboration Environment) products that run on current Macintosh systems with the updated System 7 Pro. Applications recompiled for the PowerPC Architecture can take further advantage of the increased performance available by running on PowerPC-based systems.

Current Macintosh applications can run on the first PowerPC-based Macintosh models, and developers are rapidly porting their products to the PowerPC platform. In particular, applications that do not require floating-point capability that follow Macintosh programming guidelines should run using 68LC040 emulation. Applications that require floating-point operations must be recompiled, and should run much faster using the faster instruction throughput of the FPUs on PowerPC processors.

A great many software developers, such as Adobe Systems, Inc., ACIUS Inc., Aldus Corporation, Claris Corporation, Deneba Software, Frame Technology, Insignia Solutions, Inc., Microsoft Corporation, Quark Inc., Specular International, and WordPerfect Corporation are preparing native versions of their software to run on PowerPC-based Macintoshes. Apple is actively working with hundreds of other developers to speed the conversion process for other software packages to take full advantage of PowerPC processor performance.

Corporate Macintosh users with custom applications can upgrade their computer installations to PowerPC-based Macintoshes, if those applications adhere to current Macintosh programming guidelines. Developers should make sure that software is 32-bit compliant and should write in ANSI C or C++, ensure that data structures are aligned, isolate and minimize use of low-memory global calls, isolate and eliminate the use of internal Toolbox calls, and isolate dependencies on 80-bit extended-format numeric types. Developers should also not depend on the 680x0 run-time model, specific interrupt levels, and patching traps.

Developers who want to produce native PowerPC applications can choose from among the Apple-provided solutions and a number of third-party solutions. Apple provides a software developer's kit, "Macintosh on PowerPC SDK," which supports editing, compiling, and linking on a 680x0-based Macintosh and execution and debugging on a PowerPC system.

Apple expects the transition to native PowerPC applications to be graceful, and native applications will be released alongside versions that are native for 680x0-based Macintoshes.

Also, PowerPC-based Macintosh systems will continue to support all drivers (including print drivers), INITs, CDEVs, and other utility software.

Although Apple is developing system software that will incorporate preemptive multitasking and protected memory, initial systems will ship with the current System 7, which uses cooperative multitasking without memory protection.

Meanwhile, Apple and IBM continue to promote the development of Taligent, a jointly funded corporation that is creating an object-oriented operating system due in the mid-1990s. Taligent software will run on Apple's PowerPC-based Macintosh systems.

IBM and Operating Systems

IBM's first PowerPC-based systems, four desktop systems released as part of the RISC System/6000 series, take advantage of the 601's POWER compatibility and run the AIX/6000, Version 3.2.5, operating system.

IBM's first systems to take full advantage of the PowerPC Architecture are scheduled to become available in mid-1994. These systems will run Windows NT, AIX, Solaris, and IBM's Workplace OS. The Taligent operating system will be added and possibly a version of Macintosh System 7.

The version of Windows NT that IBM will offer with its PowerPC systems is being developed by IBM and Motorola under a licensing agreement with Microsoft, who will market it to other PowerPC-system designers. The product also will be available in retail stores.

IBM's PowerPC-based systems also will support applications written for 16-bit operating systems, such as DOS, Windows, and MAC, by way of the compatibility support provided by the 32-bit operating systems described earlier.

IBM also is developing the Workplace OS, which will support OS/2 for the PowerPC Reference Platform. DOS and Windows applications will be supported on the Workplace OS using the same type of Multiple Virtual DOS Machines as is provided on OS/2 2.1. For systems running AIX, DOS applications are supported.

AIX and Solaris use the Windows Application Binary Interface (WABI), which combines aspects of emulation with native execution for Windows. Most portions of Windows can achieve native performance.

The PowerPC version of Windows NT supports Windows applications in the same way that other versions of Windows NT do.

MAC applications will be supported on AIX using a MAC emulator, which is an optional component of the PowerOpen environment.

Applications written for 32-bit OS/2 can run natively after being recompiled by using a cross-compiler. A conversion tool is being made available for converting 16-bit calls to 32-bit calls.

The current installed base of AIX applications will run native as will OS/2, Solaris, and Windows NT applications that have been recompiled for the PowerPC Reference Platform.

Initially, UNIX-based systems will run MAC and DOS applications, and Workplace OS-based systems will run DOS and Windows applications at speeds comparable to PCs, although this is very likely to improve as software is updated.

IBM has been actively and successfully recruiting support from among other 32-bit operating system providers and many independent software developers will recompile or otherwise port their applications to run natively on the platform. Because the number of developers is expected to grow, the Power Personal computers will provide strong support for existing 16-bit applications as well as a platform for growth for the personal computer, workstation, and human-centered applications of the future. This software support is an important factor in determining the success of these computers in the marketplace.

The PowerOpen Association

To address the problems that users and developers face in the very disjointed world of UNIX, the three corporations in the PowerPC alliance—Apple, IBM, and Motorola—have joined forces with other companies to ensure a foundation of open systems that will provide both a unified operating system (the PowerOpen environment) and a means of certifying PowerOpen-compliant software.

The problems that PowerOpen seeks to avoid are summed up by Mark Hevesh, PowerOpen marketing manager. "The UNIX world is fractured—independent software vendors who want to penetrate a sizable market have to provide multiple ports. Primarily, it is the software developers who pay. They have to have different proprietary UNIXes and different documentation and different part numbers and inventories. Users have to make decisions. They can either get involved with one particular vendor or they can have a heterogeneous environment, but they have to take extra steps to make things talk to each other or similar applications or the same application residing on different platforms. There's a lot you have to do to make things work."

The PowerOpen Association is an international organization, incorporated by Apple, Bull, IBM, and THOMSON-CSF, in February 1993 with the expressed goal of providing a RISC-based open systems environment, and the association has actively and successfully been recruiting additional members. PowerOpen has produced the PowerOpen Application Binary Interface (ABI) specification, which provides specifications that allow developers to generate products that are binary-compatible. This interface allows system designers independence in choosing a bus interface.

The PowerOpen Environment provides a high-performance platform for users and software developers across the widest range of systems from notebooks to super computers. The PowerOpen environment will allow users to choose a graphical interface based either on Macintosh or on OSF/Motif or a character-based interface.

Figure 4.1 shows the relationships between the PowerOpen programming environment, the PowerOpen ABI, the PowerPC Architecture and the body of applications that will be supported by PowerOpen.

As shown in Figure 4.1, at the lowest level is the PowerPC processor itself. The next level up is the PowerOpen application binary interface, or ABI, which defines the structure of the application in the PowerOpen environment. The ABI defines such low-level elements as linking and loading conventions, object formats, the execution environment, and networking infrastructure.

The next level up is the application programming interface, which defines the set of system calls, library functions, header files, commands, and utilities that an application programmer must use in order to be compliant. The API adheres to common industry standards such as POSIX and X/Open.

Figure 4.1
The PowerOpen
environment.

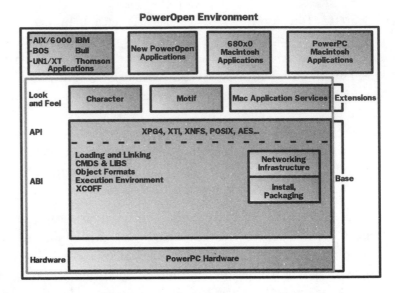

The PowerOpen extensions provide an interface between application programs and the API. The PowerOpen extensions include services, such as OSF/Motif, Macintosh application services, and character-based interfaces, that will allow a variety of different applications to run as if they were in their native environment.

PowerOpen is developing the following resource tools:

- *Verification test suites.* These tools are used to certify both application programs and platforms. Developers can use the application test suite to verify retail software products, and the system vendors can use the platform test suite to verify a large application portfolio.

- *Application Binary Interface (ABI).* The development of the ABI, which defines conventions such as register assignments and other resources not prescribed by the PowerPC Architecture, can allow software developers to generate products that can run on multiple platforms yet remain consistent within the PowerOpen environment.

- *System Information Library.* This will be a publicly available reference library provided for use by system platform developers in creating ABI-compliant operating systems.

IBM's Workplace OS

Workplace OS is a general operating system, designed to be portable to a variety of hardware platforms, that is comprised of the following:

- The IBM Microkernel

- Personality Neutral Services

- Multiple Personalities. Initially, this includes OS/2 and DOS and will later include UNIX.

The portability of the Workplace OS is largely due to its being based on the IBM microkernel—a small nucleus that passes messages to the operating system. The microkernel, which encapsulates processor and system hardware dependencies, supports the surrounding operating system through a set of applications, called servers.

The microkernel supports system services such as virtual memory management, I/O communications, management of interrupts, tasks, and threads.

The initial release provides the functionality of OS/2 2.1. Workplace OS supports any PowerPC processor running at supported frequencies with being proportionate to processor speed and larger internal caches.

Summary

This chapter has looked at the somewhat complicated picture concerning operating system support for PowerPC processors. With the many new OS products on the horizon, it appears that the picture will continue to become more complex in the coming decade. The PowerPC Architecture, however, stands to benefit well from the advances in OS technology.

The next chapter takes a step back and examines the origins of RISC architecture. It traces the technology as it has evolved from being the architecture of choice for high-end workstations to being suitable for a broader range of systems, including general-purpose desktop and portable computers.

Chapter 5

The Genesis of the PowerPC RISC Architecture

This chapter traces the development of RISC architecture, showing the evolution of basic concepts, such as register-to-register operations and the use of simplified, uniform-length instructions. These instructions made it easier to design more efficient processors that could take better advantage of techniques such as instruction parallelism and pipelining.

Mainframes, Microprocessors, and Everything In Between

The one thing about computers that you can take for granted is that you can't take anything for granted. To illustrate that point, consider the ever-narrowing gap between our concepts of mainframe computers and personal computers. Twenty years ago, that gap seemed unbreachable. Mainframe computers were required to do all of the hard work, and the upstart personal computers were but small chips off very monumental blocks. The early personal computers were dedicated to serving their mainframe parents and too puny to ever stand on their own two feet.

The gap between mainframes and microprocessor-powered computers quickly began closing from both sides. On one hand, personal computing has greatly exceeded its perceived potential on virtually every account and has replaced

This chapter discusses major steps in the development of the PowerPC Architecture:

- IBM's seminal experimental design intended for a telephone-switching system

- The first prototype computers developed by IBM and by the academic com-munity

- The first commercially produced RISC processors

the mainframe in many environments. Meanwhile, mainframes, minicomputers, and super computers have taken advantage of transistor miniaturization and other technological leaps.

As higher-end workstations met the need for mainframe computers, many mainframe design principles proved suitable for microprocessor implementations, and many of these principals are embodied in RISC architecture. The PowerPC Architecture stands poised to close the gap.

This chapter traces IBM's development of the RISC processor, from its beginnings as a very special-purpose device, through the experimental 801 minicomputer, to the POWER architecture intended for multiple-chip implementations for high-end workstations and servers. PowerPC Architecture— the culmination of these development efforts—is useful for mainframe-type systems as well as desktop systems and battery-powered, very portable, computers and other devices.

Changing Perspectives: Personal Computing Comes of Age

Twenty years ago, when personal computing was beginning to catch on, it seemed powerful enough to accomplish its intended purpose. The PC was a handy appliance that helped smaller businesses maintain simple databases and perform basic calculations for managing budgets and inventories. Gradually, as prices came down, the personal computer made its way into the home, where it proved a useful tool for writing letters and (maybe even more importantly) playing games.

Twenty years ago, when personal computing was beginning to catch on, the PC was regarded as a handy appliance that helped smaller businesses maintain simple databases and perform basic calculations for managing budgets and inventories. Gradually, as prices came down, the personal computer made its way into the home, where it proved a useful tool for writing letters and (maybe even more importantly) playing games.

Science fiction maintained its love affair with the mainframe and supplied endless images in which the mainframe occupied an entire room, its important-looking lights and banks of reel-to-reel tape storage devices humming soberly as it gnawed away inexorably at some inscrutable master plan.

Some visionaries had big ideas about the role personal computers could play in the future; but these notions, too, were fed as much by science fiction as by science.

For a while, the personal computer remained a stepchild in the computer industry. Space, power, and cost restrictions kept it in its assigned place. Few believed that this little box born with a 640K operating system and a relatively ineffectual 4- or 8-bit address bus would ever challenge the massive, powerful, multiple-user mainframe computers. The limitations of personal computing were many, and each seemed insurmountable. Clock speeds were too slow, and fabrication technology seemed incapable of producing small, affordable, and usable semiconductors. Consider that it wasn't that long ago that 1M of memory cost $1,000, and a 20M hard drive cost twice that much (if you had room on your desk for it).

Personal computers have been closing in on mainframes in stages, and the development of RISC microprocessor architectures has been a critical step in that evolution. Other factors in that evolution include the following:

- The incredible popularity of the personal computer fueled technology in virtually every aspect. Power-hungry users have helped finance much of the miniaturization and competition that now make a more efficient RISC architecture practical for personal computing.

- As the demand for faster processors in personal computers increased, processor designers were forced to place the greatest emphasis on faster clocks, wider data and address buses, and further integration of on-chip resources such as caches and *floating-point units*. Designers also developed more sophisticated methods of working around the basic shortcomings of CISC architectures.

  Floating-point unit (FPU)
  Performs very precise arithmetic for scientific, engineering, and graphical applications. Earlier computers implemented floating-point arithmetic in separate math coprocessor chips.

- Advances in networking made it possible for personal computers to communicate with one another and to share resources. Less-powerful client computers freely connected to faster, more powerful systems to share databases and applications. LAN-based systems proved themselves to be easy-to-manage and expandable.

- Personal computers have largely replaced the dedicated terminals and gateways that provide links between the user and larger host systems.

- Many advanced CPU design techniques developed for mainframe computing were suitable for new microprocessor designs. IBM's seminal efforts in RISC design were picked up by the academic community and quickly gained a broad acceptance. By the late 1980s, RISC processors began to dominate the higher-end workstation market.

■ Further miniaturization and advances in process technology in the second generation of RISC processors made single-chip implementations feasible.

Just as the unexpected popularity of the personal computer has funded technological innovations, it also has presented a critical stumbling block to bringing microprocessor architecture up-to-date. The personal computer industry has prospered by rationing innovation; consumers must pay the price for each small advancement. A wider address bus, a faster clock, or an on-chip math coprocessor represent enough extra computing power to make the last year's model worth considerably less.

Although all processors designed from scratch in the last five years are RISC designs, the CISC philosophy remains at the core of the personal computer. CISC designs, however, have been relegated to remodeling a 20-year-old architecture that is ill-equipped for modern conveniences such as 64-bit addressing, multiprocessing, and on-chip caches, MMUs, and FPUs.

RISC Architecture: Its Mainframe and Minicomputer Ancestry

Execution unit
A unit that executes instructions within the processor. Includes integer units (IUs) to perform integer calculations, and floating-point units (FPUs) to perform floating-point arithmetic.

Although RISC architecture dates back only to the mid-1970s, many of its basic principles came into use a decade earlier. Mainframe, minicomputers, and supercomputers exploited the advantages of parallel processing, pipelining, and register-to-register operations. Most notable in this context is the CDC 6600 supercomputer, built in 1964.

The design of the CDC 6600 represented a radical departure from other computers, and used techniques that are shared by RISC architecture, such as the following:

■ The CDC 6600 strongly emphasized parallel processing, incorporating ten independent *execution units*.

- It incorporated a large complement of registers that provided source and destination operands for arithmetic instructions.

- It limited the number of instruction formats.

- The instruction format provided for nondestructive results (that is, the instructions could specify separate source and destination registers so results didn't automatically overwrite source data).

- It took advantage of instruction pipelining.

Although these techniques do not define RISC architecture, they are techniques that are common to most RISC processors. In many respects these techniques represent the motivation behind the RISC philosophy, which defines instructions and other aspects of processor design in such a way that they can take advantage of such techniques.

In many ways, the CDC 6600 is unlike RISC processors (in particular, the CDC 6600 uses an unusual implicit method of reading and writing to memory and the use of variable-length instructions), but the CDC 6600 convincingly demonstrates the efficiency of a computer design based on the techniques described above.

The CDC 6600 represents a special case in which price mattered less than performance. With a massively parallel organization, the CDC 6600 was intended to eliminate bottlenecks and to be an extremely fast scientific supercomputer. Many of the same techniques we associate with RISC architecture, however, were implemented in other mainframe and minicomputers. The VAX 8600 and 8800 and IBM's System/360 Model 91, for example, implemented pipelining. Many special-purpose computers, such as the ILIAC IV and Thinking Machines' CM-1 and CM-2 demonstrated the advantages of parallel processing.

The development of RISC architecture has run parallel to the trend toward miniaturization that has pervaded every aspect of computers. The design techniques feasible only on mainframe computers in the 1960s were implemented on multiple-chip processors by the 1980s, and in the 1990s, this power has become available to desktop, and even battery-powered, hand-held computers.

The Birth of RISC Architecture—IBM's Phone Switching Computer

Despite its elegant simplicity and its suitability for personal computing implementations, RISC architecture was not created in an attempt to solve the fundamental problems of general-purpose computing or to provide a common architecture for a wide spectrum of processor requirements. Instead, its basic principles arose from an IBM project intended to solve a very specific problem.

In 1974, IBM engineers needed a system to manage a telephone-switching network that could execute more than 20,000 instructions per call and 300 calls per second. No off-the-shelf computer of the period met this sort of real-time design criterion. Without these capabilities, arithmetic operations would quickly pile up waiting to get access to the memory bus to store their results to memory; the memory bus would become a tremendous bottleneck with loads competing with stores.

This latency also affected the ability to perform the arithmetic operation quickly. The arithmetic operation and the store operation were like Siamese twins; when one half encountered a stall, the other half was affected. Chip resources were forced to remain idle when work badly needed to be done.

The phone-switching project had no need for most of the instructions implemented in general-purpose processors. Instead, it required a lean and fast instruction set that performed integer addition, manipulation and combination of bits in registers, loads and stores, and input/output operations. To meet the project's demanding specifications, IBM's designers envisioned a machine with simple instructions and extensive and well-placed, on-chip memory—two fundamental characteristics of RISC technology.

Simpler instructions were more predictable and allowed for more flexible dispatching, execution, and completion schemes. Complicated operations were broken down into simpler tasks. The most significant example of this was the definition of a separate set of instructions that handled all load and store operations. Arithmetic instructions accessed registers to obtain source data and to record results. Having separate load and store instructions helped prevent arithmetic instructions from being affected by time required to access systemn memory, so once the arithmetic was done, the arithmetic logic unit (ALU) was free to begin work on the next arithmetic calculation.

Although tasks required a greater number of instructions, the division of responsibilities enabled the ALU to begin work on a new instruction without waiting for the memory access to complete. More importantly, the new arrangement provided a greater degree of control over memory accesses.

To further reduce the time required to access memory (memory *latency*), the design incorporated separate instruction and data caches on the chip. So competition for the cache did not interfere with instruction-fetching (and vice versa).

Latency
The time taken to perform an operation. Instruction latency is the time taken to execute an instruction. Memory latency is the time taken to access memory.

All instructions in this phone-switching computer were the same length, which greatly simplified many design aspects. For example, all instruction buffers and stages in the processor could be the same size, and sequential instruction fetching and decoding required less logic.

The First Prototype RISC Computers

Although IBM's telephone switching system was never built, IBM's processor designers went on to further explore the possibilities presented by the project. The concept of a fast load/store processor also created excitement in academic circles. By the mid-1970s there were several design projects underway:

- IBM further developed the design principles of its telephone switching system to the design of the IBM 801 minicomputer. The 801 was developed by John Cocke in the mid-1970s at IBM's T. J. Watson Research Center.

- David Patterson and his colleagues at the University of California at Berkeley developed the RISC-I and RISC-II processors (and coined the term RISC).

- John Hennessy and his colleagues at Stanford University were developing the Stanford MIPS machine.

All three projects exploited the principles of IBM's telephone-switching design by taking advantage of simple, fixed-length instructions. (Although the first 801 design did not have fixed-length instructions, the second version had 32-bit-word-length instructions, which greatly simplified decoding and dispatch.) RISC offered an exciting alternative to the prevailing philosophy of processor design, complex instruction-set computing, or CISC, which was suffering from a sort of urban sprawl.

The success of these designs spawned considerable interest on the part of major established computer makers. The university projects brought RISC design principles out of the laboratories and into the research and development efforts of commercial chip manufacturers.

General-purpose registers (GPRs)
Provide an on-chip resource for operands. Load and store instructions transfer data to and from memory; other instructions access these registers as source data and record the execution results.

IBM's second-generation 801 chip developed the processor's emphasis on on-chip registers. For example, in a superscalar processor handling conditional branch instructions requires special care. Whether a branch is taken depends on the results of other instructions, typically recorded in a condition register. For the conditions to be properly recorded, it must appear to do so sequentially, which can create a bottleneck. The 801 was able to base a branching decision on a bit setting in any of the 32 *general-purpose registers (GPRs)*. The state of the condition register could be saved in a GPR, reducing the potential bottleneck. The flexibility of the register design and its focus on reuse (rather than destruction) of register contents became important elements in subsequent designs.

Many types of implementations incorporate RISC design principles. Currently, however, RISC design is most closely associated with a handful of microprocessor manufacturers, (such as IBM, Motorola, Sun Microsystems, Hewlett-Packard, and DEC) whose products are intended mostly for use in high-end workstations.

RISC design continues to mature and take hold in more environments, and RISC designers have capitalized on other technological advances. As manufacturing processes continue to improve and transistor miniaturization makes possible many more transistors per square millimeter, RISC processors have moved from multiple-chip designs to single-chip processors with caches, FPUs, and MMUs on board the same chip. As a result of these advances, RISC design is available to desktop and, with the PowerPC 603 processor, even low-power battery operated systems such as notebook and palm-top computers. Further, the availability of devices with faster response times have made it possible to build chips with higher and higher clock frequencies.

IBM's RS/6000 and the POWER Architecture

Developers quickly applied to commercial products the technological gains that resulted from the 801 research projects. Most important among those products was the RISC System/6000 (or RS/6000) computer announced in 1990. The design of the RS/6000 is worth examination. Many of the principles of its design are incorporated in the PowerPC 601 processor, the first PowerPC chip to be released. More importantly, the RS/6000 implements the POWER architecture, which is the basis of the PowerPC Architecture.

The POWER architecture has the following fundamental RISC criteria:

- The POWER ISA consists of uniform-length instructions with simple and consist encodings.

- The POWER instructions perform simple, multi-purpose operations that generally have the same instruction latency.

- All arithmetic instructions use a large complement of registers for source operands and for storing results.

- The POWER ISA includes a separate set of load/store instructions that transfer data between memory and the general-purpose register files.

- The POWER ISA implements relatively simple addressing modes.

- The POWER ISA uses non-destructive instruction formats that provide separate registers for multiple source operands (usually two) and the destination operand.

The designers of the RS/6000 incorporated in its design principles many of the lessons learned from the 801 project. To answer the needs of scientific and graphical applications, however, the RS/6000 incorporates a floating-point processor chip (FPU) that is tightly interlocked with the *branch processing unit* (BPU) and the *integer unit* (IU). Although the FPU may seem out of place in a RISC processor design, it is essential for meeting the demands of scientific and graphics-intensive software applications and has become a common feature in RISC designs.

Branch processing unit (BPU)
Handles operations to process branch instructions. BPUs test conditions that determine when a branch is taken; some implement sophisticated branch prediction mechanisms.

Integer unit (IU)
An execution unit that performs integer arithmetic. Performs fixed-point arithmetic, such as required for financial calculations.

Exception
An event that occurs when a problem or special situation occurs that requires special handling by the operating system.

Most of the instructions in the POWER instruction set are simple, single-cycle instructions that do not duplicate functionality (that is, the instruction set is largely orthogonal). The POWER architecture also includes several special-purpose instructions:

- *Load/store string/multiple instructions*. These instructions provide an efficient way to save and restore registers during context-switching and *exception* handling.

- *Floating-point accumulate instructions*. These instructions perform floating-point multiply-add, multiply-subtract, negative-multiply-add, and negative-multiply-subtract operations. These instructions are particularly useful for matrix algebra, because they perform both a multiply and an add operation in half of the time required to execute separate multiply and add instructions. Further, because rounding occurs only once (instead of twice, as in the case of separate instructions), greater accuracy is maintained.

- Instructions for manipulating bits within registers.

- Optional updating of the condition register by certain integer and floating-point instructions.

Figure 5.1 shows a block diagram of the RS/6000 processor.

Figure 5.1
RS/6000 Block Diagram.

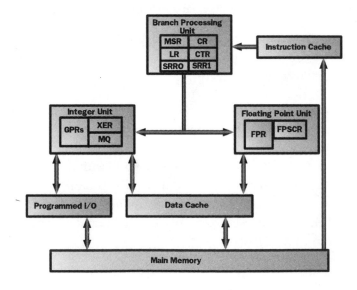

Figure 5.1 shows instructions can be fetched from the instruction cache and dispatched in pairs to the two execution units (the IU and FPU). The FPU and IU are shown to contain the registers that are most closely associated with floating-point and integer operations, respectively. The most important of these of course are the 32 FPRs, which hold source and destination operands for floating-point instructions, and the 32 GPRs, which provide source and destination operands for integer operations. The FPU is pipelined so that a series of floating-point instructions can execute with a throughput of one instruction every other clock cycle. Although such techniques as pipelining and superscalar dispatch are not intrinsic to the definition of RISC, they are a common design goal. The POWER architecture is explicitly intended to facilitate superscalar implementations.

In a manner similar to the 801, the RS/6000 implements a Harvard architecture cache design—that has separate instruction and data caches. The PowerPC Architecture is also designed to permit both Harvard-architecture and unified cache implementations.

Having separate instruction and data caches allows each cache to be optimized according to the respective needs of data and instructions. For example, since all instructions are the same size, the cache system can be designed with that in mind; data caches, however, may contain data in various sizes (bytes, half-words, words, and double words), which may require a more complex implementation. Also, typically only the instruction fetching mechanism needs to read an instruction cache, while many resources on the chip (such as the FPU, the IU, and the memory management unit) require access to data.

Using separate caches reduces contention for cache resources; instruction fetches do not need to compete with load/store instructions to the data cache.

The RS/6000 incorporates the 801's flexible implementation of the condition register. Instead of saving the register to a GPR, however, the POWER architecture divides the 32-bit condition register into eight, four-bit fields. The first field is used by integer instructions, and the second is used by floating-point instructions. The values in those two fields can be saved to the remaining four-bit fields. The PowerPC Architecture implements the condition register in the same way.

POWER and PowerPC

The PowerPC Architecture is modeled closely on the POWER architecture, and IBM's first PowerPC-based systems are an extension of their RS/6000 series. The transition to the PowerPC Architecture has been largely a matter of adapting POWER features for single-chip implementations and providing a flexible architectural definition that will enable a smooth transition to subsequent generations of PowerPC-based computers.

The PowerPC Architecture adopts the POWER programming model; it uses the same instruction encoding schemes, effective address generation, and nondestructive instruction format.

Although it does not implement a number of POWER instructions, the PowerPC Architecture is designed to guarantee compatibility with POWER applications. The PowerPC Architecture follows essentially the same model as the POWER architecture. For example, the BPU is incorporated into the instruction unit, and the integer and floating-point units are tightly coupled to support superscalar dispatch and parallel execution. Moreover, the PowerPC floating-point and integer instruction set remains close to that of the POWER architecture. For example, the floating-point instruction set definition favors a model in which the multiply-add instructions for the basis for other operations. Both the POWER and the PowerPC Architectures support the industry-standard specifications for floating-point operations defined by the Institute of Electrical and Electronic Engineers (IEEE). This standard (referred to as IEEE 754) defines how floating-point numbers are represented in memory, how numbers are rounded, and other details regarding floating-point arithmetic.

Other modifications to the POWER architecture include the following:

- The definition of the programming model and instruction set to include 64-bit addressing. This definition supports 64-bit (double-word) data for integer instructions and requires some registers to be widened to accommodate 64-bit addresses and data types (in particular the GPRs, the link register, and several of the registers used to save and restore the processor state when exceptions are taken and control is passed to the operating system).

- This definition allows the processor to improve performance by offering a more flexible set of rules for bus operations. For example, load and store accesses do not need to occur in program order—this is referred to as a weakly-ordered storage model.

- The ability to perform single-precision floating-point calculations. The POWER architecture supports only double-precision arithmetic.

- The removal of several of the more complex instructions, such as the Load String and Compare Byte instruction.

- The definition of bits (in the machine state register) to configure the processor to perform big- and little-endian byte ordering.

- The definition of resources to support power-saving modes for battery-powered implementations.

Note

The relation between POWER and PowerPC is discussed in greater detail in Chapter 11, "The RS/6000 POWER Connection."

Summary

This chapter has provided a brief history of RISC processing, emphasizing in particular how the development of this technology is closing the gap between mainframes and personal computers.

The next chapter takes a closer look at the PowerPC Architecture. Some of the technical information discussed include the three levels of the PowerPC Architecture, the differences between 32- and 64-bit implementation, and the nature of the architecture.

Chapter 6

Building a Flexible RISC Architecture

If you ask most computer users if they can identify the architecture that their computer uses, most users say they don't know, and a few might tell you the name of the chip used in their system, or the name of the computer manufacturer. Very few people know the answer.

This chapter provides a general overview of aspects of the PowerPC Architecture that are described more thoroughly in subsequent chapters. Some of the technical information discussed includes the three levels of the PowerPC Architecture, the differences between 32- and 64-bit implementation, and the nature of the architecture.

The notion of an architecture is far removed from everyday computing. The architecture is the framework, the underlying conceptual rules for making the machine that the chip maker, the system designer, the programmer, and the user set into motion. Architecture is so pervasive that it seems invisible.

Architectures can be flexible or specific and rigid. If an architectural definition is too rigid, performance improvements become much more expensive when the architecture is outgrown. The cost of implementing a wider bus, or of incorporating an on-chip math coprocessor into an architecture not intended for them, typically requires complicated solutions. Moreover, if the architecture is too restrictively designed, it is much more difficult to maintain software compatibility with previous generations of processors, some of which are long extinct.

With that in mind, the PowerPC Architecture is designed to be flexible enough to allow ease of implementation across a wide range of

This chapter teaches you about the following:

- The PowerPC register set
- Memory conventions
- The PowerPC instruction set
- The PowerPC exception model
- The PowerPC cache model
- The PowerPC memory management model

price/performance trade-offs, as well as to provide a graceful means of taking the next major step to a 64-bit addressing scheme. So, the PowerPC Architecture says little about the actual hardware required in a PowerPC processor— rather, it defines the instructions and various conceptual models to which each implementation should adhere.

In particular, the PowerPC Architecture is a RISC architecture that defines conventions to ensure software compatibility among applications written for the range of PowerPC-compatible devices using a single-chip microprocessor. Notice that the PowerPC Architecture does not preclude the possibility of multiple-chip processor designs.

Design Criteria

The PowerPC Architecture was designed to provide an efficient and practical design platform across a wide range of implementations, from battery-powered hand-held devices and embedded controllers to main-frame-style multiprocessing implementations. With these goals in mind, the PowerPC architects began recasting the POWER architecture, which was created for multi-chip implementations in IBM's RISC System/ 6000 workstations, into an architecture more suitable for a broader range of single-chip implementations.

Flexibility of the PowerPC Architecture Specification

One of the most significant characteristics of the PowerPC Architecture is its flexibility. This flexibility is important for several reasons:

- A flexible architecture offers a wider assortment of price/performance trade-offs while still software compatibe.

- Flexibility allows the subsequent generations of processors to take better advantage of technological advances, both predicted and not predicted.

- The PowerPC Architecture is scalable; it includes specifications for both 32- and 64-bit implementations to ensure software compatibility between today's 32-bit PowerPC processors and the next generation of 64-bit processors.

■ Similarly, the PowerPC ISA is defined in such a way that binary compatibility is ensured with existing AIX software provided for POWER-based RS/6000 workstations.

Perhaps the most noteworthy aspect of the flexibility of the PowerPC Architecture is the inclusion of both 32- and 64-bit definitions, ensuring that applications written for 32-bit processors run on 64-bit processors without enforcing awkward and restrictive backward-compatibility solutions as the demands for 64-bit addressing increase. This also greatly simplifies the design of the next generation of processors.

The Three Levels of the PowerPC Architecture

Another aspect of the PowerPC Architecture's flexibility is that it is defined in three levels:

■ *The user instruction set architecture (UISA).* This includes the user application-level instructions and the registers accessed by these instructions. The UISA also defines instruction-related parameters, such as addressing modes and instruction formats.

■ *The virtual environment architecture (VEA).* The VEA defines aspects of the memory model—especially the cache model—and the time base. The VEA defines resources primarily used by compilers.

■ *The operating environment architecture (OEA).* The OEA defines the memory management model, and the exception model. The OEA defines resources used primarily by operating systems.

Implementations are allowed to adhere to the architecture at different levels. An implementation can be UISA-compatible without complying to the other levels. Likewise, a VEA-compliant implementation need not adhere to the OEA, but it must adhere to the UISA for parallel construction.

Because the PowerPC Architecture is intended for a broader range of implementations than was the POWER architecture (which is intended primarily for high-powered workstations), the PowerPC Architecture implements an additional set of single-precision floating-point instructions. Typically, single-precision floating point instructions have a shorter execution latency than their double-precision counterparts. This provides faster floating-point operation when accuracy is less important than speed.

The PowerPC Architecture also provides additional space in the instruction set for implementation-specific instructions, additional register space for implementation-specific special-purpose registers, and additional space in the exception vector table for implementation-specific exceptions.

> **Note**
>
> The PowerPC allows optional implementation of certain bits within registers and functionality of some exceptions.

Another way in which the PowerPC Architecture is flexible lies in the variable role that software and hardware can play in the implementations. For example, the FPU is tightly linked in the design, and some implementations can choose to implement all floating-point instructions and every aspect of execution, such as rounding and denormalization, in hardware. However, PowerPC processors intended for less number-intensive systems can be designed so that some or all floating-point instructions are implemented wholly or partially in software. Also, the architecture (OEA) defines exceptions for certain conditions, however, an implementation may choose to handle the condition in hardware instead of invoking an exception handler. For example, the 601 processor handles certain alignment conditions in hardware that are allowed to cause exceptions in other PowerPC processors.

> **Note**
>
> Also, the 601 processor performs all page translation table search operations in hardware, whereas the 603, which has a more streamlined and lower-power design intended for portable implementations, uses software to do this, and defines additional register resources and exceptions to perform this task.

Much of the flexibility of the PowerPC Architecture lies in what it does not specify. For example, the architecture does not specify bus signals or bus protocol, although it is likely that many implementations will use a similar set of signals, as is the case with the 601 and 603 processors. This is not prescribed by the architecture. The architecture can refer to a signal in a general way, as is the case for certain signal-driven interrupt exceptions. It is left to the designers of a particular implementation to specify the signal or signals that trigger the exception.

Along with the system interface, the architecture specifies other hardware aspects only in the most general sense. Although the architecture defines, in a general way, the cache implementation and instructions that are used with controlling a split-cache implementation, it does not specify the size, the set associativity, whether a unified cache is employed, and in fact whether a cache is implemented at all. Also, although it is anticipated that most processors employ *snooping* and the MESI *cache coherency* protocol, this is not prescribed by the architecture.

The flexibility of the architecture is clearly illustrated by the cache implementations of the 601 and the 603 processors. The 601 implements a unified 32KB, eight-way set associative unified cache, whereas the 603 implements separate 8KB two-way set associate caches. The 601, which is intended for both single and multiple processor systems, provides separate ports into the cache tag arrays to prevent snooping from interfering with other bus activity; whereas the 603, which is intended for single processor systems, has less hardware support for snooping than the 601 does and enforces only a subset of the MESI protocol. (The 601 does not support the shared state (S), because a cache block is never shared by multiple processors.)

Other Internal Microarchitecture Issues

The PowerPC Architecture does not prescribe which execution unit is responsible for executing a particular instruction. It also does not define details regarding the instruction fetching mechanism, how instructions are decoded and dispatched, and how write-back is handled. Dispatch and write-back can occur in or out of order. Also, although the architecture specifies certain registers, such as the GPRs and FPRs used for providing source and destination operands for integer and floating-point instruction, respectively, some implementations may choose to implement rename registers to reduce the impact of register contention.

The PowerPC Architecture was designed according to the following criteria:

- The PowerPC Architecture follows the methodology of RISC architecture; arithmetic instructions use a large complement of register files as source and destination operands (GPRs for integer instructions and FPRs for floating-point instructions).

- Separate instructions are implemented for integer and floating-point load and store operations. These instructions carry data (in byte to double-word length units) between memory (caches or system memory) and the register files.

Snooping
A means by which cache coherency is enforced in a multiprocessor system. When an address for a memory access is put on the memory bus, other caches snoop that address to see if it is a reference to data in its cache. If the address is not there (a snoop miss), the snooping cache does require any action.

Cache coherency
A term used to indicate that all caching devices that share external memory have an accurate view of memory.

- Instructions are of uniform length with uniformly short latencies.

- Instructions are mostly simple and the instruction set is largely orthogonal. There are relatively few addressing modes and instruction formats are consistent.

- Instructions employ nondestructive addressing modes for arithmetic instructions in which the second and third (and rarely a fourth) operand, specify source registers, and the destination is specified by the first operand.

Certainly, a central motivation for designing a RISC architecture is to allow implementations to take advantage of more efficient strategies of instruction processing—in particular, superscalar dispatch, parallel processing, and instruction pipelining.

Although it is important to note that the PowerPC Architecture definition is deliberately flexible and does not specify hardware details for each implementation, the PowerPC ISA is designed according to a conceptual model, shown in Figure 6.1. The ISA is formed around this model, ensuring that superscalar dispatch, parallel processing, and other optimizing schemes are at the basis of the architectural design.

In the past decade, compiler technology has improved such that compiler designers can reschedule code to take fullest advantage of these design considerations. This efficiency is passed on to user-level applications.

Figure 6.1

The PowerPC Architecture conceptual processor model showing the role of parallel execution in the architectural design.

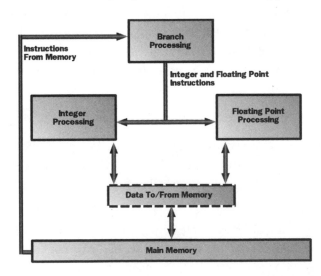

As shown in Figure 6.1, the branch processing unit (BPU) is closely tied with the instruction unit. This allows a wide range of schemes to minimize the effect on throughput caused by branch instructions. Uniform instruction length makes it easier to buffer instructions, which in turn makes it easier to perform branch look-ahead operations.

The BPU can quickly provide the branch target instruction address when a branch is predicted taken, or fetch from the correct instruction path when a branch prediction is incorrect. The ISA also provides for a variety of branch prediction mechanisms, and, in particular, the architecture specifies a programmable bit in conditional branch encodings for static branch prediction.

Note

The architecture allows, but does not prescribe, various speculative branch operations, such as dispatch, decoding, and execution.

The processor model (see fig. 6.1) includes two execution units, which are issued instructions using a superscalar dispatch mechanism. This model specifies a floating-point unit (FPU) and an integer unit (IU), although the architecture does not prescribe the hardware definition of individual implementations. Implementations can have more instruction units; such as a separate load/store unit (LSU), or additional FPUs or IUs, or a processor may choose not to implement either (or both!) the FPU or IU in hardware. For example, some implementations may be geared toward systems that do not require floating-point capabilities (like many older CISC processors). These processors must, however, support all floating-point instructions in software in order to be PowerPC compliant.

The processor model includes a tightly-coupled FPU, even though, in the strictest definition, a dedicated FPU strays somewhat from the single-clock latency instructions of a purely RISC architecture. However, because of the widespread and growing demand to perform floating-point operations in graphical and scientific applications (a demand that is spreading to lower-end systems as more audio-visual resources become popular), the PowerPC Architecture (and the POWER architecture for that matter) assumes a closely integrated FPU. The FPU conceptually incorporates the FPRs, which provide source and destination operands for floating-point instructions (both arithmetic and load store instructions). Again, it is important to note that the architecture does not prescribe that the FPRs physically reside in the FPU because implementations may implement multiple FPUs or additional execution units that need ready access to the FPRs. The FPU defines support for IEEE 754 floating-point operations, although processors have the option of implementing a non-IEEE mode for faster performance.

Perhaps even more important is that the PowerPC Architecture does not even require that the FPU be implemented in hardware. For example, the price/performance criteria of a particular implementation can make it practical to execute floating-point instructions partially— or entirely—in software.

The instruction set includes several floating-point "accumulate" instructions:

- Floating-Point Multiply Add

- Floating-Point Multiply Subtract

- Negative Floating-Point Multiply Add

- Negative Floating-Point Multiply Subtract

These operations performed by these instructions are basic to matrix algebra, which is an integral part of the kind of computations that are required by graphical, engineering, and scientific applications.

These instructions distinctly diverge from the basic RISC concepts, such as simple primitive instructions and instruction-set orthogonality. However, they are incorporated in the PowerPC Architecture (and in the POWER architecture) because the FPU is implemented in such a way that these instructions have the same latency as other floating-point instructions, at little additional hardware expense, and because they shorten the instruction path. That is, this compound instruction can execute two operations in half of the time it takes to perform these operations as separate floating-point multiply and floating-point add instructions.

Moreover, because rounding occurs only once, the results of the single instruction are more accurate than those of separate instructions. Note again, that although it may be common among PowerPC processors to implement an FPU that provides single-cycle throughput for these instructions, the architecture does not prescribe this design.

The integer unit (see fig. 6.1) operates in parallel with the FPU and incorporates the GPRs, used for calculating addresses for both integer and floating-point load/store instructions.

The PowerPC Architecture also assumes a weakly-ordered memory model. Loads and stores can occur out of order, which reduces the restrictions and memory latency of a strongly-ordered interface. To support this type of bus operation, the architecture defines a set of synchronized instructions when strongly-ordered operations are necessary.

Because load and store operations can occur out of order, these operations can be prioritized. For example, the 601 and 603 processors can be configured to give certain cache-to-memory store operations higher priority over conventional loads and stores.

Like the POWER architecture, the PowerPC Architecture defines a Harvard-style cache implementation—separate caches for instructions and data. The architecture (VEA and OEA) defines additional instructions to perform address-only operations that can selectively invalidate, flush, or clear instruction or data caches. These instructions are especially useful in multiprocessor implementations.

The architecture provides additional cache "touch" instructions that can be used (typically by a compiler) to make data available to a processor's cache before it is actually requested by a program. These instructions generate low-priority bus transactions that occur only if the bus is otherwise idle. This way, when the instruction that needs the data is available, there is no need to wait for the memory access. Touch operations are low-priority because any advantages gained by getting this data early would be lost if explicitly requested bus activity is affected. These instructions do not cause exceptions if there is an error related to the bus activity, and may be implemented as no-ops on some PowerPC processors.

The architecture also makes other provisions for multiprocessor implementations, such as aspects of coherency. For example, the architecture allows blocks and pages of memory to be configured as write-back or write-through, cacheable or noncacheable, and coherency enforced or not enforced. Another bit indicates whether the block or page is guarded. The architecture also defines a pair of load/store with reservation instructions, used as primitives for various operations (such as "test and set"), that are useful in multiprocessor implementations.

One of the major obstacles to compatibility in the PC world lies in a very subtle fact. Typically, the smallest unit of data that can be accessed from memory is the byte, and this is the unit with which data is addressed.

However, data can be stored in various-sized data types. For example, PowerPC instructions are each one word (four-bytes) long. Floating-point operands can be either 32-bit (for single-precision values) or 64-bit (for double-precision values). Systems can arrange the bytes in memory in one of two different ways:

- The byte can be placed in the most-significant byte position (big-endian). This is the typical configuration for a PowerPC processor.

- The byte can be placed in the least-significant byte position (little-endian).

The PowerPC Architecture allows the processor to be configured in either big- or little-endian mode, a feature of critical importance for compatibility among existing hardware and software. For example, this allows PowerPC systems to be configured to support Windows NT, which is designed for little-endian systems.

The PowerPC Architecture Definition

The PowerPC Architecture defines the following aspects of processor design:

- *Instruction set*. The PowerPC Architecture defines the functionality, instruction size, encodings, address modes, and other aspects of the instruction set.

- *Programming model*. The programming model provides the programmer with a consistent conceptual model that ensures compatibility among PowerPC processors. The PowerPC Architecture defines the registers used for instruction execution, exception handling, memory management, and time keeping. The programming model also defines conventions for how data is store in memory and details regarding the bit- and byte-ordering.

- *Memory model*. The memory model defines the size of addressable memory and memory attributes as they pertain to cache implementations (such as whether memory is defined as write-back or write-through, cacheable or noncacheable, and whether coherency is enforced). The memory model also defines operating system-level

memory management unit (MMU) resources that determine how
logical-to-physical address translations are performed, and what
mechanisms are used for saving and searching for address translations.

- *Exception model*. The exception model defines the PowerPC exceptions
  and the conditions that cause them. Each exception is assigned a specific vector offset, and each exception defines how register contents are
  saved.

Notice that the definitions for these parameters typically fall into more than
one level of the architecture. For example, the UISA, VEA, and OEA each
define instructions and registers.

The Levels of the PowerPC Architecture

The PowerPC Architecture is defined in three levels, which correspond to
three programming environments.

User Instruction Set Architecture (UISA)

UISA defines the user-level instruction set and registers used by those instructions, such as the FPRs and GPRs that are used for source and destination
operands, the count, link, and condition registers (which are used for branch
instructions), and the integer exception register and the floating-point status
and control registers used by integer and floating-point instructions. The
UISA also defines addressing modes, instruction encoding, and instruction
formats.

Virtual Environment Architecture (VEA)

The VEA defines the cache model and specifies the memory model for a multiprocessor environment. The VEA also defines the time-keeping facility—the
time base—from a user perspective.

Operating Environment Architecture (OEA)

The OEA specifies the model for PowerPC memory management units, for
which it provides several register resources, such as the Block Address Translation registers (which define characteristics of memory blocks), the segment
registers, and others. The other important specification included in the OEA

is the exception model. The OEA also provides a mechanism for writing to the time-base facility.

Implementations are allowed to adhere to the architecture at different levels. An implementation can be UISA-compatible without complying to the other levels. Likewise, a VEA-compliant implementation need not adhere to the OEA, but must adhere to the UISA.

64-Bit and 32-Bit Architecture Definitions

The PowerPC Architecture is defined for both 32-bit and 64-bit addressing.

The 32-bit PowerPC architectural provides 32-bit effective addresses and 32-bit integer data types. In the 32-bit implementation, all registers are 32-bits wide, except for the FPRs, which are 64-bits wide. The memory model defines a 52-bit virtual address space and uses segment registers instead of the segment table.

The 64-bit extension to the PowerPC Architecture definition provides 64-bit effective addresses and 64-bit integer data types. Several of the registers are 64-bits wide, in particular the GPRs (which hold 64-bit integer values), the MSR, and all registers that are required to hold addresses (such as SRR0, the link register, and SDR1). The 64-bit architectural definition provides a somewhat different MMU model to allow for 64-bit addressing, including an 80-bit virtual address space and the ASR (which holds the physical address of the segment table).

Note

The 64-bit architectural definition includes additional instructions, most of which are integer instructions that take advantage of the double-word data types. There also are instructions used in conjunction with the 64-bit MMU model to control segment lookaside buffers.

The 64-bit definition also provides a 32-bit mode, which is enabled by clearing MSR[SF]. This mode allows software written for 32-bit implementations to run on 64-bit implementations. All instructions provided for 64-bit implementations are available in both 64- and 32-bit modes.

PowerPC Register Set

The programming model incorporates 32 GPRs, 32 FPRs, special-purpose registers (SPRs), and several miscellaneous registers. Likewise, each implementation can have its own unique set of hardware implementation (HID) registers.

PowerPC processors have two levels of privilege that roughly correspond with the levels of the architecture. All instructions and registers defined by the UISA are accessed by user-level software. The VEA provides user-level read access to the time base registers. The remaining registers, all defined by the OEA, are accessed only by supervisor-level software (typically operating systems). These registers include registers with exception handling (saving and restoring registers and condition determination), memory management (segment registers, block address translation (BAT) registers, and the table search descriptor register 1 (SDR1)). The OEA also defines the clocking-related registers, the decrementer register (DEC), and the supervisor-definition of the time-base registers (which are read by user-level software, but are written to only by supervisor level software).

User-Level Registers

All UISA registers can be accessed by all software with either user or supervisor privileges. The user-level register set includes the following:

■ Registers that support integer operations:

General Purpose Registers (GPRs)

Integer Exception Register (XER)

■ Registers that support floating-point operations:

Floating-Point Registers (FPRs)

Floating-Point Status and Control Register (FPSCR)

■ Registers that support branch operations:

Condition Register (CR)

Link Register (LR)

Count Register (CTR)

Some registers are accessed explicitly either as operands (such as the GPRs and FPRs) or as a side-effect of instruction execution (such as the XER, FPSCR, and CR). Some registers, identified as special-purpose registers, or SPRs, are read or written to explicitly by using a Move from Special-Purpose Register (mfspr) instruction or Move to Special-Purpose Register (mtspr) instruction. These include the LR, CTR, and XER.

Registers that Support Branch Processing

The *condition register* (CR) is defined as a 32-bit register in both 32- and 64-bit implementations and is modeled after the CR defined in the POWER architecture. The CR reflects the results of certain arithmetic operations to provide a mechanism for testing and branching. Like the CR defined by the POWER architecture, the PowerPC Architecture divides the CR into eight four-bit fields, CR0 through CR7, to reduce the effects of contention and to increase flexibility. Bits in the CR are set implicitly by CR update forms of integer and floating-point instructions, indicated by a period at the end of the instruction. The first three bits of CR0 are set by an algebraic comparison of the result to zero and the fourth bit of CR0 is copied from XER[SO]. Update forms of floating-point instructions set bits in the CR1 field (bits 4 through 7) using bits 0 through 3 of the FPSCR to provide information about floating-point exception conditions.

The CR also can be altered by the following instructions:

- Integer or floating-point compare instructions can specify a CR field to store the result.

- Move to Condition Register Field instructions (mtcrf) updates CR fields by writing bits from a specified GPR.

- Move to Condition Register from XER instructions (mcrxr) updates a specified CR field by writing bits from the XER.

- Move to Condition Register from FPSCR instructions (mcrfs) updates a specified CR field by writing bits from the FPSCR.

- Move Condition Register Field instructions (mtcrf) move data from one CRx field to another.

- Condition register logical instructions perform logical operations on individual bits.

The bits in the CR are interpreted by branch conditional (bc), Branch Conditional to Link Register (bclr), and Branch Conditional to Count Register (bcctr) instructions, which specify one of the bits (with the BI operand in the instruction) in the CR as the branching condition. The target instruction is specified either as an operand, as in bc instructions, or by an address in the LR or CTR by the bclr and bcctr instructions, respectively.

The link register (SPR8) provides the branch target address for the Branch Conditional to Link Register (bclr) instruction, and can optionally be used to hold the logical address of the instruction that follows a branch and link instruction, typically used for linking to subroutines. Because the LR must hold addresses, it is 32 bits wide in 32-bit implementations and 64 bits wide in 64-bit implementations.

The count register (SPR9) can hold a loop count that is decremented during execution of Branch Conditional or Branch Conditional To Link Register instruction (this is specified by selecting a value of the BO operand such that BO[2] = 0). The CTR can also hold the branch target address for the Branch Conditional to Count Register (bcctr) instruction. Like the LR, because the CTR must hold an address, it is 64 bits wide in 64-bit implementations and 32 bits wide in 32-bit implementations.

Registers that Support Integer Operations

The integer unit contains (at least conceptually) thirty-two general purpose registers (GPRs) designated as GPR0 through GPR31. The GPRs are 32 or 64 bits wide depending on the implementation. Integer instructions specify a destination operand (using the format **r**A) or source operands (**r**B and **r**C and occasionally **r**D), where A, B, C, and D refer to a number 0 through 31. The architecture does not define conventions that assign specific programming functions to particular registers.

The integer exception register XER (SPR1) registers overflow and carries for integer operations. It is set implicitly by many computational instructions when overflow or carries occur. The mcrxr instruction is used to copy the value in the XER to a field in the condition register.

Registers that Support Floating-Point Operations

The floating-point register (FPR) file consists of thirty-two 64-bit FPRs designated as FPR0 through FPR31, which serves as the data source or destination for all floating-point instructions. These registers can contain data objects of either single- or double-precision floating-point format.

The floating-point status and control register (FPSCR) is a user-level register that contains all floating-point exception signal bits, exception summary bits, exception enable bits, and rounding control bits needed for compliance with the IEEE 754 standard.

Time-Base Registers (User-Level Readable)

The time-base registers are defined by the VEA and OEA. The VEA defines how the registers are read, and the OEA defines how the registers are written. The two 32-bit time-base registers (TBU and TBL) together form a 64-bit counter that contains a 64-bit unsigned integer value. This value is incremented at a frequency determined by each implementation. These registers are read by using the mftb instruction.

Supervisor-Level Registers

The registers that are accessed only by supervisor-level software are all defined by the OEA. These registers are used by the operating system for system configuration and in conjunction with memory management, exception handling, and time keeping. All of these registers except the MSR and the segment registers are SPRs.

- System Configuration and Status

    Machine State Register (MSR)

- Registers Used for Exception Handling

    Machine Status Save/Restore Register 0 (SRR0)

    Machine Status Save/Restore Register 1 (SRR1)

    DAE/Source Instruction Service Register (DSISR)

    Data Address Register (DAR)

- Registers Used for Memory Management

    Segment Registers

    Table Search Descriptor Register 1 (SDR1)

    Address Space Register (ASR)

    BAT Registers (IBATs and DBATs)

■ Registers Used for Time Keeping

> Time Base Registers (TBU and TBL)
>
> Decrementer Register (DEC)

■ Miscellaneous Registers

> General SPRs (SPRG0_SPRG3)
>
> External Access Register (EAR)
>
> Processor Version Register (PVR)

The machine state register (MSR), which is 64-bits wide in 64-bit implementations and 32-bits wide in 32 bit implementations, is used to configure the processor. For example, it contains bits that determine whether byte addressing is big- or little-endian, whether floating-point exceptions are treated as precise, imprecise, or disabled, whether decrementer and external interrupt exceptions are masked, and if machine check and system reset exceptions are enabled. The MSR is modified by the Move to Machine State Register (mtmsr), System Call (sc), and Return from Exception (rfi) instructions. It is read by the Move from Machine State Register (mfmsr) instruction. When an exception occurs, bits from the MSR are saved to the machine status save/restore register 1 (SRR1).

Registers Used for Exception Handling

The machine status save/restore register 0 (SRR0) SRR0 register (SPR26) is used for saving machine status on exceptions and restoring machine status when an rfi instruction is executed. Typically, when an exception occurs, SRR0 contains the next instruction to be executed after the exception handling is complete. This may be either the instruction that caused the exception or next instruction in program order. This register is 64 bits wide in 64-bit implementations and 32 bits wide in 32-bit implementations.

The machine status save/restore register 1 (SRR1) (SPR27) is used to save bits from the MSR as well as implementation-specific information when an exception occurs. This information is restored when an rfi instruction is executed. This register is 64 bits wide in 64-bit implementations and 32 bits wide in 32-bit implementations.

The DAE/source instruction service register (DSISR) (SPR18) identifies the instruction that caused an alignment for data access exceptions, the

DSISR indicates the type of exception. The DSISR is 32-bits wide in all implementations.

The Data address register (DAR) (SPR19) holds the effective address generated by the instruction that caused a data access or an alignment exception.

The General SPRs (SPRG0-SPRG3) registers (SPR272-SPR275) are provided for operating system use, typically as a scratch register or for holding addresses that point to memory space to be used by an exception handler. Because these registers are expected to hold addresses, are 32 bits wide in 32-bit implementations and 64 bits wide in 64-bit implementation.

Registers Used for Memory Management

Segment registers (SR) are 32-bit implementations of the PowerPC Architecture that implement sixteen 32-bit segment registers (SR0-SR15). The fields in the segment register are interpreted differently depending on the value of SR[T] (bit 0), but in general they contain information about access-level protection, and typically hold the virtual segment ID.

The table search descriptor register (1SDR1) register (SPR25) specifies the page-table base address for virtual-to-physical address translation.

The address space register (ASR) register (SPR280) holds the 64-bit physical address of the segment table in 64- bit implementations.

Block-address translation (BAT) registers. The OEA defines four pairs of instruction BATs (IBAT0U-IBAT3U and IBAT0L-IBAT3L), designated as SPR528-SPR535; and four pairs of data block-address translation registers (DBAT0U-DBAT3U and DBAT0L-DBAT3L), designated as SPR536-SPR543. These registers hold information about memory configuration and protection.

Registers Used for Time Keeping

The Decrementer register (DEC) (SPR22) is a 32-bit decrementing counter. A decrementer exception occurs after the value in the DEC register changes from all zeroes to all ones. The value in the DEC is set by using the mtspr instruction. Each implementation determines the decrementer frequency as a subdivision of the processor clock.

The time base registers (TBU and TBL) are used to maintain a running count from which the time-of-day can be determined. The OEA specifies the supervisor-level portion of the time-base facility and defines the supervisor-level

SPRs-TBU (SPR284) and TBL (SPR285). The time-base counter is written only by supervisor-level software, but can be read by user-level software.

Miscellaneous and Optional SPRs
The processor version register (PVR) (SPR286) is a read-only register that identifies the processor's version (model) and revision level.

The external access register (EAR) (SPR282) is an optional register that supports the optional eciwx and ecowx instructions.

Hardware Implementation Registers
The PowerPC Architecture defines SPR register space for each processor to define registers for specific, implementation-specific purposes. For example, the 603 defines registers to support the power-saving modes. Note that some of these registers are common among PowerPC processors even though they are not defined by the PowerPC Architecture.

Data Organization in Memory and Data Transfers

Bytes are numbered consecutively starting with 0. Each number is the address of the corresponding byte.

Memory operands can be bytes, half words, or words. Double-word operands are used for double-precision floating-point operands and for double-word integer operations, available in 64-bit implementations. Load/store string instructions specify a sequence of bytes and load/store multiple word instructions specify a sequence of words. The address of a memory operand is the address of its first byte (that is, of its lowest-numbered byte).

Operands are aligned according to the operand length. An operand is aligned if the address is an integer multiple of the size of the operand.

Floating-Point Conventions

The UISA defines that single-precision arithmetic instructions use single-precision source operands and always produce single-precision results. Double-precision arithmetic instructions can use single-precision operands, but must produce double-precision results.

Big- and Little-Endian Byte Ordering

The default byte-ordering is big-endian; however, the OEA defines two bits in the MSR for specifying byte-ordering. MSR[LE] specifies the mode that the processor enters at start up; MSR[ELE} specifies the mode when an exceptions is taken. For both bits, 0 specifies big-endian mode and 1 specifies little-endian mode.

PowerPC Instruction Set and Addressing Modes

PowerPC instructions are grouped according to the following criteria:

- If they are accessible by user- or supervisor-level software.

- If they are defined by the UISA, VEA, or OEA. All instructions defined by the OEA are supervisor-level instructions. All instructions defined by the UISA and the VEA are accessible by user-level software, although typically VEA defined instructions are not used by typical applications. They are more likely to be used by compilers.

- All optional instructions are guaranteed to trap to the illegal instruction error handler, if they are not implemented.

User-level Instructions

The PowerPC instructions are divided into the following categories. Note that these categories do not indicate which execution unit executes a particular instruction.

The UISA and VEA portions of the PowerPC Architecture define instructions that can be accessed by user-level software. The instructions defined by the VEA are typically used by compilers to optimize the use of the caches and to access the time-of-day resources.

Load/Store Instructions. Load/store instructions are defined by the UISA and transfer data between system memory and the register files (GPRs for integer instructions and FPRs for floating-point instructions). The UISA defines a variety of load/store instructions, which are described as follows:

- *Integer load and store instructions.* These instructions move data between system memory (which can be a cache) and the GPRs.

- *Integer load/store multiple/string instructions.* These instructions load and store multiple integer values.

- *Floating-point load and store.* These instructions move data between system memory (which can be a cache) and the FPRs.

- *Floating-point move instructions.* These instructions move values from one FPR into another FPR.

- *The load/store with reservation instructions.* Instructions (lwarx/ldarx and stwcx/stdcx) which are provided as primitives for constructing atomic memory operations. These are more properly treated as memory synchronization instructions.

Integer instructions. These instructions, which are defined by the UISA, include computational and logical instructions that use GPRs for source and destination operands. Some integer instructions also affect the condition register and the integer exception register. The UISA defines the following integer arithmetic instructions:

- *Integer arithmetic instructions.* These instructions perform basic integer arithmetic—addition, subtraction, multiplication, and division.

- *Integer compare instructions.* These instructions compare two integer values and write the results to a specified field in the CR.

- *Integer logical instructions.* These instructions perform Boolean logic operations, such as AND, OR, XOR, and NAND, and write the results to a specified GPR.

- *Integer rotate and shift instructions.* These instructions rotate and shift values in specified GPRs and write the results to a specified GPR.

Floating-Point Instructions. Floating-point instructions are defined by the UISA. Computational instructions use FPRs for source and destination registers. Some floating-point instructions also affect the condition register and the floating-point status and control register (FPSCR).

- *Floating-point arithmetic instructions.* These operations perform basic arithmetic—addition, subtraction, multiplication, and division. There are single- and double-precision versions of these instructions.

- *Floating-point multiply/add instructions.* These instructions are compound instructions, which is atypical of RISC instruction-set architectures. In most PowerPC implementations, such as the 601 and 603, these instructions perform with the same latency as floating-point add or multiply instructions. These instructions are especially useful for performing vector calculations.

- *Floating-point rounding and conversion instructions.* These instructions round double-precision operands to single-precision values and convert floating-point operands to integer operands.

- *Floating-point compare instructions.* These instructions compare two FPR values and write the results to a specified field in the CR.

- *Floating-point status and control instructions.* These instructions manipulate bits in the FPSCR.

The UISA defines a number of instructions for branching and for trapping to the exception handler. These are referred to as program flow instructions, as follows:

- *Branch instructions.* These instructions include Branch (b) (unconditional), Branch Conditional (bc), Branch Conditional to Link Register (bclr), and Branch Conditional to Count Register (bcctr) instructions. Conditional branch instructions provide an operand to predict whether the branch is taken or not taken. An operand bit in bc and bclr instructions is used to treat the CTR as a decrementing counter.

- *Trap instructions.* These instructions trap exception handlers on specified words and double words.

- *Condition register logical instructions.* These instructions perform logical operations on bits within the CR.

- The *System Call* (sc) *instruction* is used to invoke the exception handler. This instruction is further defined by the OEA.

The UISA defines several *memory synchronization instructions* for synchronizing memory operations and forcing strongly-ordered memory accesses. These are especially useful for multiprocessing systems:

■ *Load Word/Double Word and Reserve Indexed (lwarx and ldarx) and Store Word/Double-Word Conditional Indexed (stwcx and stdcx)*. These provide primitives for synchronization operations such as test and set, compare and swap, and compare memory.

■ *The Synchronize instruction* (sync) synchronizes load and store operations on a multiprocessor memory bus.

Move to/from Special-Purpose Register Instructions (mtspr and mfspr) are defined by the UISA, however, the registers that are accessed depend on the level at which an SPR is defined. For example, the UISA defines these instructions as being able to access UISA-defined registers (such as the link register), the VEA defines the instructions as being able to access VEA-defined registers (namely the time base registers), and the OEA defines the instructions as being able to access OEA-defined registers (such as those required in exception handling, like SRR0, SRR1, and DSISR, and those required for memory management, like the IBAT and DBAT registers).

User-Level Instructions Defined by the VEA

The VEA defines mtspr and mfspr instructions for accessing VEA-defined registers and two instructions used for memory synchronization:

■ *Instruction Synchronize (isync)*. The isync instruction causes the processor to discard all prefetched instructions, wait for any preceding instructions to complete, and then branch to the next sequential instruction. This effectively clears the pipeline behind the isync instruction.

■ *Enforce In-Order Input/Output (eieio)*. The eieio instruction is used instead of the sync instruction when only memory references seen by I/O devices have to be ordered.

The VEA defines several memory-control instructions:

■ *Cache management instructions*. These instructions are used to ensure cache coherency in multiprocessor implementations.

Supervisor-Level Instructions Defined by the OEA

The OEA defines instructions typically for use by the operating system for configuring the processor and memory resources, providing software and hardware diagnostics, and handling exceptions.

The OEA defines mtspr and mfspr instructions for accessing OEA-defined registers and the Move to/from Machine State Register instructions (mtmsr and mfmsr) for accessing the MSR.

The OEA defines two flow-control instructions for entering and returning from supervisor level:

- *System Call (sc)*. Although this instruction is provided in the UISA, the OEA further defines details of how this instruction operates with respect to the PowerPC exception model.

- *Return from Interrupt (rfi)*. This instruction is used by exception handlers to indicate that exception handling is complete and control is returned to an interrupted process.

The OEA defines several memory control instructions:

- *Data Cache Block Invalidate (dcbi)*. This instruction invalidates cache blocks in the data cache.

- Instructions for invalidating TLB contents and SLB contents (in 64-bit implementations)

- *Segment register manipulation instructions* (in 32-bit implementations). These instructions are used to read and write to the segment registers.

- *Translation lookaside buffer (TLB) management instructions*. Like cache control instructions, these instructions are used to invalidate entries in the TLBs.

The OEA defines two optional external control instructions for use with special input/output devices:

- External Control Input Word Indexed (eciwx)

- External Control Output Word Indexed (ecowx)

Effective Addresses

The logical or *effective address (EA)* is the 32-bit address computed by the processor when executing a memory access or branch instruction or when fetching the next sequential instruction. The MMU translates this address to a physical, or real, address to access memory, which includes RAM and caches, which are physically-addressed as defined by the PowerPC Architecture.

The PowerPC Architecture supports two simple memory addressing modes:

Effective address
The address generated to access data or instructions. This address identifies a memory location within the address space as viewed by the program, called the logical address space.

- Register indirect with immediate index (the index is an immediate value):

    ```
    EA = (rA¦0) + offset (including offset = 0)
    ```

- Register indirect with index (the index is provided in a GPR):

    ```
    EA = (rA¦0) + rB
    ```

The operand (rA|0) is a convention that indicates that when GPR0 is specified (r0), a value of 0 is provided rather than the actual contents of GPR0. This convention is followed for all load, store, addi, and addis instructions.

PowerPC Cache Model

As previously noted, the PowerPC Architecture does not provide specific details about hardware implementation, so the PowerPC cache model does not prescribe cache size, set associativity, the mechanism that ensures cache coherency, whether the cache is unified or Harvard architecture, or whether a cache is present at all. However, the PowerPC Architecture does define basic details about memory configuration that affect the cache implementation:

The VEA defines memory according by the following criteria:

- *If a page or block is cacheable.* Memory-mapped I/O should not be cached. This is determined by the I bit in the BAT or PTEG.

- *If a page or block is write-back or write-through.* Write-back memory allows write operations to update a memory location in cache without having to update memory. This is determined by the W bit in the BAT or PTEG.

- *If a page or block requires enforcement of memory coherency.* If a page or block does not require coherency to be enforced, it is more efficient to mark this area of memory as not memory coherent. This is determined by the M bit in the BAT or PTEG.

The PowerPC Architecture specifies that the caches are physically addressed and it defines that coherency is maintained on a per-cache block-basis. Typically, a cache block is identical to a cache line; however, in the 601 a cache block is eight words long, half of a 16-word line . Cache control instructions perform operations, such as flushing (writing modified cache blocks back to memory and invalidating the cache block) and clearing (setting all bits to zero) cached data on a cache-block basis. As described earlier in the section on instructions, data cache block touch operations speculatively load a cache block from memory before a memory access instruction is executed. This allows more efficient scheduling of bus activity. The OEA defines the Data Cache Block Invalidate instruction, dcbi, which invalidates a data cache block.

Although the PowerPC Architecture defines the notion of coherency, it does not define the mechanism that enforces coherency. The 601, which supports multiprocessing systems, implements a full MESI cache-coherency protocol with separate read ports in the cache for snooping. The 603, which is not intended for multiprocessor systems, only implements the MEI states of MESI protocol and requires a separate bus operation for snooping.

PowerPC Exception Model
The OEA defines the PowerPC exception mechanism. Exceptions can occur for various reasons, either in the regular course of system management or when a problem is encountered. As an example of the former, a decrementer exception occurs when the value in the decrementer register passes through zero. The operating system may depend on the decrementer exception handler to enable the system to swap between multiple processes. A machine check exception is an example of the latter. This exception is taken usually as the result of a serious hardware problem, such as a data parity error, and the processor may not be able to continue processing.

When exceptions occur, information about the state of the processor is saved to SRR0 and SRR1, the values in the machine-state register are reset, and the processor begins to operate in supervisor mode to execute the exception handler software that resides at the unique address specified for the exception by the OEA. In some cases additional information about the exception is saved in exception-related registers (such as the DSISR or the DAR), which the exception handler uses to determine the source of the exception.

The PowerPC Architecture requires a precise exception model. Although it is not prescribed by the architecture, typically, instruction-caused exceptions are taken in program order so the processor can resume execution with the next instruction when exception handling is complete. The architecture does allow the optional implementation of two floating-point imprecise modes (recoverable and nonrecoverable). Any incomplete instructions ahead of the excepting instruction (in program order) must be allowed to complete execution and present their results, which can mean updating memory, or GPRs or FPRs, and handling any exception associated with those instructions.

In a parallel implementation, this requires sufficient logic to be able to restore program order even though instructions execute in separate pipelines. The architecture does not prescribe the mechanism that restores program order.

Only one exception is handled at a time, although exceptions can occur while the operating system is handling an exception. If a single instruction causes multiple exceptions, those exceptions are handled sequentially.

The OEA architecture supports four types of exceptions, *synchronous* (caused by instructions) or *asynchronous* (initiated by signals). Synchronous exceptions are either precise or imprecise.

Precise exceptions require that all instructions issued prior to the exception complete execution and that no instructions after the exception have begun. The PowerPC Architecture allows partially executed instructions for data access and alignment exceptions. The affected instructions are allowed to be restarted, which gives the effect of being precise.

- *Synchronous, precise exemptions.* Instruction-caused exceptions are handled precisely. The machine state at the time the exception occurs is known and is restored after the exception handler issues the rfi instruction. When these exceptions are taken, the address of the next instruction to be fetched is saved in SRR0. For most exceptions, this is the instruction that caused the exception. This ensures that no execution results are lost. Trap and system call exceptions save the address of next instruction in the instruction flow.

- *Synchronous, imprecise exceptions.* The PowerPC Architecture defines two optional imprecise floating-point exception modes, recoverable and nonrecoverable. These modes are selected through setting MSR[FE0] and MSR[FE1].

Synchronous exceptions

Synchronous exceptions are generated by the program itself, either when an illegal operation is attempted or when software provided by the exception handler is required to complete a particular operation.

Asynchronous exceptions

Asynchronous exceptions are generated by an event outside of the current program, and are typically triggered by a signal.

■ *Asynchronous, maskable exceptions.* The external interrupt and decrementer exceptions are maskable asynchronous exceptions that are handled precisely. These exceptions provide a mechanism for handling system resources. When these exceptions occur, their handling is postponed until all instructions, and any exceptions associated with those instructions, complete execution. These exceptions are masked by setting the MSR[EE] bit.

■ *Asynchronous, nonmaskable exceptions.* The nonmaskable asynchronous exceptions, system reset and machine check exceptions, are typically initiated by signals, and although these exceptions may not be fully recoverable, implementations can provide a limited degree of recoverability to allow diagnostic operations.

Additional exceptions are defined for each processor. For example, the 603 implements the hardware interrupt exception—an additional maskable, asynchronous exception used in conjunction with power management.

The exceptions defined by the PowerPC Architecture are described in table 6.1.

Table 6.1 Exceptions Defined by the PowerPC		
Exception	**Offset ***	**Explanation**
Reserved	00000	
System reset	00100	This exception is typically used to force the processor to restart and is initiated by an implementation-defined signal or signals. If the processor state is so corrupted that the contents of SRR0 and SRR1 are no longer valid or the processor cannot reliably resume execution, the processor sets MSR[RE]
Machine check	00200	Initiated by an implementation-defined signal or signals. The causes for machine check exceptions are implementation-dependent, but typically these causes are related to conditions such as bus-parity errors or attempting to access an invalid real address. The machine check exception is disabled by clearing MSR[ME] , in which case a machine check exception condition causes the processor to go into checkstop state.

Exception	Offset *	Explanation
Data access	00300	A data access exception occurs when a load/store, memory, or cache control instruction fails for any of the following reasons: 1. The effective address cannot be translated. 2. The access violates memory protection. 3. The instruction is invalid for an I/O controller interface segment. 4. The instruction causes an I/O controller interface exception. 5. The cause of a data access exception is determined by the bit settings in the DSISR.
Instruction access	00400	An instruction access exception occurs when an instruction fetch fails for any of the following reasons: 1. There is a page fault for this portion of the effective address translation, so an instruction access exception must be taken to retrieve the translation from a storage device such as a hard disk drive. 2. The fetch access violates memory protection. Areas of memory are configured to prohibit read access; attempts to fetch instructions from such areas generate an exception. 3. An attempt is made to fetch an instruction from an I/O controller interface segment.
External interrupt	00500	An external interrupt occurs when an implementation-defined external exception signal is asserted and external interrupts are enabled (MSR[EE] = 1.
Alignment	00600	An alignment exception can occur when the processor cannot perform a memory access for one of the following reasons: 1. The operand of a lmw, stmw, lwarx, stwcx. or double-word load or store operation is not word-aligned. 2. The operand of a floating-point load or store operation is in an I/O controller interface segment (SR[T]=1). 3. The operand of a ldarx or stdcx. instruction is not double-word aligned. 4. An lmw or stmw operand crosses a segment or block boundary. 5. The operand of a load instruction crosses a protection boundary. 6. The operand of a Data Cache Block Set to Zero (dcbz) instruction is in a page specified as write-through or cache-inhibited for a page-address translation access.

(continues)

Table 6.1 Continued		
Exception	**Offset ***	**Explanation**
		Notice that the PowerPC Architecture allows implementations to perform the operation without causing the exception.
Program	00700	There are several types of program exceptions: 1. A floating-point enabled exception occurs when either exceptions are enabled and FPSCR[FEX] is set because of an exception condition. 2. An illegal instruction program exception occurs when an instruction of code is not supported by an implementation. These include unimplemented optional instructions, POWER instructions not present in the PowerPC ISA, and 64-bit instructions issued to a 32-bit implementation. 3. A privileged instruction program exception occurs when a user-level program attempts to execute a privileged instruction 4. A trap exception occurs when a trap instruction executes successfully.
Floating-point unavailable	00800	A floating-point exception when a floating-point instruction is attempted when the floating-point available bit is disabled, MSR[FP]=0.
Decrementer	00900	The decrementer exception occurs when the most significant bit of the decrementer (DEC) register transitions from 0 to 1 and the decrementer exception is not masked.
Reserved	00A00	Some PowerPC implementations use this as an I/O controller interface error exception.
Reserved	00B00	
System call	00C00	A system call exception occurs when a System Call (sc) instruction is executed.
Trace	00D00	The trace exception is optional. Either the MSR[SE]=1 and any instruction (except rfi) successfully completed or MSR[BE]=1 and a branch instruction is completed.
Floating-point assist	00E00	The optional floating-point assist exception provides software assistance for floating-point operations such as denormalization.

Exception	Offset *	Explanation
Reserved	00E10_00FFF	
Reserved	01000_02FFF	Reserved, implementation-specific.

* The vector address is x'FFF...F*nnnnn*' or x'000...0*nnnnn*' where *nnnnn* is the hexadecimal offset. The prefix is determined by the setting of the MSR[EP] bit.

PowerPC Memory Management Model

The OEA portion of the PowerPC Architecture determines how effective (logical) addresses generated by software programs for instruction and explicit memory accesses (load and store instructions) are translated to the physical (real) addresses required to access system memory (including the physically addressed caches that are defined by the PowerPC cache model). The memory management model also defines how recently used translations are stored on the chip and how the search for translations is performed (table-search operations).

The memory management model also defines how memory is organized in pages, blocks, or segments, and provides access protection on a block or page basis.

The memory management model differs somewhat between 32- and 64-bit implementations.

The 64-bit PowerPC memory model provides 2^{64} bits of logical address space. The 64-bit implementations employ a 2^{80}-bit interim virtual address.

The 32-bit PowerPC memory model provides 2^{32} bits (4G) of logical address space. The 32-bit implementations employ a 2^{52}-bit interim virtual address.

Both 32- and 64-bit implementations allocate 4K pages and 256M segments. The block address translation (BAT) mechanism translates large blocks of memory with blocks selectable from 128K to 256M. Hashed page tables help generate the physical addresses for both 32- and 64-bit implementations.

Segment and page tables are used to locate the logical-to-physical address mapping. To provide flexibility in a wide range of processors, the methods by which segment or page table information is saved on-chip vary from implementation to implementation.

Typically, processors use on-chip translation look-aside buffers (TLBs) to save recently used address translations for reuse. The 64-bit architecture definition describes segment look-aside buffers (SLBs), which contain recently-used segment table entries. As with the caches, the architecture does not prescribe specific details about the TLBs and SLBs, such as their size and set-associativity.

Summary

This chapter has provided an overview of the PowerPC Architecture, placing special emphasis on how the architectural definition is flexible to allow for a wide variety of PowerPC processors.

The flexibility of the PowerPC Architecture is illustrated by taking a closer look at the first two PowerPC processers, which are described in the next chapter.

Chapter 7

Introducing the PowerPC Processor Family

As described earlier, flexibility and scalability were essential criteria in the specification of the PowerPC Architecture, making RISC performance available across a wide range of system implementations and offering ample room for an easy transition into the next generation of 64-bit processors.

This chapter provides a basic introduction to the PowerPC processors, describing the criteria and the price/performance trade-offs that determined the design of each processor. This chapter also provides basic information about those parts, and, in particular, points out significant characteristics concerning the unique way in which a processor realizes the PowerPC Architecture or implements features that are optional to the PowerPC Architecture.

The breadth of the PowerPC Architecture is clearly demonstrated by the first four chips announced by the PowerPC consortium:

- The 601 processor has a 64-bit data bus and a 32-bit address bus and is optimized for desktop and workstation implementation, including multiprocessing workstations.

- The 603 processor has a 64-bit data bus and a 32-bit address bus and is optimized for battery-powered systems.

In this chapter you learn:

- The criteria that determined the designs of the first PowerPC processors

- The basic features of the PowerPC 601 and 603 processors

- Examples of how the flexibility of the PowerPC Architecture is exploited in each design to provide a common software platform

- The 604 processor has a 64-bit data bus and a 32-bit address bus and also is optimized for desktop and workstation implementation, including multiprocessing workstations, but offers faster performance than the 601.

- The 620 processor has a 64-bit data bus and is the first PowerPC processor to have 64-bit address bus. The 620 is optimized for high-end server and workstation implementations.

> **Note**
>
> More detailed information about each processor is provided in Chapter 16, "The PowerPC 601 RISC Processor"; Chapter 17, "PowerPC 601 RISC Processor Instruction Timing"; and Chapter 18, "The PowerPC 603 RISC Processor."

PowerPC—The Chips

To understand the differences among the initial four PowerPC processors, it is useful to look at them from the perspectives of the flexibility and expandability of the PowerPC Architecture. That flexibility allows processors to be designed to meet a variety of markets and needs without cumbersome solutions that compromise either efficiency or functionality.

Big- and little-endian byte mode
How bytes are ordered within a larger unit of memory. Systems addressing the most-significant byte are big-endian, and systems addressing the least-significant byte are little-endian.

The PowerPC Architecture has been designed specifically for a broad assortment of implementations, and the first four chips announced by the Apple/IBM/Motorola consortium address the broadening range of microprocessor environments. They were designed to take advantage of the further miniaturization of personal computing, and the growing number of possibilities to tie personal computing with other media and household electronics while retaining the capability to meet the massive demands of corporate computing and special scientific and graphics computing.

Another example of the flexibility of the PowerPC Architecture is the support for big- and little-endian byte addressing. PowerPC processors are configurable to run in *big- or little-endian mode*. This flexibility allows much greater flexibility for running software from different environments. The PowerPC endian-switching mechanism is described in Chapter 12, "PowerPC Memory Conventions."

> **Note**
>
> The PowerPC Architecture offers expandability and flexibility in several ways.
>
> Taking into account the current pace of technology, the PowerPC architects have provided headroom into the architecture. Even though it is not anticipated that 64-bit addressing will become commonplace in personal computing for a number of years, the PowerPC Architecture was designed to make the transition effortless. The PowerPC user instruction set architecture (UISA) defines additional instructions (these mostly allow integer operations to take advantage of double-word operations). The 64-bit implementations provide a 32-bit mode to accommodate 32-bit applications, and the additional 64-bit instructions are guaranteed to trap on 32-bit implementations, so software is completely compatible.

Degrees of Architectural Compatibility

The PowerPC Architecture defines three layers of architecture: the user instruction set architecture (UISA), the virtual environment architecture (VEA), and the operating environment architecture (OEA). VEA-compliant implementations are necessarily UISA compliant, and OEA-compliant implementations are necessarily compliant with the other levels of the architecture.

While the four announced processors that are jointly designed comply with all three levels of the architecture, it is possible to design processors that only support the PowerPC user instruction set. This further extends the range of implementations available to the PowerPC Architecture and compatible with PowerPC software.

The PowerPC Architecture does not define which functionality must be provided in hardware and which can be provided in software. Some implementations may have little or no need for floating-point operations, while other implementations may depend on them heavily. The PowerPC Architecture allows microprocessors to implements floating-point instructions wholly or partially in software.

A single implementation may implement more than one unit. It may, for example, employ multiple FPUs to support high resolution animation, or it may employ multiple IUs for a processor designed for use in server systems where the IU bears a great deal of traffic.

> **Note**
>
> The PowerPC Architecture provides a conceptual model of a branch-processing unit, a floating-point unit, and an integer unit. These units may vary greatly from implementation to implementation.

A single implementation may employ more specific types of execution units. It may be desirable to have one FPU for single-precision operations and another for double-precision operations. Multiple integer units may be implemented to handle logical instruction, simple integer calculations, and longer latency integer instructions.

Implementations can define additional execution units. For example, the load/store unit in the 603 handles all integer and floating-point load/store operations.

Processors can define additional hardware facilities—such as buffers, reservation stations, rename buffers, and feed-forwarding paths—to reduce data dependencies and to reduce stalls, or at least reduce the effect of stalls. Such optimizing hardware can vary greatly in complexity.

In addition to hardware optimization schemes that are directly related to executions units, designers are provided a wide latitude of options to tune a processor to the price/performance needs of the systems they are intended. This is particularly noticeable in the wide range of cache implementations possible. The PowerPC Architecture supports the use of independent caches for instructions and data, but processors are free to implement unified caches or no caches at all.

There are many, more subtle differences possible. For example, because the 601 processor can be used in multiprocessing implementations, *cache snooping* (which is performed to ensure that all caches have an accurate view of memory) is implemented in hardware. The 603 processor, on the other hand, is not optimized for multiprocessor implementations, but it may still share the system bus with other devices (such as direct-memory addressing, or DMA, devices). There is still a concern that another bus device may need to know when a *cache block* has been modified in the 603 cache. So, the 601 provides a separate port for snooping addresses broadcast on the system bus so the act of snooping itself does not interfere with memory accesses on the system bus—although if a snoop hit occurs, additional bus activity is

Cache snooping

A mechanism used to ensure cache coherency in a multiprocessing environment. Caching devices monitor, or snoop, addresses that are broadcast on the bus by other devices.

Cache block

The cacheable unit of data. In the 601 and 603 processors, this is 8 contiguous words of data. In both processors, coherency is maintained on a cache block basis.

required to ensure MESI memory coherency. Details regarding the PowerPC cache implementation is described in Chapter 14, "PowerPC Cache Implementation Model."

However, because snooping is less important to single-processor systems, no extra ports are provided in the 603 and snooping is performed on the bus. And because the 603 is not optimized to share system memory with other 603s, there is no need to implement full MESI cache coherency. Specifically, it is assumed that there is no other caching device on the bus, and there is no need to implement the shared state, so less logic is required to implement an MEI state machine.

The 601

The 601 processor was the first available PowerPC processor. The 601, aimed at the workstation and desktop market, offers a 32-bit address bus and 64-bit data bus. It contains three independent execution units—a branch processing unit (BPU), an integer unit (IU), and a floating-point unit. The initial release of the 601 included 50 and 66 MHz versions, and has become available as a 80 MHz processor.

The 603

The 603 processor, announced in October 1993, also features a 32-bit address bus and 64-bit data bus. The 603 is designed for system implementations with low-power demands, such as notebook and hand-held computers. The 603 also is optimized for use in single-processor implementations, but allows multiple system bus masters (such as a DMA device) and supports a subset of the MESI cache coherency protocol.

Table 7.1 summarizes the differences between the PowerPC 601 and 603 processors.

Table 7.1 The PowerPC 601 and 603 Processors		
Feature	**601**	**603**
Address bus width	32 bit	32 bit
Data bus width	64 bit	64 bit
Execution units	Three (Branch processing unit, integer unit, floating-point unit)	Five (Branch processing unit, integer unit, floating-point unit, load/store unit, system resource unit)

(continues)

Table 7.1 Continued		
Feature	**601**	**603**
MMUs	One (unified)	Two (one for instructions and one for data)
Cache	Unified, 32KB	Separate 8KB instruction and data caches
Cache coherency	MESI protocol. Caches are dual-ported to support zero-cycle snooping	MEI protocol. Caches are single-ported
Die size	11mm x 11 mm	7.4 mm x 11.5 mm
Transitors	2.8 million	1.6 million
DC voltage	3.6V	3.3V
Power dissipation	8.5W to 9.5W (80 MHZ)	ca. 3W (80MHz)
Process	0.6μm complementary metal-oxide semiconductor (CMOS)	0.5μm CMOS
Packaging	304 pin	240 pin
Processor frequencies	50MHz, 66MHz, 80MHz	Currently 80MHz
Metal layers	4	4

The following sections provide overviews of the major features of the released parts. In-depth discussions are provided in Chapter 16, "The PowerPC 601 RISC Processor"; Chapter 17, "PowerPC 601 RISC Processor Instruction Timing"; and Chapter 18, "The PowerPC 603 RISC Processor."

601 Overview

The 601 processor implements the 32-bit subset of the PowerPC Architecture and is intended for desktop, workstation, and server implementations. A die photo of the 601 showing the major functional units is shown in Figure 7.1.

Although the PowerPC Architecture allows varying degrees of hardware support for floating-point operations, the 601 fully implements floating-point operations in hardware, and the FPU is tightly linked to the processor core—optimizing performance for number-intensive workstation implementations.

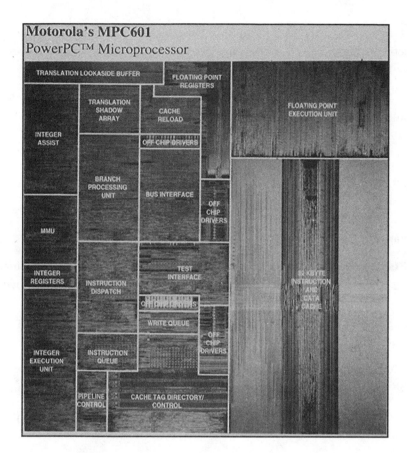

Figure 7.1

The PowerPC 601 processor with layout of major functional units.

The 601 is fully pipelined and incorporates many features to optimize pipeline performance and reduce the effect of pipeline stalls.

The 601 instruction-fetching logic takes advantage of the fact that PowerPC instructions are all the same length (32 bits) and implements a large instruction queue that enables the branch processor to detect and handle branch instructions early. It also provides out-of-order superscalar dispatch to the three executions units.

Floating-point instructions, for example, can be dispatched to a buffer when there is a stall in the floating-point pipeline. There are also numerous feed-forwarding mechanisms. For example, the results of an integer arithmetic calculation are made available directly to a subsequent integer instruction at the same time it is written to the destination GPR. This is particularly useful because an integer instruction can use the result of the previous integer instruction without incurring the one-clock delay that would have been required had the second instruction had to wait for the result to be written to the destination GPR.

Because the 601 is intended for multiprocessing systems, it includes extensive support for multiprocessing, such as hardware snooping support and full MESI cache coherency protocol.

Major features of the 601 are covered in the following sections. These include particular details about the instruction set, general information about instruction timing, and an overview of the cache and memory management implementations.

601 Instruction Set. The 601 implements the PowerPC instructions defined for 32-bit addressing as well as numerous POWER instructions not provided in other PowerPC processors for full compatibility with IBM RS/6000-based AIX applications. The 601 also supports the eciwx and ecowx optional instructions.

The 601 provides a subset of the functionality of the instruction and data cache instructions appropriate for the 601's unified cache implementation.

Most 601 instructions can execute with a throughput of one instruction per clock.

601 Instruction Dispatch. The 601's superscalar instruction dispatch mechanism demonstrates many of the advantages of the RISC PowerPC Architecture. Most important is the flexibility that fixed-length instructions provide with respect to the capability to fetch a large number of instructions at a time, which in turn provides the capability to pre-emptively detect and handle branching instructions, reducing the performance degradation that branches cause. Fixed-length instructions greatly simplify this fetching scheme and the preliminary decoding required for branch look-ahead.

The instruction unit can fetch as many as eight instructions (a full cache block) per clock from the cache and place those instructions in the eight-entry instruction queue. The large instruction queue both reduces the likelihood of running out of instructions available for dispatch (starvation) and makes it easier to implement look-ahead capability for detecting, predicting, and resolving branches. Likewise, when a branch is taken, it is possible to fetch an entire cache block of instructions into the instruction queue.

Branch and floating-point instructions can be dispatched from any of the four bottom slots in the IQ (IQ0-IQ3). Integer instructions are dispatched from IQ0. In most cases, an integer instruction can be decoded while it is in the IQ0 stage. The 601 can dispatch as many as three instructions per clock—one to each of the three execution units. The 601 implements out-of-order dispatch and completion. Although instructions may actually write back their results out of order, they appear to complete in order—that is, all data dependencies are observed.

601 Execution Units. The 601 implements the three execution units as they are presented conceptually by the PowerPC Architecture—an integer unit (IU), a floating-point unit (FPU), and a branch processing unit (BPU). The BPU is closely linked to the instruction unit for quick resolution of branch instructions, as is described in the discussion of the instruction unit. Branch instructions can be folded (replaced by the target instruction or the next sequential instruction) as long as there are no data dependencies.

The BPU also performs condition register (CR) look-ahead operations and provides programmable static branch prediction on unresolved conditional branches. Static branch prediction is performed by setting a bit (defined by the architecture) in a conditional branch instruction.

The IU contains thirty two 32-bit GPRs to provide source and destination operands for integer arithmetic instructions. The IU also performs both integer and floating-point load and store operations, transferring data between memory and the GPRs and FPRs, respectively. The IU also executes logical instructions as well as instructions that read and write data to and from architected registers, such as the special purpose resisters, the machine state register, the condition register, and others.

The FPU, which is tightly integrated into the 601, complies with the industry standard for floating-point operations defined by the Institute of Electrical and Electronics Engineers (IEEE) for both single- and double-precision operations. These specifications are published as IEEE 754. The FPU incorporates thirty two 64-bit FPRs for single- or double-precision source and destination operands. Operands in the FPRs are stored in double-precision format regardless of whether they are to be used for single- or double-precision calculations.

The FPU is pipelined, allowing most single-precision instructions to execute with a throughput of one instruction per clock cycle and most double-precision operations to execute with a throughput of one instruction every other clock cycle.

There are three execute stages of the FPU that allow a single-precision floating-point multiply-add instruction (fmadds) to execute with a throughput of one instruction per clock. That is, the floating-point stages can execute the mathematical expression Ax + B with a single-cycle throughput. Simpler floating-point multiply and add instructions essentially execute a floating-point multiply-add instruction, but with one of the variables held constant. For example, a floating-point add instruction (fadds) treats the variable A as a 1, or (1*x)+B, and a floating-point multiply (fmuls) treats the variable B as a zero, or Ax + 0.

> ### Note
>
> While fmadds is not a typical RISC instruction, it can be implemented at no additional cost, and with the same single-cycle throughput as simpler instructions.

601 Cache Implementation. The 601 incorporates a 32KB, eight-way set-associative, unified cache. Each cache line in the 601 consists of two eight-word cache blocks (also called *cache sectors*). The PowerPC specifies that cache coherency is maintained on a cache-block basis. The cache is physically addressed.

Because the 601 is suitable for multiprocessing systems, the 601 implements full MESI cache coherency protocol. That is, because more than one 601 may share system memory, and because caches are typically configured to allow memory to be updated in the cache without being written through to memory (this is called *write-back mode*), it is necessary that each processor have an accurate view of memory. So, if processor A has updated a cache block and has not updated the corresponding location in system memory (the cache block is said to be Modified, in MESI parlance), processor B needs to be able to determine that the most recent data resides in processor A's cache. This coherency is maintained by the implementation of snooping addresses as they are broadcast on the system bus, and the 601 has additional ports to the caches so such snooping is done at no expense to the bus performance.

Note

For a more in-depth discussion of MESI cache coherency, see Chapter 17, "PowerPC 601 RISC Processor Instruction Timing."

When all eight possible cache locations available to hold a cache block are full and a new cache block must be added (typically as the result of a memory reference that misses in the cache), the least-recently used cache block must be cast out to system memory to make room for the new data. This is referred to as a *least-recently used (LRU) replacement algorithm.*

The main reason to implement a cache is to reduce time-consuming bus operations, which is especially significant for systems in which the bus frequency can one third slower than the processor frequency. For this reason it is typical for the cache to operate in write-back mode; that is, the 601 operates out of the cache, and modifies data in the cache without updating system memory. Through the memory configuration performed by the MMU, pages or blocks can be configured to inhibit or allow caching (memory defined for I/O operations would typically be defined as cache inhibited), write-back or write-through, or coherency enforced or not enforced (typically, coherency does not need to be enforced for memory areas that contain instructions).

There are a number of resources on the 601 that arbitrate for cache access— load and store operations generated by the IU and MMU operations and by instruction-fetching logic, which constantly attempts to update the instruction queue. To reduce the impact of cache contention, the 601 implements a non-blocking cache on cache misses and on burst loads.

Note

When a memory access misses in the cache, the cache is not forced to remain idle while the data is transferred to or from external memory.

When a cache miss occurs, the data that was requested (a byte, half word, word, or double word) resides within the first quad word transferred in the first two beats of data read from system memory. These two beats transfer a quad word (half of the eight-word cache block). This quad word is referred to as the *critical quad word.* The memory unit also provides a quad-word buffer

Critical quad word

The quad word that contains the data requested on a cache miss.

that holds this critical word, and this entire buffer is written to the cache in a single clock cycle. While the remaining quad-word is being transferred (in the final two data beats), the cache is free to handle other cache accesses.

The memory unit is shown in Figure 7.2.

Figure 7.2

The PowerPC 601 memory unit.

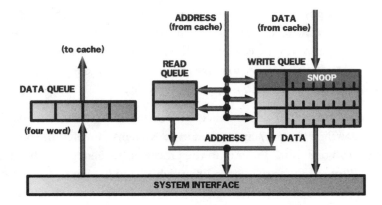

601 Memory Unit. The memory unit helps isolate the 601 from the effects of bus activity. The memory unit provides a means for posting write operations, freeing the processor to do other work, and the memory unit also helps reorder bus operations to take advantage of the weakly ordered storage model.

Read queue

Bus transactions that read data from external memory are first buffered (queued) in the read queue. This queue holds the address of the data to be read.

Write queue

Bus transactions that write data to external memory are first buffered in the write queue. This queue holds the address and the data to be written.

The memory unit contains a two-element *read queue* that buffers address for read operations, and a three-element *write queue* that buffers addresses and data for write operations.

The write queue can hold as much as an entire eight-word cache block of data. The write queue can contain modified data (for example, when a modified cache block is cast out because of the LRU algorithm), so it also participates in snooping addresses on the bus to ensure coherency.

The write queue also is used to buffer smaller units of data, such as those generated by store instructions. This data is not snooped in the write queue. To maintain coherency, write operations also generate a special address-only operations that invalidate any other caches in which this cache block is present.

As mentioned in the discussion of the non-blocking cache, the memory unit maintains a quad-word buffer, allowing the critical quad-word to be made available to be loaded into the cache in a single clock cycle.

601 System Bus. Although hardware details of the system bus are not defined by the PowerPC Architecture (for example, there are no specific signals that are identified in the architecture, even though many such signals may be common to a wide assortment of PowerPC processors). Nonetheless, the system bus is well tuned to the performance needs of single-chip RISC implementation.

The 601 clocking scheme is configurable to allow the bus to run at integer divisions of the processor clock frequency—1:1, 1:2, 1:3, and so forth—although it is unlikely that the bus would need to run at much slower frequencies.

> **Note**
>
> The most common type of bus transaction on the PowerPC 601 is the four-beat data burst (which can transfer an entire cache block), followed by single-beat transactions that can transfer as many as two words per beat.

The 601 system bus supports a weakly ordered storage model—that is, loads and stores do not need to occur in order, which improves bus performance.

The system bus consists of a 32-bit address bus and a 64-bit data bus. Typically, bus transactions consist of memory accesses—loads and stores—which require an address tenure followed by a data tenure. The system bus also may broadcast a variety of address-only transactions, which can be either explicit (by executing a data cache block flush, dcbf) instruction, or implicit (as in the case when a single-beat write is passed to the system bus, as described above).

In much the same way that it is advantageous to make arithmetic instructions independent from load/store instructions, having independent address and data tenures greatly increases the flexibility of system bus operation. In the 601, two address tenures may be broadcast before the first data tenure is begun. This is referred to as *one-level pipelining*.

The PowerPC Architecture also defines data cache block touch instructions that can be used to speculatively load a cache block before it is actually needed. This means that a cache block that will be needed by the processor at a later point can be scheduled as a low-priority bus operation. It is a low-priority operation so that it does not interfere with normal, non-speculative bus activity.

Multiprocessor implementations can take further advantage of this independence by allowing an address tenure from a second processor to occur before the data tenure of the first processor has begun. This type of bus is referred to as a *split-transaction bus*.

601 Memory Management Unit (MMU). The MMU translates effective (logical) addresses, generated by software into the physical addresses required for accessing memory—both the system memory accessed through the system bus, and the on-chip, physically addressed cache. The MMU also defines memory regions as 4KB pages, 256MB segments, and variable blocks (128KB to 8MB).

The MMU incorporates a four-entry, first-level instruction translation lookaside buffer (ITLB) and a 256-entry, two-way set-associative unified TLB (UTLB). If translations miss in the TLBs, the search for the translation proceeds as a translation table search through hashed page tables in physical memory. This table searching (also referred to as *table walking*) is implemented in hardware in the 601.

The address translation mechanism provides an intermediate 52-bit virtual address space, which maps to the 32-bit physical address space.

The BAT registers and the page table also define aspects of memory that pertain to the cache implementation. In particular, bits are provided to specify whether a block or page is cacheable, whether the cache is write-back or write-through, and whether coherency is enforced.

Likewise, the MMU also specifies whether a block or page can be accessed only by supervisor-level software or by user-level software.

601 Multiprocessing Support. Because the 601 can be used in multiprocessing systems implementations, the 601 provides extensive hardware support for enforcing the four-state cache coherency protocol (MESI), including separate ports to the cache tag array so snooping does not directly affect bus operations.

The PowerPC Architecture also provides a set of instructions for manipulating caches and TLBs.

The architecture also provides the load/store with reservation instructions (lwarx/stwcx) that provide a set of primitives for a number of operations useful for synchronization in multiprocessing operations.

The 601 system bus also supports split transactions, so address and data tenures from separate devices on the bus can occur out of order.

601 Testability. The 601 provides in-system testability and debugging features through boundary-scan capability.

603 Overview

The 603 processor is the first RISC processor aimed at low-power implementations such as battery-powered lightweight notebooks and hand-held computers. Because of its low-power demands and its fast throughput, including floating-point operations, the 603 is especially suitable for the growing range of applications that incorporate audio, video, and voice recognition, as well as pen computing.

A die photo of the 603, showing the major functional units, is shown in Figure 7.3.

The design requirements of the 603 force it to take a different approach to instruction processing than the 601. In addition to the BPU, FPU, and IU, the 603 implements additional execution units. Whereas dispatch and write back can be out of order on the 601, the 603 dispatches and completes instructions in order.

The 603 is intended for low-power systems, which determines many aspects of the design, including additional registers, exceptions, and instructions specifically intended to support the *nap*, *doze*, and *sleep* modes.

The space and power requirements of the 603 and the fact that it is not intended for multiprocessor implementations lend it to performing more tasks in software. Table search operations for page or block translations are performed by hardware on the 601 and by software with hardware assistance in the 603.

Also, whereas the 601 provides additional hardware for snooping, this hardware is not implemented in the 603 because it is not designed for multiprocessor implementations. Therefore, snooping is less apt to affect overall performance.

Doze
All functional units of the 603 are disabled exept the time base/ decrementer registers and bus-snooping logic.

Nap
Further reduces power consumption by disabling bus snooping, leaving only the time base register and the PLL in a powered state.

Sleep
Reduces power consumption to a minimum by disabling all internal functional units, after which external system logic may disable the PLL and SYSCLK.

Figure 7.3
The PowerPC 603
processor with
layout of major
functional units.

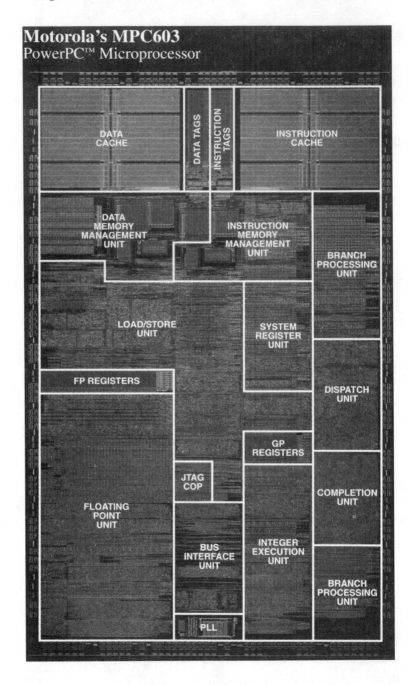

The following sections summarize the basic features of the 603 processor.
These include particular details about the instruction set, general information
about instruction timing, and an overview of the cache and memory management implementations.

603 Instruction Set. The 603 implements the PowerPC instructions defined for 32-bit addressing. The 601 also supports the optional eciwx, ecowx, and tlbsync instructions used in conjunction with the external control facility. The 603 also implements the following optional floating-point instructions:

- Floating-Point Select (fsel)

- Floating-Point Reciprocal Estimate Single-Precision (fres)

- Floating-Point Reciprocal Square Root Estimate (frsqrte)

- Store Floating-Point As Integer Word (stfiwx)

Most 603 instructions can be executed with a throughput of one instruction per clock.

603 Instruction Dispatch. The great flexibility allowed among implementations is demonstrated in the different approaches that the 603 and the 601 take to instruction dispatch.

Like the 601, the 603 instruction dispatch mechanism is pipelined and superscalar; however, while the 601 allows instructions to be dispatched out of order, the 603 provides in-order dispatch of as many as two instructions per clock cycle to any of the 603's five independent execution units. Like the 601, the 603 takes advantage of the instruction set's uniform-length instructions to implement a large (six-entry) instruction queue that facilitates the ability to avoid performance degradation usually caused by branch instructions.

The 603 processor implements a separate instruction cache, typically from which as many two instructions are fetched into the six-entry instruction queue per clock. The address of the next instruction to be fetched is determined by the sequential fetcher, the BPU, exception logic, and the completion unit.

Fetching continues sequentially unless an exception occurs, in which case fetching begins at the exception vector, or if the instruction sequence includes a branch instruction, in which case the BPU predicts the next instruction to be fetched based on a programmable bit in the branch instructions. (Unconditional branches do not require branch prediction.) If the branch prediction is incorrect, the next instruction is determined by the completion logic. In most cases, the branch instruction can be removed from the instruction flow and replaced by the target instruction (if the BPU predicts that the branch will be taken) or the next sequential instruction (if the BPU predicts that the branch will not be taken).

The dispatch unit issues as many as two instructions per clock to any of the five execution units.

603 Execution Units. The 603 incorporates five independent execution units with large register files as defined by the PowerPC Architecture:

- The 603's branch processor unit (BPU) works closely with the instruction unit to provide early detection of branch instructions, and a programmable static branch prediction mechanism.

Branch folding
Refers to the ability to remove the branch instruction from the instruction flow, replacing it with the predicted instruction.

Most branch instructions can be replaced by the next predicted instruction—either the target instruction or the next sequential instruction. This is called *branch folding*.

The BPU provides programmable static branch prediction on unresolved conditional branches. This capability is provided by setting a bit in the conditional branch instructions, as specified by the PowerPC Architecture.

The BPU also performs condition register (CR) look-ahead operations for early detection and handling of conditional branch instructions.

- The 603's integer unit (IU) incorporates the thirty two 32-bit GPRs, which provide source and destination data for all integer calculations. The IU is fully pipelined, and most integer instructions execute in one clock cycle.

- The floating-point unit (FPU) is fully IEEE 754-compliant for both single- and double-precision operations. The FPU incorporates the thirty two 64-bit FPRs defined by the PowerPC Architecture. The FPU is pipelined so one single-precision multiply-add instructions can be issued and retired every clock cycle. The FPRs hold data in double-precision format, regardless whether the data is used for single-or double-precision instructions.

- The load/store unit (LSU) executes integer and floating-point loads and store instructions, transferring data between the data cache and GPRs and FPRs.

■ The system resource unit (SRU) executes condition register (CR) and the move to/from special-purpose register (SPR) instructions.

Note

Feed-forwarding paths reduce instruction delays due to data dependencies.

---

603 Cache Implementation. The 603 implements separate 8KB instruction and data caches, which are fully supported by the PowerPC Architecture. Both caches are two-way set-associative and physically addressed. The caches employ a least recently used (LRU) replacement algorithm for updating the cache—that is, the least recently used cache block is replaced when a cache block is updated.

The caches can be configured as write-back/write-through, cacheable/non-cacheable, and coherency enforced/not enforced on a per page or per (memory) block basis.

Coherency for the data cache is enforced through a subset of the MESI protocol—Modified, Exclusive, and Invalid cache states. The shared state is not supported because the processor is not designed for multiprocessor implementations. Coherency is not required for the instruction cache.

603 Memory Management Units (MMUs). The 603 incorporates separate (and identical) MMUs for instruction and data following the specifications provided in the OEA portion of the PowerPC Architecture. The MMUs perform effective to physical address translations, define memory in pages or blocks, and provide memory protection on a page and block basis. The use of separate MMUs prevents delays due to data and instructions competing for address translation resources.

Whereas the 601 used the integer unit to generate effective addresses for load/store instructions, the 603 implements a separate load/store unit to serve this purpose. Like the 601, however, the instruction unit calculates the effective addresses for instructions. Unless translation is disabled in the MSR, these addresses must be translated by the appropriate MMU to access the correct locations in physical memory.

The effective-to-physical address translation uses a 52-bit virtual address space and a 32-bit physical address space.

The MMUs also enforce the protection hierarchy programmed by the operating system in relation to the supervisor/user privilege level of the access and in relation to whether the access is a load or store.

Each MMU contains a 64-entry, two-way set-associative translation look-aside buffer (DTLB and ITLB) on chip. The TLBs support demand-paged virtual memory address translation and variable-sized block translation. The TLBs hold the most recently used address translations, and are replaced using an LRU replacement algorithm.

For instruction accesses, the MMU looks up an address in both the 64 entries of the ITLB and in the instruction BAT array. If the address is in both places, the IBAT array translation takes priority. Data accesses cause a lookup in the DTLB and DBAT array for the physical address translation. In most cases, the physical address translation resides in one of the TLBs, and the physical, address bits are readily available to the on-chip cache.

The 603 provides hardware assistance, not defined by the PowerPC Architecture, to support software search through memory for translation tables when an address translation is not present in the TLBs. These include the following:

- IMISS and DMISS registers for saving the missed effective instruction and data address, respectively

- HASH1 and HASH2 registers, which store the primary and secondary hashed physical address of the page table entry group (PTEG). The HASH data is generated from the contents of the IMISS or DMISS register, depending on whether the last miss was an instruction or data address.

- The physical page address (PPA) register that matches the format of the lower word of the PTE

- Buffers, or shadows, for GPR0-GPR3, used only for servicing TLB misses

- Two TLB access instructions (tlbli and tlbld) that are used to load an address translation into the instruction or data TLBs

System Interface

The system interface uses a 32-bit address bus and a 64-bit data bus (which can be configured to work as a 32-bit bus). The 603 bus supports single-beat and burst data transfers for memory accesses. Burst transfers are used to transfer entire cache blocks of data to and from memory. Clocking for the system bus is programmable and supports processor/bus clock ratios of 1/1, 2/1, 3/1, and 4/1.

The 603 supports one-level address pipelining—that is, two address tenures can be outstanding before the first data transaction is initiated. The system bus is weakly ordered—that is, bus transactions can occur out of order, unless order is explicitly enforced. The 603 system bus supports memory-mapped I/O and I/O controller interface addressing.

603 Integrated Power Management

The 603 uses low-power, 3.3-volt CMOS process technology and is fully compatible with TTL devices. The 603 supports three static power-saving modes—doze, nap, and sleep. The 603 also supports a dynamic power management mode—it automatically enters a low-power mode when functional units remain idle after a preset time.

603 Testability

The 603 provides in-system testability and debugging features through JTAG boundary-scan capability

The block diagram shows the 603's five execution units—IU, FPU, BPU, LSU, and SRU—which operate independently and in parallel.

Summary

In this chapter, you have learned more about the first PowerPC processors. In particular, you have learned how the PowerPC 601 and 603 processors take advantage of the wide range of price and performance options offered by the flexibility of the PowerPC Architecture.

The next two chapters look at the first computer systems developed by IBM and Motorola based on the PowerPC 601 processor.

Chapter 8

Apple's PowerPC Systems

In the spring of 1994, Macintosh offered its first systems built with PowerPC processors:

- The Power Macintosh 6100/60, which uses a 60MHz PowerPC 601 processor, is aimed at small-to-medium businesses, and to users who have the need to run both Macintosh, DOS, and Windows programs.

- The Power Macintosh 7100/66, which uses a 66MHz PowerPC 601 processor, is intended for business, educational, educational installations, and professional users.

- The Power Macintosh 8100/80, which uses a 80MHz PowerPC 601 processor, is aimed at the publishing, engineering, and multi-media industries.

Simultaneously, Apple is providing a wide range of upgrade options for most systems that are currently manufactured.

Overview of the Power Macintosh Systems

There have been few births in the personal computer industry more eagerly awaited than the arrival of Apple's first PowerPC-based systems. As with any birth, the most often asked questions are: What is the name and who does it look like?

This chapter teaches you the following about Apple's first PowerPC products:

- An overview of the first three Power Macintoshes

- An overview of the PowerPC upgrade options

- The options provided with the first Power Macintoshes

- Software support for the first Power Macintoshes

- A brief look at the role PowerPC is playing in Apple's future

The new PC line was named Power Macintosh to make the point that these new systems have the look and feel of the familiar 680x0-based Macintoshes. Users who are comfortable with the Macintosh user interface will feel at home with the new systems. But the 680x0 functionality of the Power Macintosh is actually a subset of what the new systems can do, and in fact each of the new Macintoshes includes a ROM chip (68LC040) that supports emulation of the existing 680x0-based software.

Although the new systems have kept the Macintosh family name, Apple has adopted a new naming convention—indicating the processor frequency in the system name, a practice common in the personal computer industry. So, the Power Macintosh 6100/60 uses a 60MHz PowerPC 601 processor, the Power Macintosh 7100/66 uses a 66MHz 601, and the Power Macintosh 8100/80 uses an 80MHz 601.

The following list summarizes the features that all three systems have in common:

- All three systems ship with System 7 (7.1.2), which is enhanced to make some native calls to the PowerPC 601. Subsequent releases of System 7 will take more advantage of native calls to the PowerPC processors.

- All three systems run both existing Macintosh software in 680x0 emulation as well as native software for the PowerPC 601.

- All three systems are available in AV models. These systems provide support for audio and video features.

- All three systems support Insignia's SoftDOS and SoftWindows emulation products.

- The new systems all support Apple's NuBus expansion slots.

- The disk drives support both Macintosh and DOS diskettes.

In addition, the first three systems have the following common hardware features:

- On-board EtherNet with DMA channel and AAUI connector

- 16-bit stereo audio I/O with DMA

- Two serial ports—LocalTalk and GeoPort—that are compatible with DMA channel

- Apple Desktop Bus (ADB) for input devices

- Standard DRAM video

- Support for high speed asynchronous SCSI devices

The following sections look more closely at each Power Macintosh.

The Power Macintosh 6100/60

It seems inevitable that the Power Macintosh 6100/60 will be compared to Apple's original Macintosh, which revolutionized the computer industry a decade ago. In terms of raw features, there is hardly a contest. For the same amount of money that you would spend on the old system with its 128KB RAM, 9-inch black-and-white monitor, and single-sided 400KB floppy drive, you can now purchase a system with a 14-inch color monitor, 8MB of RAM (expandable to 72MB), at least a 160MB hard drive, and a disk drive that can read either Macintosh or DOS diskettes.

Figure 8.1 shows the Power Macintosh 6100/60.

Figure 8.1
The Power Macintosh 6100/60.

The Power Macintosh 6100/60 has the following features:

- 60MHz PowerPC 601 processor

- 68LC040 ROM provided for 680x0 emulation. Current 680x0-based software runs approximately as fast as it does on a fast 68030- to 68040-based system.

- Native software runs two to four times faster than a 33MHz, 68040-based system

- Support for an optional second-level cache

- 8MB DRAM standard with capacity for 72MB

- Base hard-drive configuration 160MB to 250MB

- One 1.4MB disk drive with DMA (drive reads both standard Macintosh and DOS diskettes)

- CD-ROM optional. New CD ROMs do not require the CD caddy on older models.

- Support for high-speed asynchronous SCSI devices

- EtherNet on-board with DMA channel, AAUI connector

- 16-bit audio stereo I/O with DMA

- Two serial ports—LocalTalk and GeoPort compatible with DMA channel

- Apple desktop bus (ADB for input devices)

The Power Macintosh 7100/66

The Power Macintosh 7100/66 is aimed toward business, educational, and professional environments, and uses a PowerPC 601 processor running at 66MHz. The 7100/66 has more room for expansion, with capacity for 136MB of DRAM (compared to the 6100/60's maximum 72MB). The Power Macintosh 7100/66 also has three full-size NuBus expansion slots and ships with 1MB video RAM, expandable to 2MB.

Figure 8.2 shows the Power Macintosh 7100/66.

The Power Macintosh 7100/66 has the following features:

- 66MHz PowerPC 601 processor

- 68LC040 ROM provided for 680x0 emulation

Figure 8.2
The Power
Macintosh
7100/66.

■ Native and emulated software runs 25 percent faster than the Power Macintosh 6100/60.

■ Slot for an optional second-level cache

■ 8MB DRAM standard with capacity for 126MB

■ Base hard-drive configuration 250MB to 500MB

■ One 1.4MB disk drive with DMA (drive reads both standard Macintosh and DOS diskettes)

■ CD-ROM optional. New CD ROMs do not require the CD caddy on older models.

■ Support for high-speed asynchronous SCSI devices

■ EtherNet on-board with DMA channel, AAUI connector

■ 16-bit audio stereo I/O with DMA

■ Two serial ports—LocalTalk and GeoPort compatible with DMA channel

■ Ships with hardware support and connections for two monitors

■ Apple desktop bus (ADB for input devices)

The Power Macintosh 8100/80

The Power Macintosh 8100/80 is a tower system and is designed for use in performance-critical professional situations, in particular in engineering and publishing (including CD-ROM publishing) installations. The 8100/80 uses a PowerPC 601 processor running at 80 MHz and its system memory is expandable to 264MB. The 8100/80 ships with 2MB of VRAM, which is expandable to 4MB.

Figure 8.3 shows the Power Macintosh 8100/80.

Figure 8.3
The Power
Macintosh
8100/80.

The features of the Power Macintosh 8100/80 are summarized as follows:

- 80MHz PowerPC 601 processor

- 68LC040 ROM provided for 680x0 emulation

- Native and emulated software runs nearly twice fast as the Power Macintosh 6100/60.

- Standard 256KB second-level cache

- 8MB DRAM standard with capacity for 264MB

- Base hard-drive configuration 250MB to 1GB

- One 1.4MB disk drive with DMA (drive reads both standard Macintosh and DOS diskettes)

- CD-ROM optional. New CD ROM do not require the CD caddy on older models.

- Support for high-speed asynchronous SCSI devices. Dual SCSI channels

- EtherNet on-board with DMA channel, AAUI connector

- 16-bit audio stereo I/O with DMA

- Two serial ports—LocalTalk and GeoPort compatible with DMA channel

- Ships with hardware support and connections for two monitors

- Apple desktop bus (ADB for input devices)

Table 8.1 summarizes the basic features of the three Power Macintosh systems.

Table 8.1 The Power Macintosh System—Functionality Matrix

Power Macintosh	6100/60	7100/66	8100/80
Processor	PowerPC 601	PowerPC 601	PowerPC 601
Speed	60MHz	66MHz	80MHz
L2 Cache	Supported/		
Optional	Supported/		
Optional	256KB standard		
Performance: Native applications	2 to 4 times 68040@33MHz	25% faster than 6100/60	Nearly twice as fast as 6100/60
Performance: Emulated applications	Fast 68030 to 68040-based Macintosh	25% faster than 6100/60	Nearly twice as fast as 6100/60
Standard DRAM	8MB	8MB	8MB
DRAM capacity	72MB	136MB	264MB
SIMM slots	2	4	8
Standard Hard Drive	160MB to 250MB	250MB to 500MB	250MB to 1GB
Standard Diskette Drive	1.4MB with DMA	1.4MB with DMA	1.4MB with DMA

(continues)

Table 8.1 Continued			
Power Macintosh	**6100/60**	**7100/66**	**8100/80**
CD-ROM	Optional	Optional	Optional
DRAM Video	Standard	Standard	Standard
VRAM Video		1MB standard	2MB standard
VRAM expansion		2MB	4MB
Standard support	1 monitor	2 monitors	2 monitors
SCSI	High-speed asynchronous	High-speed asynchronous	High-speed asynchronous
Dual SCSI channels			
Networking	EtherNet onboard with DMA channel, AAUI connector		
Other built-in features	16-bit audio stereo I/O with DMA Two serial ports—LocalTalk and GeoPort compatible with DMA channel Apple desktop bus (ADB for input devices)		

Power Macintosh AV Models

The three Power Macintosh systems also are available in AV models. The basic characteristics are the same as the base models, but they require additional hardware to support video input and output. This hardware enables the user to use a television or VCR as input or output. AV models also provide telephone integration and voice recognition, which also are available as options on the non-AV models.

Apple's PowerPC Upgrade Options

Along with the Power Macintosh systems, Apple is offering a wide range of upgrade options for existing systems. Some systems can upgrade logic boards to make them equivalent to the new Power Macintosh systems. Apple also offers a user-installable upgrade card. The upgrade options are described in the following sections.

Power Macintosh Logic Board Upgrades
The first three Power Macintosh systems, described in this chapter, use the same form factors of previous systems, which allows current 680x0-based

systems to be easily upgraded to Power Macintoshes. Logic board upgrades allow users of existing systems to upgrade their current Macintosh to the newer Power Macintoshes by replacing the current logic boards with the newer logic boards.

Apple is providing logic board upgrades for both their base models and the AV models of all three Power Macintosh systems. The features and requirements are summarized as follows:

- Upgrade support provided for all three Power Macintosh systems.

- Power Macintosh 6100/60 upgrades are available for Centris/Quadra 660AV and Centris/Quadra 610 systems.

- Power Macintosh 7100/66 upgrades are available for Centris/Quadra 650, Macintosh IIvx, Macintosh IIvi, and Performa 600 systems.

- Power Macintosh 8100/80 upgrades are available for Quadra 840AV and Quadra 800 systems.

- Upgrades include 8MB DRAM and the same interface connectors and audio/video supports as the Power Macintosh model.

- The logic boards offer the same DRAM and VRAM expandability options as the Power Macintosh models. DRAM must be 72-pin, 80 nanoseconds or faster, and installed in pairs.

- Upgrade includes the following software—System 7.1.2 operating system with AppleScript, PC Exchange, and QuickTime.

- AV upgrades include the following video-in features—NTSC, PAL, and SECAM; a resizable video in window; and frame and video capture.

- AV upgrades include NTSC and PAL video-out features.

- AV upgrades include S-video for video input/output and include composite (RCA) adapters.

Power Macintosh Upgrade Cards

The Power Macintosh upgrade card allows some Macintosh users to upgrade their processor to a PowerPC 601. The upgrade cards are available for Quadra 700, 800, 900, and 950 models and Centris/Quadra 610 and 650 models, and can be installed by the user.

The upgrade card fits into the Motorola 68040 Processor Direct Slot (PDS) on the host system.

The features and requirements of the Power Macintosh upgrade cards are summarized as follows:

- The processor speed is twice the clock speed of the host mother board.

- The upgrade card includes 1MB of static RAM (SRAM) memory.

- A minimum of 8MB on the host motherboard is required.

- The adapter card does not provide additional interfaces; all interfaces on the host system can be used.

- The adapter card requires a NuBus slot in line with the 68040 PDS to be available.

- Upgrade includes System 7.1.2 operating system software with AppleScript, PC Exchange, and QuickTime.

- Upgrades system can boot off of the Motorola 68040 or the PowerPC 601.

The following optional Power Macintosh accessories also are available:

- Power Macintosh 6100/60 NuBus Adapter

- 256K SRAM cache card

- HDI-45 to DB-15 video display adapter

- 4-, 8-, 16-, and 32MB DRAM expansion kits

- 7100/66 and 8100/80 VRAM expansion kits

- GeoPort Telecom adapter

Table 8.2 summarizes the Power Macintosh upgrade options.

Table 8.2 Macintosh PowerPC Upgrade Options

Host Macintosh system	Logic Board Upgrades		Upgrade Card
	6100/60 6100/60AV	7100/66 7100/66AV	8100/80 8100/80AV
Quadra 900 950		Yes	
Quadra 840AV		Yes	
Quadra 800		Yes	Yes
Quadra 700			Yes
Centris/ Quadra 660AV	Yes		
Centris/ Quadra 650		Yes	Yes
Centris/ Quadra 610	Yes		Yes
IIvx, IIvi, Performa 600		Yes	

Monitor Options

Table 8.3 summarizes the monitor configurations available for the Power Macintosh systems.

Table 8.3 Power Macintosh Monitor Options

Monitor	Standard DRAM	1MB VRAM	2MB VRAM	4MB VRAM
12" color	16-bit	24-bit	24-bit	24-bit
14" color	16-bit	24-bit	24-bit	24-bit
13" VGA	16-bit	24-bit	24-bit	24-bit
15" portrait	8-bit	8-bit	8-bit	8-bit

(continues)

Table 8.3 Continued

Monitor	Standard DRAM	1MB VRAM	2MB VRAM	4MB VRAM
16" color	8-bit	16-bit	24-bit	24-bit
19" color	Unavailable	8-bit	16-bit	24-bit
21" color	Unavailable	8-bit	16-bit	24-bit

Summary

In this chapter, we have looked at the first Macintosh systems based on PowerPC Architecture—systems whose performance and functionality benefit directly from the RISC design. And over the next year, Apple will add a broader assortment of systems, both larger and smaller, that further exploit the opportunities made possible with PowerPC Architecture.

The next chapter takes a step back and looks at PowerPC Architecture's ancestry in IBM's POWER architecture—an architecture intended primarily for high-powered workstation and server systems.

Chapter 9

The RS/6000 POWER Connection

The POWER architecture is IBM's first fully implemented RISC architecture and is based on results of the experimental 801 minicomputer. The POWER architecture is intended as a multi-chip processor implementation and was developed for IBM's successful line of RS/6000 workstation and server systems.

The POWER architecture is the direct predecessor of the PowerPC Architecture, which refines many details of the POWER architecture making it more suitable for a wider range of single-chip implementations. The PowerPC Architecture retains binary compatibility with the POWER architecture, enabling it to run the large installed base of AIX software developed for the RS/6000.

Although the basic RISC design philosophy forms the core of the POWER design, some aspects of the POWER architecture diverge somewhat from the orthodox RISC methodology as it is strictly defined. But the POWER architecture is designed around a register-to-register model and with separate arithmetic and load/store instructions that are the primary characteristics of RISC processing. The POWER architecture extends away from the purest RISC concepts mainly in the inclusion of several compound, non-orthogonal instructions included in the instruction-set architecture (ISA) for greater efficiency, greater precision, or to provide greater control over register resources.

But it is the RISC nature of the architecture that provides the RS/6000 with a lean, efficiently running processor explicitly intended to take the fullest

This chapter touches on the following:

- Design criteria of IBM's POWER architecture on which the PowerPC Architecture is based

- Technical details of the POWER architecture

- Characteristics that are in common to both architectures

benefit of pipelining, superscalar dispatch, and parallel execution. These underlying considerations are clear by looking at the conceptual processor model upon which the ISA is based (see fig. 9.1).

Figure 9.1
POWER architecture model showing relationships between basic units.

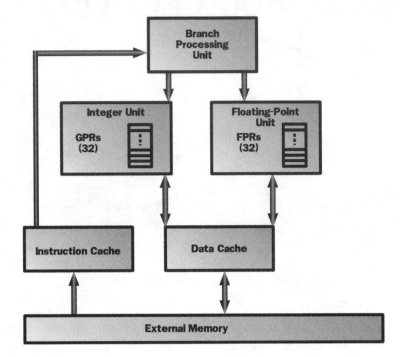

Notice in Figure 9.1 the importance that superscalar dispatch has in forming the basis for the instruction set. The conceptual model of the BPU contains branch-related registers (such as the CR, LR, and CTR), and it passes the remaining instructions on to the integer and floating-point execution units, which respectively contain the GPRs and FPRs that provide source and target registers. The integer and floating-point units have direct access to the data cache for integer and floating-point load and store instructions. Notice, however, that memory can be configured so that blocks or pages of memory may be specified as non-cacheable or write-through, so memory accesses can be forced to bypass the caches.

The POWER architecture adheres to the fundamental RISC precepts in the following respects:

- The POWER ISA consists of uniform-length (32-bit) instructions.

- The POWER instructions are implemented with simple and consistent encodings.

- The POWER ISA consists mainly of simple, multi-purpose instructions that mostly have the same instruction latency.

- All arithmetic instructions use the large complement of registers for source operands and for storing results instead of reading and writing data directly to memory.

- The POWER ISA includes a separate set of load/store instructions that transfer data between memory (including the caches) and the two register files (GPRs for integer operations and FPRs for floating-point operations).

- The POWER ISA implements relatively simple addressing modes.

- The POWER ISA uses non-destructive instruction formats that provide separate registers for multiple source operands and destination operand. Most instructions specify two source registers and one destination register.

Although the POWER architecture is centered around the basic RISC architectural tenets, it diverges the strictly orthodox RISC principles for practical reasons, most of which are consistent with the design goals seen in the conceptual model shown in Figure 9.1.

Most significant is the extensive and integrated support for floating-point instructions. Floating-point instructions tend to have longer latencies, and extended series of floating-point instructions can limit the effectiveness of highly parallel implementations, which violates a basic premise of RISC design; that is, that instructions should have the same latency. Typically, the floating-point pipeline can become the critical path for extended periods of time, forcing lower latency pipelines (such as an integer or load/store pipelines) to remain idle, which can be offset by additional resources and optimizing compilers that can reschedule instructions to reduce such impact.

However, the demand for floating-point functionality is essential to high-end workstations and is becoming more and more essential to the broader array of personal computers. While many processors (both RISC and CISC) implement floating-point instructions as a separate math coprocessor, the FPU in the POWER architecture is treated as an integral part of the machine, and the superscalar dispatch mechanism is designed with efficient, parallel floating-point operations in mind.

> **Note**
>
> The POWER architecture defines a separate condition register for branching. The use of a single resource that must be accessed by many instructions can create a bottleneck, which the POWER architecture avoids by making the condition register update optional (indicated with a period at the end of the instruction mnemonic, and by dividing the condition registers into eight, four-bit fields (CR0-CR7). CR0 is updated by integer instructions and CR1 is updated by floating-point instructions. Bits in the CR can be accessed and manipulated by several instructions. The PowerPC Architecture implements the condition register in a similar manner.

Zero-cycle branching
The ability to replace an instruction stream.

In the POWER architecture, the condition register is implemented in such a way that *zero-cycle branching* can be achieved; that is, conditional branch instructions can be resolved early and the branch instruction can be replaced in the instruction stream by either the branch target instruction or by the next sequential instruction, depending upon how the branch instruction is resolved.

The POWER architecture also supports complex instructions for handling special situations, such as the following:

- The load/store multiple/string instructions are useful primarily for saving and restoring registers across a procedure call.

- For most load and store operations, instructions are provided that automatically update the address register.

- The ISA defines a set of compound floating-point accumulate instructions—Multiply-Add, Multiply-Subtract, Negative Multiply-Add, Negative Multiply-Subtract. These compound instructions, which are especially useful in matrix algebra, can execute more quickly and with greater precision than if the operations were performed by separate instructions.

- Instructions are provided for manipulating bits within registers (particularly the condition register).

The conceptual model in Figure 9.1 is reflected in the more detailed functional block diagram of the RS/6000 processor shown in Figure 9.2.

Like the 801, the RS/6000 implements a Harvard-architecture cache design—that is separate instruction and data caches. Likewise, the PowerPC

Architecture is designed to permit both Harvard-architecture and unified cache implementations. Having separate instruction and data caches allows each cache to be optimized according to the special needs of data and instructions. For example, coherency typically is not an issue with instruction caches because most processors do not implement self-modifying code. Therefore, snooping logic and coherency checking need only be implemented in the data cache. Also, implementing separate caches reduces contention for cache resources—instruction fetches do not need to compete with load/store instructions to the data cache.

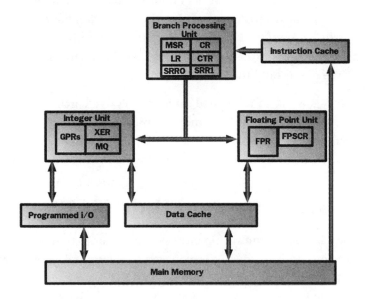

Figure 9.2
RS/6000 block diagram showing parallel instructions units, cache structure, and register resources.

The data and instruction caches in the RS/6000 are different from one another and are optimized for their individual needs. The instruction cache is a two-way set associative 8KB cache with a 64-byte line size. The instruction cache can pass as many as four instructions to the instruction buffer (assuming they are in the cache, they fall within the same 4KB page, and there are no instructions stalled in the instruction buffer). The instruction cache unit (ICU) can dispatch as many as four instructions from the instruction buffer—two internally (branch and condition register instructions) and two instructions in any combination to the IU and FPU.

The data cache is a four-way set associative 64KB cache (implemented as four 16KB chips) with a line size of 128 words. The RS/6000 can optionally be run with two data cache chips (for 32KB of data cache). The four-chip version provides a four-word bus to system memory, a double-word bus to the FPU (the width of an FPR, so an entire double-precision operand can be transferred in a single clock), a single-word connection to the integer unit (the width of a GPR, so an entire integer operand can be transferred in one clock), and a double-word connection to the instruction cache unit.

The instruction cache unit incorporates the branch processing unit (BPU), which plays an essential role in determining the address of the next instruction to be fetched; that is, if a branch is encountered, the BPU determines the address of the predicted target instruction for speculative fetching. Instructions from the predicted path are placed in the instruction buffer, but they are not dispatched until the branch is resolved. This is unlike the 601, which speculatively executes instructions from a predicted branch, but does not write back the results until the branch is resolved.

As shown in Figure 9.1 and discussed earlier, the POWER architecture is optimized to facilitate superscalar implementations. The instruction unit dispatches instructions in pairs to the FPU and to the IU in any combination (two floating-point instructions, two integer instructions, or one of each).

The System Control Unit (SCU)

Because the RS/6000 is a multi-chip processor, communication between the component chips is required. This is managed by the central system controller. The SCU acts as the processor's memory and I/O bus master and controls communication between the CPU (which consists of the IU, FPU, and the data cache unit), main memory, and I/O.

Execution Units

Instructions issued from the ICU/BPU are dispatched in pairs to the IU and the FPU, Each execution unit sees both instructions but discards instructions intended for the other execution unit. So, although the BPU can dispatch both instructions to the same execution unit, the most efficient combination is to dispatch one instruction apiece to each execution unit.

The notion of out-of-order execution may seem a bit contradictory—certainly a programmer must be careful about the order in which instructions are specified in the program, so it would seem that the processor should not be allowed to mix the order of those instructions at will. It doesn't. Operations that do not have some serial dependency are allowed to complete, but those operations that do require certain events to occur in a strict order are serialized by the processor. Therefore, instructions execute in parallel, but resources (such as register renaming) are provided to reduce interdependencies among the units and to allow instructions to complete out-of-order. From a programming perspective, though, instructions appear to complete in order.

The integer unit executes all integer arithmetic instructions, and like the 601, the integer unit also executes both integer and floating-point loads and store instructions.

The integer unit contains the arithmetic logic unit (ALU) and the general-purpose registers (GPRs). The GPRs are implemented in such a way that arithmetic instructions, which use the GPRs for specifying source and destination operands, can be pipelined with integer load/store instructions. That is, both instructions have similar latencies. However, there is a single-cycle delay between an integer load instruction and a subsequent instruction that depends on the load data.

Because the IU executes floating-point load and store instructions, floating-point load instructions are less apt to cause delays to dependent floating-point instructions. This is due to the fact that the IU is typically ahead of the FPU. There is no delay if the dependent instruction is a floating-point store instruction.

To help with address translations for load/store operations, the IU also contains the 128-entry, two-way set-associative data table look-aside buffers (DTLBs). The DTLBs contain the most recent translations used to translate the effective (logical) addresses into the physical addresses necessary for accessing memory. The DTLBs also contain information about page protection and data locking. The IU contains the 16 segment registers used to generate the 52-bit virtual address, which is similar to the effective/virtual/physical memory translation scheme used by the 601.

The IU contains the integer exception register (XER), which is also defined by the PowerPC Architecture, and the MQ register, required by certain integer instructions. The MQ register is implemented in the 601 processor, but is not defined by the PowerPC register.

The integer pipeline has four stages:

- *Instruction decode.* Instructions are decoded and operand data is retrieved from the GPRs.

- *Integer execute.* Arithmetic calculations are performed on ALU instructions and addresses are generated for all load/store instructions.

- *Cache access.* Data is fetched from the data cache to the GPRs and FPRs.

- *Writeback.* Integer arithmetic results are written to the GPRs.

Not all integer instructions must pass through each stage in the integer pipeline.

Most floating-point instructions have a latency of two clock cycles. The FPU contains the 32, 64-bit FPRs, which store all data in double-precision format. The FPRs can be locked, which effectively prevents the execution of floating-point instructions.

The FPU also contains the floating-point status and control register, which is used to enable floating-point exceptions and to indicate the source of those error conditions.

The FPU conforms to the IEEE 754 floating-point standard. Because the POWER architecture is intended for high-end workstation implementations it supports only double-precision floating-point operations. On the other hand, the PowerPC Architecture is intended for a wider range of system implementations, including lower-end desktop and portable systems, so the PowerPC Architecture provides an additional set of single-precision floating-point instructions that provides faster execution when the greater accuracy provided by double-precision arithmetic is not required.

The floating-point pipeline consists of six stages:

- *Predecode.* To avoid stalls due to resource contention, FPR dependencies are noted in preparation for FPR register renaming.

- *Remap.* The registers specified by the floating-point instructions (both arithmetic and load/store instructions) are mapped to physical registers.

- *Floating-point decode.* Instructions are decoded and data from the FPRs is available to floating-point instructions.

- *Two execute stages*. In two clock cycles the execution stages can perform a complete multiply-add calculation—(A*B)+C=D. (This operation is not only atypical because it is a compound operation, but also because it specifies three source registers instead of two.)

- *Floating-point writeback*. Results of arithmetic instructions write back their results to the FPRs.

Not all floating-point instructions must pass through every floating-point pipeline stage. To preserve a precise exception model (that is, to be able to keep an instruction from writing back its results ahead of an instruction that causes an exception), the four stages of the integer pipeline and the first four stages in the floating-point pipeline function in lock step.

The FPU also contains a five-entry pending-store queue and a four-entry store data queue, which allows floating-point store instructions to pass through the integer pipeline without stalling even though the FPU has not yet produced the store data. The IU, which typically runs ahead of the FPU, is able to generate the effective address, handle TLB and cache operations, and check for data protection for the floating-point store without stalling for lack of floating-point data, therefore allowing subsequent instructions in the integer pipeline to execute.

Table 9.1 describes the registers implemented in the RS/6000.

Table 9.1 RS/6000 RegistersTable 9.1 RS/6000 Registers	
Register	**Description**
User-Level Registers	
General-Purpose Registers (GPRs)	Thirty-two 32-bit registers used to provide source and destination operands for integer arithmetic instructions and integer load/store instructions. Also used for calculation of effective addresses for load/store instructions.
Floating-Point Registers (FPRs)	Thirty-two 64-bit registers used for source and destination registers for floating-point arithmetic instructions.
Condition Register (CR)	Divided into eight four-bit fields (CR0–CR7). CR0 is updated by integer instructions, and CR1 is updated by floating-point instructions. The condition register is used for determining directions for conditional branch instructions.

(continues)

Table 9.1 Continued	
Register	**Description**
User-Level Registers	
Count Register (CTR)	Holds loop counter value for Branch to Count Register Instructions.
Link Register (LR)	Holds target address for Branch to Link instructions and return address.
Multiply Quotient (MQ)	Used for shift with MQ, multiply, and divide instructions and for arithmetic instructions that require extended precision.
Integer Exception Register (XER)	Indicates exception condition sources (such as overflows and carries) for integer arithmetic instructions.
Floating-Point Status and Control Register (FPSCR)	Records status that results from floating-point operations and provides bits for enabling and disabling floating-point exception conditions, such as invalid-instruction, overflow, and zero-divide conditions.
Exception-Related Registers	
Machine State Register (MSR)	The MSR is used to specify operational modes of the processor.
Save Restore Register 0 (SRR0)	Saves the address of the next instruction to be executed after returning from an exception.
Save Restore Register 1 (SRR1)	Holds the contents of the MSR that defines the configuration before an exception is taken.
External Interrupt Summary Register (EIS)	Holds information that identifies the source of an external interrupt.
External Interrupt Mask Register (EIM)	Provides bits for enabling and disabling conditions that can generate external interrupts.

POWER Instruction Set

The tables in this section show the relationship between the POWER and PowerPC instruction sets.

The POWER instructions that are implemented in the PowerPC Architecture are listed in Table 9.2.

Table 9.2 POWER Architecture Instructions Implemented in PowerPC Architecture			
POWER		**PowerPC**	
Mnemonic	**Instruction**	**Mnemonic**	**Instruction**
ax	Add	addcx	Add Carrying
aex	Add Extended	addex	Add Extended
ai	Add Immediate Carrying	addic	Add Immediate
ai.	Add Immediate and Record	addic.	Add Immediate Carrying and Record
amex	Add to Minus One One Extended	addmex	Add to Minus One Extended
andil.	AND Immediate Lower	andi.	AND Immediate
andiu.	AND Immediate Upper	andis.	AND Immediate Shifted
azex	Add to Zero Extended	addzex	Add to Zero Extended
bccx	Branch Conditional to Count Register	bcctrx	Branch Conditional to Count Register
bcrx	Branch Conditional to Link Register	bclrx	Branch Conditional to Link Register
cal	Compute Address Lower	addi	Add Immediate
cau	Compute Address Upper	addis	Add Immediate Shifted

(continues)

Table 9.2 Continued

POWER		PowerPC	
Mnemonic	**Instruction**	**Mnemonic**	**Instruction**
caxx	Compute Address	addx	Add
cntlzx	Count Leading Zeros	cntlzwx	Count Leading Zeros Word
dclz	Data Cache Line Set to Zero	dcbz	Data Cache Block Set to Zero
dcs	Data Cache Synchronize	sync	Synchronize
extsx	Extend Sign	extshx	Extend Sign Half Word
fax	Floating Add	faddx	Floating-Point Add
fdx	Floating Divide	fdivx	Floating-Point Divide
fmx	Floating Multiply	fmulx	Floating-Point Multiply
fmax	Floating Multiply-Add	fmaddx	Floating-Point Multiply-Add
fmsx	Floating Multiply-Subtract	fmsub	Floating-Point Multiply-Subtract
fnmax	Floating Negative Multiply-Add	fnmaddx	Floating-Point Negative Multiply-Add
fnmsx	Floating Negative Multiply-Subtract	fnmsubx	Floating-Point Negative Multiply-Subtract
fsx	Floating Subtract	fsubx	Floating-Point Subtract
ics	Instruction Cache Synchronize	isync	Instruction Synchronize
l	Load	lwz	Load Word and Zero
lbrx	Load Byte-Reverse Indexed	lwbrx	Load Word Byte-Reverse Indexed

POWER		PowerPC	
Mnemonic	**Instruction**	**Mnemonic**	**Instruction**
lm	Load Multiple	lmw	Load Multiple Word
lsi	Load String Immediate	lswi	Load String Word Immediate
lsx	Load String Indexed	lswx	Load String Word Indexed
lu	Load with Update	lwzu	Load Word and Zero with Update
lux	Load with Update Indexed	lwzux	Load Word and Zero with Update Indexed
lx	Load Indexed	lwzx	Load Word and Zero Indexed
mtsri	Move to Segment Segment Register Indirect	mtsrin	Move to Register Indirect*
muli	Multiply Immediate	mulli	Multiply Low Immediate
mulsx	Multiply Short	mullwx	Multiply Low
oril	OR Immediate Lower	ori	OR Immediate
oriu	OR Immediate Upper	oris	OR Immediate Shifted
rlimix	Rotate Left Immediate then Mask Insert	rlwimix	Rotate Left Word Immediate then Mask Insert
rlinmx	Rotate Left Immediate then AND	rlwinmx	Rotate Left Word Immediate then AND with Mask
rlnmx	Rotate Left then AND with Mask	rlwnmx	Rotate Left Word then AND with Mask
sfx	Subtract from	subfcx	Subtract from Carrying
sfex	Subtract from Extended	subfex	Subtract from Extended

(continues)

Table 9.2 Continued

POWER		PowerPC	
Mnemonic	**Instruction**	**Mnemonic**	**Instruction**
sfi	Subtract from Immediate	subfic	Subtract from Immediate Carrying
sfmex	Subtract from Minus One Extended	subfmex	Subtract from Minus One Extended
sfzex	Subtract from Zero Extended	subfzex	Subtract from Zero Extended
slx	Shift Left	slwx	Shift Left Word
srx	Shift Right	srwx	Shift Right Word
srax	Shift Right Algebraic	srawx	Shift Right Algebraic Word
sraix	Shift Right Algebraic Immediate	srawix	Shift Right Algebraic Word Immediate
st	Store	stw	Store Word
stbrx	Store Byte-Reverse Indexed	stwbrx	Store Word Byte-Reverse Indexed
stm	Store Multiple	stmw	Store Multiple Word
stsi	Store String Immediate	stswi	Store String Word Immediate
stsx	Store String Indexed	stswx	Store String Word Indexed
stu	Store with Update	stwu	Store Word with Update
stux	Store with Update Indexed	stwux	Store Word with Update Indexed
stx	Store Indexed	stwx	Store Word Indexed
svca	Supervisor Call	sc	System Call

POWER		PowerPC	
Mnemonic	**Instruction**	**Mnemonic**	**Instruction**
t	Trap	tw	Trap Word
ti	Trap Immediate	twi	Trap Word Immediate *
tlbi	TLB Invalidate Entry	tlbie	Translation Lookaside Buffer Invalidate Entry
xoril	XOR Immediate Lower	xori	XOR Immediate
xoriu	XOR Immediate Upper	xoris	XOR Immediate Shifted

* Supervisor-level instruction

Table 9.3 lists the instructions that are part of the POWER architecture that have been deleted from the PowerPC Architecture.

Table 9.3 POWER Instructions Deleted from PowerPC Architecture	
Mnemonic	**Instruction**
abs	Absolute
clcs	Cache Line Compute Size
clf	Cache Line Flush
cli	Cache Line Invalidate
dclst	Data Cache Line Store
div	Divide
divs	Divide Short
doz	Difference or Zero
dozi	Difference or Zero Immediate
lscbx	Load String and Compare Byte Indexed
maskg	Mask Generate

(continues)

Table 9.3 Continued	
Mnemonic	**Instruction**
maskir	Mask Insert from Register
mfsrin	Move from Segment Register Indirect
mul	Multiply
nabs	Negative Absolute
rac	Real Address Compute
rlmi	Rotate Left then Mask Insert
rrib	Rotate Right and Insert Bit
sle	Shift Left Extended
sleq	Shift Left Extended with MQ
sliq	Shift Left Immediate with MQ
slliq	Shift Left Long Immediate with MQ
sllq	Shift Left Long with MQ
slq	Shift Left with MQ
sraiq	Shift Right Algebraic Immediate with MQ
sraq	Shift Right Algebraic with MQ
sre	Shift Right Extended
srea	Shift Right Extended Algebraic
sreq	Shift Right Extended with MQ
sriq	Shift Right Immediate with MQ
srliq	Shift Right Long Immediate with MQ
srlq	Shift Right Long with MQ
srq	Shift Right with MQ
svcx	Supervisor Call, with SA = 0

Summary

This section has taken a closer look at the POWER architecture, emphasizing in particular the relationships between the POWER and the PowerPC Architectures.

The next several chapters take a closer look at details of the PowerPC Architecture, describing in some detail aspects of the register set, instruction set, memory conventions, exception model, and the cache and memory management models.

Chapter 10

The PowerPC Register Set

IBM's earliest experiments that lead to RISC architecture was the telephone switching device described in Chapter 5, "The Genesis of the PowerPC RISC Architecture." One of the most important things learned from that experiment was the increased performance that can be achieved by decoupling the load and store operations from the arithmetic calculations. To reduce both the number of accesses to memory and the interdependence between memory accesses and arithmetic operations, the processor needs a large amount of space on the chip to keep operands that can be accessed both by the execution units and by system memory.

This use of a large flexible register file, or general-purpose register file, is a primary, common characteristic of RISC processors, and also is central to the PowerPC Architecture. Rather than having an instruction write its results back to memory, that operation is given to separate load instructions. Also, operands are maintained in a set of registers instead of being pushed and pulled from a stack or maintained in an accumulator. The PowerPC Architecture defines register-to-register operations for all computational instructions, and the term register-to-register architecture is often used interchangeably with RISC architecture.

The PowerPC Architecture fully supports both single- and double-precision floating-point operations, and implements a separate set of 32 64-bit floating-point registers for floating-point arithmetic. Having separate register files reduces contention for register resources, and in 32-bit implementations, integer and single-precision floating-point arithmetic requires only 32-bit operands, while double-precision operands require 64-bit operands, as specified by the IEEE floating-point specifications.

This chapter teaches you the following:

- A full description of the organization and functionality of the PowerPC register set

- Information regarding how registers can be read or written

- Distinctions between how the 32- and the 64-bit registers are implemented

Register files

The registers used as source and destination registers by arithmetic instructions and for load/store instructions.

Also, by having ample *register files*, the PowerPC Architecture is able to provide a nondestructive, three-register (also called triadic) instruction format. This format allows the programmer to specify distinct target and source registers, preserving the original data for use by other instructions and reducing the number of instructions required for certain operations. Data is transferred between memory and registers with explicit load and store instructions.

The PowerPC Architecture allows additional hardware mechanisms to further reduce the contention for these resources, such as rename registers and feedforwarding paths, that allow operand results to be provided directly to a dependent instruction, saving the additional time that may be required to read the data from a GPR or FPR.

In addition to the GPRs and FPRs, the PowerPC Architecture defines other registers that support a variety of functions such as configuration, recording arithmetic error conditions, instruction flow, memory management, timekeeping, and exception handling.

Some registers are designed for holding instruction addresses to determine the instruction flow for branch instructions and exception recovery. The count register (CTR) and link register (LR) are typically used to save the return address for certain conditional branching instructions, and the save/restore register 0 (SRR0) holds the address of the next instruction to execute when a program must be interrupted to handle an exception. Other registers also are used to save the system configuration (machine state) of the interrupted process when an exception occurs, so when exception handling completes, the processor can resume operation in the proper context.

Some branch instructions use the condition register to test certain values that determine if a branch should be taken. Many floating-point and integer instructions can optionally update the condition register.

Some registers provide a way to control system resources. For example, bits in the machine state register (MSR) determine whether the processor operates in big- or little-endian mode, or whether certain exceptions will be ignored when they occur. This information helps define the machine state, and changes when an exception is taken. The PowerPC exception model is described in Chapter 15, "PowerPC Exception Model." The previous settings are saved (to the save/restore register 1) when an exception is taken, and when the exception handling software completes its work, it issues a return from interrupt instruction (rfi), which writes the saved contents of the SRR1 register back to the MSR, and the interrupted process can resume.

> **Note**
>
> Registers also are used to store status and error conditions, which is useful in exception handling. Integer error conditions are recorded in the integer exception register (XER) and floating-point exception conditions are saved in the floating-point status and control register (FPSCR).

The time-base and decrementer registers are both incremented at a frequency drawn from the processor clock. The time-base registers provide a time reference and the DEC can be used to generate periodic exceptions (useful for splitting processor time among multiple applications).

Registers fall into the following functional categories:

- *System configuration.* Machine state register (MSR) and processor version register (PVR).

- *Registers that support integer operations.* General-purpose registers (GPRs) and integer exception register (XER).

- *Registers that support floating-point instructions.* Floating-point registers (FPRs) and floating-point status and control register (FPSCR).

- *Registers that support branch operations.* The link register (LR), the count register (CTR), and the condition register (CR).

- *Registers that support memory management.* Data and instruction block-address translation registers (DBATs and IBATs), table search description register 1 (SDR1), segment registers (in 32-bit implementations), address-space register (in 64-bit implementations).

- *Registers that support exceptions.* Save/restore register 0 (SRR0), save/restore register 1 (SRR1), DAE/source instruction service register (DSISR), data address register (DAR), integer exception register (XER), and floating-point status and control register (FPSCR).

- *Time-keeping registers.* The time-base registers (TBU and TBL) and the decrementer register.

- *Miscellaneous registers.* External access register (EAR) and the general SPRs 0-3 (SPRG0-SPRG3).

The PowerPC Architecture allows registers to define additional special-purpose registers. For example, the PowerPC 603 processor has additional registers to support its power management features. Chapter 16, "The PowerPC 601 RISC Processor," and Chapter 18, "The PowerPC 603 RISC Processor," describe the registers defined specifically for those registers.

How Registers Are Accessed

Registers can be read or written in a variety of ways. Accesses are either implicit or explicit. An implicit access is an ancillary action that occurs as part of another operation such as when an arithmetic instruction accesses the FPRs or GPRs in the course of fetching or storing operand data. For example, the GPRs and FPRs are accessed implicitly as sources and destinations for calculations. If an integer calculation causes an overflow, the XER is updated implicitly. The save/restore registers, SRR0 and SRR1, are updated implicitly when an exception is taken.

An explicit access is the result of the execution of a specific instruction designed to read or write to a specific register or group of registers. Some registers are implemented as special-purpose registers and can be written to by using the Move to Special-Purpose Register (mtspr) instruction and read by using the Move from Special-Purpose Register (mfspr) instructions. Similar instructions are provided for accessing other registers that are not SPRs, such as the machine-state register, condition register, segment registers, and the floating-point status and control register.

Some registers are accessed both explicitly and implicitly. For example, a value in the count register can be incremented implicitly as the result of the execution of certain conditional branch instructions. The CTR also can be accessed with the mfspr and mtspr instructions.

Register Set Overview

This section provides a summary of all of the register resources defined by the PowerPC Architecture. The registers are grouped by access level. User-level registers can be accessed by both user- and supervisor-level software; supervisor-level registers can be accessed only by supervisor-level software (that is, by the operating system). The registers also are grouped into functional groups, but this is an arbitrary grouping and is not defined by the PowerPC Architecture.

Figure 10.1 shows the PowerPC user-level register set.

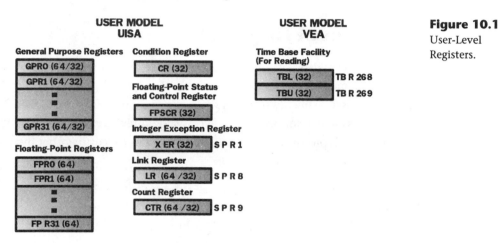

Figure 10.1
User-Level Registers.

Figure 10.2 shows supervisor-level registers.

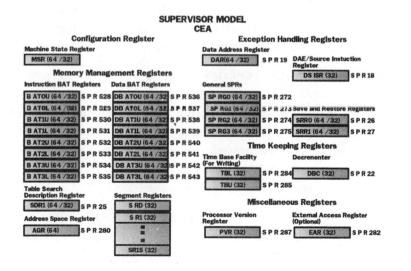

Figure 10.2
Supervisor-Level Registers.

Supervisor-level registers can only be accessed by supervisor-level software, and typically they are used for system-level operations, such as exception handling and memory management.

As shown in Figure 10.1 and Figure 10.2, some registers are 32 bits wide in 32-bit implementations and are 64 bits wide in 64-bit implementations. In most cases, the registers that are larger in 64-bit implementations are so because they are required to contain 64-bit addresses.

User-Level Registers

The user-level registers can be accessed by either user- or supervisor-level software. Some registers are defined as special-purpose registers (SPRs) and can be accessed explicitly by using the mtspr and mfspr instructions. These instructions are commonly used to access certain registers, while other SPRs may be more typically accessed as the side effect of executing other instructions.

All UISA registers can be accessed by all software with either user or supervisor privileges. The user-level register set can be grouped according to the functions they support, as described in the following sections.

Registers that Support Integer Instructions

The PowerPC Architecture defines two registers that primarily support the execution of integer instructions—GPRs and the integer exception register. Integer instructions also may interact with other registers, such as the condition register, which is described in the section on branch registers.

General-Purpose Registers (GPRs). The 32 GPRs (GPR0-GPR31) serve as the source and destination registers for integer instructions. They also are used for calculating effective addresses for both integer and floating-point load and store instructions (specified as **r**A in the instruction syntax). Conceptually, the PowerPC Architecture defines the GPRs as part of the integer unit; however, individual implementations may have multiple integer units or a separate load/store unit that also require access to the GPRs.

The critical point is that execution units that must access the GPRs should do so as efficiently as possible. GPRs are 32 bits wide in 32-bit implementations and 64 bits wide in 64-bit implementations. Although this degree of resolution is not usually required for integer arithmetic operations, the GPRs often are used for saving addresses, which are 64 bits wide in 64-bit implementations. The UISA defines additional integer arithmetic operations for double-word operands that are implemented only in 64-bit implementations.

These registers are accessed as source (**r**A and **r**B) and destination registers (**r**D) in the instruction syntax. Other instructions are defined that values in the GPRs to be written to or read from other registers; for example, the Move to/from SPR instructions.

The architecture does not assign specific functionality to the GPRs, although GPR0 has a special functionality for use in calculating effective addresses and with the addi and addis. instructions. When **r**A specifies GPR0 (indicated as (**r**A|0) in the instruction syntax), the value is assumed to be zero, eliminating the need to access the register.

The architectural definition of the GPRs is presented from the perspective of the instruction set and provides the simplest conceptual model of how the GPRs might actually be implemented. Additional hardware schemes can be implemented to optimize the use of the GPRs. Feed-forwarding paths can be used to bypass a GPR so a dependent instruction can receive data at the same time that it is written to the GPR. Register renaming can be employed, as it is in the 603, which provides buffering to the GPRs to reduce the effect of contention for a GPR resource and allows instruction execution to proceed if an operand is stalled in a GPR.

Although the registers are defined as 32-entry register files, this definition indicates only how those registers must appear to software. The actual implementation of these registers may be quite sophisticated for greater flexibility and efficiency.

Such performance enhancements can become quite elaborate, but the critical limitation is that there appear to be 32 GPRs from the perspective of the instruction set.

Integer Exception Register (XER). The XER is a 32-bit SPR (SPR1) that is primarily used to report the occurrence of overflows and carries caused by integer operations. Although it can be accessed explicitly by using the mtspr, mfspr, and the mcrxr instructions, it is more typically set implicitly as the result of executing integer arithmetic instructions that are encoded in such a way that this reporting is enabled. The XER also is used to specify the amount of data to be transferred in certain load/store string instructions.

The bit definitions for XER, shown in table 10.1, are based on the operation of an instruction considered as a whole, not on intermediate results.

For example, the result of the Subtract from Carrying (subfc) instruction is specified as the sum of three values, and is not affected if the sum of two of the values would have caused a carry.

Table 10.1 Integer Exception Register Bit Definitions		
Bits	**Name**	**Description**
0	SO	Summary Overflow—This bit is set implicitly when an instruction that causes an overflow to occur (typically an arithmetic instruction) sets the overflow bit and remains set until it is explicitly cleared by an mtspr instruction or an mcrxr instruction. If an integer instruction is encoded to update the CR (by appending the mnemonic with a period), the fourth bit in the CR0 field is set if the instruction execution sets SO.
1	OV	Overflow—This bit is set implicitly when execution of an appropriately encoded arithmetic instruction has caused an overflow. This bit is enabled by the OE bit in the instruction encoding. The OV bit can be set explicitly by the mtspr and mcrxr instructions.
2	CA	Carry—The carry bit is set implicitly when an Add Carrying, Subtract from Carrying, Add Extended, or Subtract from Extended instruction causes a carry or when a Shift Right Algebraic instruction shifts a bit out that is a binary 1 of a negative number. The CA bit can be set explicitly by the mtspr and mcrxr instructions.
3-24	—	Reserved.
25-31	SS	String size—This field specifies the number of bytes to be transferred by a Load String Word Indexed (lswx) or Store String Word Indexed (stswx) instruction.

The XER works closely with the condition register, and bits in the XER contents can be written to the CR by using the Move to Condition Register from XER (mcrxr) instruction.

Registers That Support Floating-Point Instructions

Just as integer instructions have a dedicated register file for saving operands and a separate register for reporting carries and overflows, the PowerPC Architecture specifies two similar register resources to support floating-point operations—a set of 32 FPRs that store the operands used by floating-point instructions, and the floating-point status and control registers (FPSCR), which not only reports conditions that require special handling, but also provides a means for configuring how the processor handles floating-point operations.

Floating-Point Registers (FPRs). The 32 FPRs (FPR0-FPR31) serve as the source and destination registers for floating-point arithmetic and load/store instructions. Source registers are denoted as frB, frC, (and frD in floating-point multiply-add instructions). The target register is denoted frA. FPRs are 64 bits wide in both 32- and 64-bit implementations to support the double-precision floating-point format.

All floating-point arithmetic instructions operate on data located in FPRs and, with the exception of compare instructions, place results into an FPR. Instruction status is reported to the FPSCR and in some cases, into the CR (the CR1 field) after instruction execution completes.

Load and store double word instructions transfer 64 bits of data between memory and the FPRs with no conversion. Load single instructions read single-precision floating-point values from memory and convert them to double-precision floating-point values which are placed into a specified FPR. Store single instructions read double-precision floating-point values from an FPR and convert them to single-precision floating-point values, which are stored in the specified memory location.

Both floating-point arithmetic instructions accept values from the FPRs in double-precision format. Some double-precision values cannot be representedin single-precision format, and attempting to perform single-precision arithmetic with these values causes undefined results to be recorded in the target FPR, in the FPSCR, and in the condition register if the update option is specified.

Floating-Point Status and Control Register (FPSCR). The FPSCR is a user-level register provided to allow user software to control aspects of floating-point operations, such as which conditions generate exceptions and which method of rounding is used. It also provides a way that software can record floating-point exception conditions (such as overflow or underflow) and the type of the result produced by a floating-point operation.

The FPSCR can be accessed explicitly with the following instructions:

- *Move from FPSCR (mffs).* Writes the contents of the FPSCR to a specified FPR.

- *Move to FPSCR Field Immediate (mtfsfi).* Writes an immediate value to a specified FPSCR field.

- *Move to FPSCR Fields (mtfsf).* Writes the contents of a specified range in an FPR into the FPSCR.

- *Move to FPSCR Bit 0 (mtfsb0).* Clears a specified FPSCR bit (except the summary bits, FEX or VX).

- *Move to FPSCR Bit 1 (mtfsb1).* Sets a specified FPSCR bit (except FEX or VX).

- *Move to Condition Register from FPSCR (mcrfs).* Copies the contents of a specified FPSCR field into a specified condition register field. All exception bits in the FPSCR can be copied (except FEX and VX).

Notice that most exception condition bits are sticky bits (bits 0-12 and 21-23); that is, when these bits are set, they remain set until they are cleared explicitly by an mcrfs, mtfsfi, mtfsf, or mtfsb0 instruction. The two summary bits, FEX and VX, are not sticky.

As shown in table 10.2, Bits 0-23 are status bits. Bits 24-31 are control bits. The FPSCR is updated when instruction execution completes.

Table 10.2 FPSCR Bit Settings

Bit	Name	Description
0	FX	Floating-point exception summary. Set if any floating-point instruction except mtfsfi and mtfsf causes sets any previously cleared exception bit in the FPSCR. The mcrfs, mtfsfi, mtfsf, mtfsb0, and mtfsb1 instructions can explicitly write to this bit. This is a sticky bit.
1	FEX	Floating-point enabled exception summary. Set when any of the enabled exception conditions occurs. The mcrfs, mtfsf, mtfsfi, mtfsb0, and mtfsb1 instructions cannot alter this bit explicitly. This is not a sticky bit.
2	VX	Floating-point invalid operation exception summary. Set when any invalid operation exception condition occurs. It is the logical OR of all of the invalid operation exceptions. The mcrfs, mtfsf, mtfsfi, mtfsb0, and mtfsb1 instructions cannot alter this bit explicitly. This is not a sticky bit.
3	OX	Floating-point overflow exception. Set if a floating-point overflow exception condition occurs. This is a sticky bit.
4	UX	Floating-point underflow exception. Set if a floating-point underflow exception condition occurs. This is a sticky bit.
5	ZX	Floating-point zero divide exception. Set if a floating-point zero-divide exception condition occurs. This is a sticky bit.

Bit	Name	Description
6	XX	Floating-point inexact exception. Set if a floating-point inexact exception condition occurs. This is the sticky version of FPSCR[FI].
7	VXSNAN	Floating-point invalid operation exception for SNaN. Set if an SNaN invalid operation exception condition occurs. This is a sticky bit.
8	VXISI	Floating-point invalid operation exception for _-_. Set by an attempt to subtract infinity from infinity. This is a sticky bit.
9	VXIDI	Floating-point invalid operation exception for _/_. Set on an attempt to divide infinity by infinity. This is a sticky bit.
10	VXZDZ	Floating-point invalid operation exception for 0/0. Set by an attempt to divide zero by zero. This is a sticky bit.
11	VXIMZ	Floating-point invalid operation exception for _*0. Set by an attempt to multiply zero by infinity. This is a sticky bit.
12	VXVC	Floating-point invalid operation exception for invalid compare. Set by an attempt to perform an invalid compare operation. This is a sticky bit.
13	FR	Floating-point fraction rounded. The last arithmetic or rounding and conversion instruction that rounded the intermediate result incremented the fraction. This is not a sticky bit.
14	FI	Floating-point fraction inexact. The last instruction that attempted to round the intermediate result resulted in an inexact fraction or a disabled overflow exception. The XX bit is a sticky version of the FI bit.
15-19	FPRF	Floating-point result flags. This field is based on the value placed into the target register even if that value is undefined. The flags can be interpreted as follows: C < > = ? Result value class 1 0 0 0 1 Quiet NaN (QNaN) 0 1 0 0 1 -Infinity 0 1 0 0 0 -Normalized number 1 1 0 0 0 -Denormalized number 1 0 0 1 0 -Zero 0 0 0 1 0 +Zero 1 0 1 0 0 +Denormalized number 0 0 1 0 0 +Normalized number 0 0 1 0 1 +Infinity The meanings of the individual bits are described in the following two entries.

(continues)

Table 10.2 Continued		
Bit	**Name**	**Description**
15	C	Floating-point result class descriptor. Arithmetic, rounding, and conversion instructions may set this bit with the condition code bits, FPSCR[FPCC], bits 16-19, to indicate the class of the result.
16-19	FPCC	Floating-point condition code. Floating-point compare instructions always set one of these bits and clear the rest. Arithmetic, rounding, and conversion instructions may set the FPCC bits with the C bit to indicate the class of the result, in which case the high-order three bits of the FPCC still indicate that the value is positive, negative, or zero. 16 Floating-point less than or negative (FL or <) 17 Floating-point greater than or positive (FG or >) 18 Floating-point equal or zero (FE or =) 19 Floating-point unordered or NaN (FU or ?)
20	—	Reserved.
21	VXSOFT	Floating-point invalid operation exception for software request. This is a sticky bit. This bit can be altered only by the mcrfs, mtfsfi, mtfsf, mtfsb0, or mtfsb1 instructions.
22	VXSQRT	Floating-point invalid operation exception for invalid square root. Even though the optional square root instructions may not be implemented, this bit is implemented to provide exception support for emulation of these instructions.
23	VXCVI	Floating-point invalid operation exception for invalid integer convert. This is a sticky bit.
24	VE	Floating-point invalid operation exception enable.
25	OE	Floating-point overflow exception enable.
26	UE	Floating-point underflow exception enable. This bit should not be used to determine whether denormalization should be performed on floating-point stores.
27	ZE	Floating-point zero divide exception enable.
28	XE	Floating-point inexact exception enable.
29	NI	Floating-point non-IEEE mode. This allows the processor to perform floating-point operations that may not be compliant with IEEE specification, and may be useful for performing time-critical floating-point operations. The actual implementation of this mode is implementation-specific.

Bit	Name	Description
30-31	RN	Floating-point rounding control. These bits determine which rounding algorithm is used.
		00 Round to nearest
		01 Round toward zero
		10 Round toward +infinity
		11 Round toward -infinity

The description of the condition register describes the relationship between the FPSCR and the CR.

Registers That Support Branch Instructions

There are several registers that the branch processing unit (BPU) uses to determine the instruction flow. These registers perform such functions as providing the return or target address, store condition codes that can be tested to determine when a branch should be taken, or maintain a counter for iterative looping structures.

Condition Register (CR). The 32-bit condition register consists of eight four-bit fields, CR0-CR7. Breaking the CR into eight four-bit fields, CR0-CR7, greatly increases the flexibility since it can be used for multiple purposes without having to destroy the register contents. CR0 is used to indicate conditions (such as carries and overflows) associated with integer instructions and CR1 is used to indicate conditions associated with floating-point instructions. This register provides a mechanism for testing and branching. The CR is accessed implicitly by specially-coded floating-point and integer instructions. An integer or floating-point compare instruction can specify a CR field to store its result.

The architecture also defines a set of instructions for explicitly accessing the CR.

- The Move to Condition Register Field instruction (mtcrf) updates CR fields by writing bits from a specified GPR.

- The Move to Condition Register from XER instruction (mcrxr) updates a specified CR field by writing bits from the XER.

- The Move to Condition Register from FPSCR instruction (mcrfs) updates a specified CR field by writing bits from the FPSCR.

- The Move Condition Register Field instruction (mcrf) moves data from one CRx field to another.

■ Condition register logical instructions, such as cror, crxor, and crand, perform logical operations (OR, XOR, and AND) on individual bits.

Branch instructions are provided to test individual CR bits.

Condition Register CR0—Integer Conditions. If an integer instruction is coded to update the condition register (by specifying a period at the end of the instruction), the first three bits of CR0 are set by an algebraic comparison of the result to zero and the fourth bit of CR0 is copied from XER[SO].

Table 10.3 describes the bit settings for the CR0 field in the condition register.

Table 10.3 Bit Settings for CR0	
CR0	**Description**
0	Negative (LT)—Set when the result is negative.
1	Positive (GT)—Set when the result is positive (and not zero).
2	Zero (EQ)—Set when the result is zero.
3	Summary overflow (SO)—Set to value of XER[SO] at instruction completion.

Condition Register CR1 Field Definition. Most floating-point instructions can also be coded to update the condition register by specifying a period at the end of the instruction. For example, the double-precision, floating-point multiply instruction (fmul) can be made to update the condition register by putting a period at the end of the mnemonic—fmul.

Floating-point instructions with the update option selected update the CR1 field (bits 4-7) with bits 0-3 of the FPSCR. The bit settings for the CR1 field are shown in table 10.4.

Table 10.4 Bit Settings for CR1	
Bit	**Description**
4	Floating-point exception (FX)—Set to value of FPSCR[FX] at instruction completion.

Bit	Description
5	Floating-point enabled exception (FEX)—Set to value of FPSCR[FEX] at instruction completion.
6	Floating-point invalid exception (VX)—Set to value of FPSCR[VX] at instruction completion.
7	Floating-point overflow exception (OX)—Set to value of FPSCR[OX] at instruction completion.

Condition Register CRn Field—Compare Instruction. Integer and floating-point compare instructions update fields specified in their instructions. The bits of the specified field are interpreted as shown in table 10.5.

Table 10.5 CRn Field Bit Settings for Compare Instructions	
Bit*	**Description**
0	Less than, Floating-point less than (LT, FL).
	For integer compare instructions, (rA) < SIMM, UIMM, or rB (signed comparison) or rA <U SIMM, UIMM, or rB (unsigned comparison).
	For floating-point compare instructions, frA < frB.
1	Greater than, floating-point greater than (GT, FG).
	For integer compare instructions, rA > SIMM, UIMM, or rB (signed comparison) or rA >U SIMM, UIMM, or rB (unsigned comparison).
	For floating-point compare instructions, frA > frB.
2	Equal, floating-point equal (EQ, FE).
	For integer compare instructions, rA = SIMM, UIMM, or rB.
	For floating-point compare instructions, frA = frB.
3	Summary overflow, floating-point unordered (SO, FU).
	For integer compare instructions, this is a copy of the final state of XER[SO] at the completion of the instruction.
	For floating-point compare instructions, one or both of frA and frB is not a number (NaN).

*The bit number refers to the number in each four bit field, CR0-CR7.

Link Register (LR). The link register is an SPR (SPR8) that is used primarily for branching to subroutines. It typically holds the target address for Branch Conditional to Link Register (bclr) instructions, but it also can be used to hold the effective address of the sequential instruction after a branch and link instruction. Because the LR is intended to hold addresses, it is defined as a 32-bit register in 32-bit implementations and as a 64-bit register in 64-bit implementations.

Although the two least-significant bits can accept any values written to them, they are ignored for addressing. The link register can be accessed explicitly by the mtspr and mfspr instructions.

By fetching instructions along the target path (loaded by an mtspr instruction), the programmer can load the link register well ahead of a dependent branch instruction. PowerPC processors can fetch along a target path loaded by a branch and link instruction.

Both conditional and unconditional branch instructions can use the LR to hold the effective address of the instruction following the branch instruction. This is indicated by using the version of the instruction with the optional 'l' in the mnemonic. For example, the versions of the Branch (Unconditional) instruction the save the return address in the LR are coded as bl or bla instead of b or ba. Using the 'l' option sets the LK bit in the instruction encoding.

Count Register (CTR). The count register (CTR) can maintain a loop counter that can be decremented by certain branch instructions and it can also provide the target address for Branch Conditional to Count Register (bcctr) instructions. Because it is an SPR (SPR9), an address can be loaded into the CTR which can in turn be used as a target address for a bclr instruction. Because the CTR is designed to hold effective addresses, it is defined as a 32-bit register in 32-bit implementations and as a 64-bit register in 64-bit implementations.

In branch conditional instructions, the first four bits of the five-bit BO field specify the conditions under which the branch is taken, and whether the branch instruction causes the CTR to be decremented. Bit 5 of the BO field is used by certain conditional branch instructions as an aid for predicting the branch direction.

Registers Used For Time-Keeping

The PowerPC Architecture defines a time-base facility that can be configured by supervisor-level software, but can be read by user-level software. This facility consists of two 32-bit registers, TBU and TBL, which together form a 64-bit counter that is incremented at a frequency that is a subdivision of the processor clock, and is determined for each implementation.

The time-base registers can be accessed by user-level software by using the mftb instruction.

Supervisor-Level Registers

The OEA level of the PowerPC Architecture defines registers that are used by the operating system for such system-level responsibilities as system configuration, memory management, exception handling, and time keeping. All supervisor-level registers are SPRs except for the MSR and the segment registers are SPRs.

The supervisor-level registers can be grouped according to the functions they support, as in the following sections.

System Configuration and Status Registers

This section describes the two registers that are used to configure the processor and to indicate the processor status.

Machine State Register (MSR). The MSR is used to configure the processor, controlling such parameters as whether floating-point exceptions will be precise, imprecise, or disabled and whether the processor operates in little-endian or big-endian mode. These bits are reset when an exception is taken. The MSR is 32 bits wide in 32-bit implementations and 64 bits wide in 64-bit implementations; however, the principal difference is the additional bit to allow 64-bit implementations to toggle between 32- and 64-bit modes.

The MSR can be accessed explicitly by the Move to Machine State Register (mtmsr) and implicitly by the System Call (sc), and Return from Exception (rfi) instructions. It can be read by the Move from Machine State Register (mfmsr) instruction. The MSR bits have a default value when the processor is reset, as shown in table 10.6.

When an exception is taken, the MSR values that describe the machine state of the interrupted process are saved in the save/restore register 1 (SRR1), and are replaced by default values appropriate for the exception (although the endian mode used during exception handling is determined by the ELE bit setting). Typically, the values in SRR1 are saved to memory by an exception handler to prevent destruction of these values if another exception occurs during exception handling. The saved values in SRR1 are restored to the MSR when the exception handler routine issues the Return from Interrupt (rfi) instruction. Table 10.6 describes the bits in the MSR.

Table 10.6 MSR Bit Settings			
Name		**Description**	
Bit Number		**Name**	**Description**
32-Bit	**64-Bit**		
—	0	SF	Sixty-four bit mode 0 32-bit mode. 1 64-bit mode.
0-12	1-44	—	Reserved.
13	45	POW	Power management enable 0 Power management disabled (normal operation mode). 1 Power management enabled (reduced power mode).
14	46	—	Reserved.
15	47	ELE	Exception little-endian mode. When an exception occurs, this bit is copied into MSR[LE] to select the mode for exception handling.
16	48	EE	External interrupt enable 0 External interrupt and decrementer exceptions are delayed. 1 External interrupt and decrementer exceptions are not delayed.
17	49	PR	Privilege level 0 Supervisor-level. 1 User-level.
18	50	FP	Floating-point available Determines whether floating-point instructions, including floating-point loads, stores, and moves can be dispatched 0 Floating-point instructions cannot be dispatched. 1 Floating-point instructions and floating-point enabled exceptions can be taken. How exceptions are handled is determined by the FE0 and FE1 bits.

Name		Description	
Bit Number		**Name**	**Description**
32-Bit	**64-Bit**		
19	51	ME	Machine check exceptions enable 0 Machine check exceptions are disabled. 1 Machine check exceptions are enabled.
20	52	FE0	Floating-point exception mode 0. Together with FE1 determines whether floating-point exceptions are precise, imprecise, or disabled.
21	53	SE	Single-step trace enable 0 The processor executes instructions normally. 1 The processor generates a single-step trace exception upon the successful execution of the next instruction.
22	54	BE	Branch trace enable 0 The processor executes branch instructions normally. 1 The processor generates a branch type trace exception upon the successful execution of a branch instruction.
23	55	FE1	Floating-point exception mode 1. Together with FE0 determines whether floating-point exceptions are precise, imprecise, or disabled.
24	56	—	Reserved.
25	57	EP	Exception prefix. Specifies the vector offset 0 Exceptions are vectored to the physical address x'000...0nnnnn'. 1 Exceptions are vectored to the physical address x'FFF...Fnnnnn'.
26	58	IT	Instruction address translation 0 Instruction address translation is disabled—logical address = physical address. 1 Instruction address translation is enabled.
27	59	DT	Data address translation 0 Data address translation is disabled—logical address = physical address. 1 Data address translation is enabled.

(continues)

Table 10.6 Continued			
Name		**Description**	
Bit Number		**Name**	**Description**
32-Bit	**64-Bit**		
28-29	60-61	—	Reserved.
30	62	RE	Recoverable exception (for system reset and machine check exceptions) 0 Exception is not recoverable. 1 Exception is recoverable.
31	63	LE	Little-endian mode enable 0 The processor runs in big-endian mode. 1 The processor runs in little-endian mode.

The floating-point exception mode bits (FE0-FE1) are interpreted as shown in table 10.7. Some of these modes may not be supported by all implementations.

Table 10.7 Floating-Point Exception Mode Bits		
FE0	**FE1**	**Mode**
0	0	Floating-point exceptions disabled.
0	1	Floating-point imprecise nonrecoverable. A floating-point enabled condition exception may not cause the exception to be taken until after the instruction completes execution; the instruction may not be identified and its results may have been written back and used by subsequent instructions.
1	0	Floating-point imprecise recoverable. A floating-point enabled condition exception may not cause the exception to be taken until after the instruction completes execution; however, no results will have been written back and the excepting instruction can be identified.
1	1	Floating-point precise mode. All floating-point exceptions are handled precisely.

Note

Power management is implementation-dependent.

The power-up values of the MSR are shown in table 10.8.

Table 10.8 MSR Settings at Power Up

| Bit Number | | Name | Setting |
64-bit	32-bit		
0	—	SF	1
1-31	—	—	Unspecified
32-44	0-12	—	Unspecified
45	13	POW	0
46	14	—	Unspecified
47	15	ELE	0
48	16	EE	0
49	17	PR	0
50	18	FP	0
51	19	ME	0
52	20	FE0	0
53	21	SE	0
54	22	BE	0
55	23	FE1	0
56	24	—	Unspecified
57	25	EP	1
58	26	IT	0
59	27	DT	0
60-61	28-29	—	Unspecified
62	30	RE	0
63	31	LE	0

Processor Version Register (PVR). The PVR is a read-only register that identifies the version and revision level of the PowerPC processor. This register can be read by using the mfspr instruction, but use of the mtspr instruction is not permitted.

The PVR consists of two 16-bit fields as shown in table 10.9.

Table 10.9 Processor Version Register (PVR)		
Bits	**Field**	**Description**
0-15	Version	Identifies the version of the processor and of the PowerPC Architecture.
16-31	Revision	Identifies the engineering change level, or revision, of a particular version. The format is implementation-specific.

Registers that Support Exception Handling

The OEA portion of the PowerPC Architecture defines four registers to support exception handling. The two save/restore registers are used for saving a minimum amount of information about the processor state when an exception is taken, saving the address of the next instruction to be executed and information that defines the machine state. The data address register (DAR) and the DAE/source instruction service register (DSISR) are used for problem determination. In addition to these registers, the general-purpose SPRs (SPRG0-SPRG3) can be used to aid exception handling. The XER and FPSCR registers, which are user-level registers, also are used in error determination and configuration.

Machine Status Save/Restore Register 0 (SRR0). The SRR0 register (SPR27) is used for saving the address of the next instruction to be executed when control is returned to the interrupted process (when the exception handler executes an rfi instruction). The instruction saved in SRR0 may be either the instruction that caused the exception or the next instruction in program order. This is defined for each exception, but, in general, exceptions that are caused by instructions contain the address of the instruction that caused the exception, while asynchronous exceptions typically hold the address of the next instruction that would have been executed had the process not been interrupted.

Because this register must be wide enough to hold an instruction address, it is 64 bits wide in 64-bit implementations and 32 bits wide in 32-bit implementations.

To prevent loss of this information in the case of nested exceptions, an exception handler must save this information before causing or allowing another exception to be taken.

Machine Status Save/Restore Register 1 (SRR1). When an exception is taken, the SRR1 register (SPR28) records the machine state of the interrupted process by saving bits from the MSR. The PowerPC Architecture (OEA) allows individual implementations to save additional information. This information is restored when an rfi instruction is executed. This register is 64 bits wide in 64-bit implementations and 32 bits wide in 32-bit implementations.

To prevent loss of this information in the case of nested exceptions, an exception handler must save this information before causing or allowing another exception to be taken.

DAE/Source Instruction Service Register (DSISR). The DSISR (SPR18) identifies the instruction that caused an alignment or data access exception. The DSISR is 32 bits wide in all implementations.

Data Address Register (DAR). Data address register (DAR). The DAR (SPR19) holds the effective address generated by the instruction that caused a data access exception, alignment exception, or an I/O controller interface exception. Because the DAR holds an effective address, it is 32 bits wide in 32-bit implementations and 64 bits wide in 64-bit implementations.

Registers Used for Memory Management

The OEA portion of the PowerPC Architecture defines several registers that support the memory management model. Registers such as the block address translation registers (BATs) are used in memory configuration, and the table search description register 1 and the segment registers are used to support address translation. Memory management is also affected by the MSR, which determines whether data and instruction address translation is performed and the -endian mode that is used.

Block-address translation (BAT) registers. The OEA defines four pairs of instruction BATs (IBAT0U-IBAT3U and IBAT0L-IBAT3L), designated as SPR528-SPR535; and four pairs of data block-address translation registers

(DBAT0U-DBAT3U and DBAT0L-DBAT3L), designated as SPR536-SPR544. These registers hold information used to translate large blocks of logical (effective) address space to physical address space. Address translation is described in Chapter 13, "PowerPC Memory Management Model."

The block address translation mechanism is implemented in what can be considered a software-controlled array of registers (BATs). The BAT array maintains the translation information for four blocks of instruction addresses and four blocks of data addresses. The BAT array is maintained by the system software and is implemented as a set of eight special-purpose registers (SPRs). Each block is defined by a pair of SPRs called upper and lower BAT registers. These BAT registers define the starting addresses and sizes of BAT areas.

Table 10.10 and table 10.11 describe the bits in the BAT registers in 64-bit implementations. The corresponding bits for 32-bit implementations are provided in the descriptions of each field.

Table 10.10 Upper BAT Registers (IBAT0U-IBAT3U and DBAT0U-DBAT3U)

Bits	Name	Description
0-46	BLPI	Block logical page index. This field is compared with bits 0-46 of the logical (effective) address to determine if there is a hit in that BAT array entry. This field corresponds to bits 0-14 in 32-bit implementations.
47-50	—	Reserved. This field corresponds to bits 15-18 in 32-bit implementations.
51-61	BSM	Block size mask. This field is a mask that encodes the length of the BAT area. BAT Area Length BSM Encoding 128 KB 000 0000 0000 256 KB 000 0000 0001 512 KB 000 0000 0011 1 MB 000 0000 0111 2 MB 000 0000 1111 4 MB 000 0001 1111 8 MB 000 0011 1111 16 MB 000 0111 1111 32 MB 000 1111 1111 64 MB 001 1111 1111 128 MB 011 1111 1111 256 MB 111 1111 1111 The rightmost bit of BSM is aligned with bit 14 (bit 46 for 64-bit implementations) of the logical address. A logical address is determined to be within a BAT area if the logical address matches the value in the BLPI field.

Bits	Name	Description
		The number of zeros in BSM determines the bits of logical address that participate in the comparison with BLPI. Bits in the logical address corresponding to ones in BSM are cleared for this comparison.
		Bits in the logical address corresponding to ones in the BSM field, concatenated with the 17 bits of the logical address to the right (less significant bits) of BSM, form the offset within the BAT area.
		The value in BSM determines both the length of the BAT area and the alignment of the area in both logical and physical address space. The values loaded into BLPI and PBN must have at least as many low-order zeros as there are ones in SM. This field corresponds to bits 19-29 in 32-bit implementations.
62	Vs	Supervisor state valid bit. This is bit 30 in 32-bit implementations.
63	Vu	User state valid bit. This bit interacts with MSR[PR] and the PP field to determine if there is a match. This is bit 31 in 32-bit implementations.

Table 10.11 Lower BAT Registers (IBAT0L-IBAT3L and DBAT0L-DBAT3L)

Bits	Name	Description
0-46	PBN	Physical block number. This field is used in conjunction with the BSM field to generate bits 0-14 of the physical address of the block. This field corresponds to bits 0-14 in 32-bit implementations.
47-56	—	Reserved. This field corresponds to bits 15-24 in 32-bit implementations.
57-60	WIMG	Memory access controls. W—Write through I—Caching inhibited M—Memory coherence G—Guarded storage (DBATs only) Note that bit 28 (in 32-bit implementations) and bit 60 (in 64-bit implementations) are reserved in IBATs. These bits correspond to bits 25-28 in 32-bit implementations.
61	—	Reserved. This is bit 29 in 32-bit implementations.
62-63	PP	Block protection bits. This field interacts with MSR[PR] to determine the level of protection for the block. This field corresponds to bits 30-31 in 32-bit implementations.

Table Search Description Register 1 (SDR1). The table search description register 1 (SDR1) is used to aid in searching for page translations. The bits of the 64-bit implementation of SDR1 are described in table 10.12.

Table 10.12 SDR1 Bit Settings (64-Bit Implementations)		
Bits	**Name**	**Description**
0-45	HTABORG	The high-order 46 bits of the 64-bit physical address of the page table. This constrains the page table to lie on a minimum 256 KB boundary. At least 11 bits from the hash function are used to index into the page table. The page table must consist of at least 2^{11} PTEGs of 128 bytes each.
46-57	—	Reserved.
58-63	HTABSIZE	Encoded size of table.

Table 10.13 shows the bits in the 32-bit implementation of SDR1.

Table 10.13 SDR1 Bit Settings (32-Bit Implementations)		
Bits	**Name**	**Description**
0-15	HTABORG	The high-order 16 bits of the 32-bit physical address of the page table. This constrains the page table to a minimum 64 KB boundary. At least 10 bits from the hashing function are used to index into the page table. The page table must consist of at least 2^{10} PTEGs of 64 bytes each.
16-22	—	Reserved.
23-31	HTABMASK	Mask for page table address.

The table search operations are described in Chapter 16, "The PowerPC 601 RISC Processor."

Segment Registers (32-Bit Implementations Only). The PowerPC Architecture defines sixteen 32-bit segment registers (SR0-SR15), which are used by 32-bit implementations to define memory segments. The fields in the segment register are interpreted differently depending on the value of SR[T] (bit 0), but in general they contain information about access-level protection, and typically the SR holds the virtual segment ID.

Segment registers can be accessed explicitly by using the mtsr and mtsrin instructions. The bits in the segment registers are interpreted as shown in table 10.14 and table 10.15.

Table 10.14 Segment Register Bit Settings (T = 0)		
Bits	**Name**	**Description**
0	T	T = 0 selects this format
1	Ks	Supervisor-state protection key
2	Ku	User-state protection key
3-7	—	Reserved
8-31	VSID	Virtual segment ID

The bits in the segment register when T = 1 are described in table 10.15.

Table 10.15 Segment Register Bit Settings (T = 1)		
Bits	**Name**	**Description**
0	T	T = 1 selects this format
1	Ks	Supervisor-state protection key
2	Ku	User-state protection key
3-11	BUID	Bus unit ID
12-31	—	Device specific data for I/O controller

If T = 0 in the selected segment register, the effective address indicates an ordinary memory segment. However, if an access also is translated by the block address translation (BAT) mechanism, the BAT translation is used instead of the segment register translation. If not, the 52-bit virtual address (VA) is formed by concatenating the the 24-bit VSID field from the segment register with the 16-bit page index, EA[4-19] and the 12-bit byte offset, EA[20-31].

If T = 1 in the selected segment register (and the access is not translated by a BAT), the effective address is a reference to an I/O controller interface segment. No reference is made to the page tables.

Address Space Register (ASR)—(64-Bit Implementations). The ASR is an SPR (SPR280) defined for 64-bit implementations only. It holds the 64-bit physical address of the segment table that defines the set of addressable segments. Access to the ASR is supervisor-level. It can be accessed explicitly by using the mfspr and mtspr instructions.

Time-Keeping Registers

The time base and the decrementer registers are both incremented at a frequency that is a subdivision of the processor clock. The PowerPC Architecture does not specify this frequency.

Time Base Register (TB). The time base (TB) is a 64-bit register, comprised of two separately addressable 32-bit registers (TBU and TBL). The TB holds a 64-bit unsigned integer that is incremented at a frequency related to the processor clock but determined by each processor implementation.

The time base registers can be read by user-level software, but can be written to only by supervisor-level software. The value in TB can be read into a GPR without affecting the count, and a value in a specified GPR can be written to the TB. Operating system software is responsible for initializing this value. The time base is incremented until all bits are set; the bits are cleared on the next cycle without generating an exception.

Decrementer Register (DEC). The DEC is a 32-bit decrementing counter that provides a mechanism for causing a decrementer exception after a programmable delay. On PowerPC processors, the DEC frequency is based on a subdivision of the processor clock.

The DEC register is used to generate periodic exceptions, for example, to help the operating system perform task-switching operations. An mtspr instruction can be used to write a value to the DEC; this value is decremented (at the same frequency as the time base) until the register value is all zeroes. On the next clock cycle (when DEC[0] changes from 0 to 1), the decrementer exception condition is signaled. This exception (and the external interrupt exception) can be masked by setting the EE bit in the MSR. However, the exception will be taken when EE is reset to 1.

Miscellaneous and Optional SPRs

The OEA portion of the PowerPC Architecture also defines several individual SPRs and allows implementations to define SPRs for specific purposes such as power management and debugging.

External Access Register (EAR). The EAR (SPR282) supports the optional external control facility, and is used with the optional External Control Input Word Indexed (eciwx) and External Control Output Word Indexed (ecowx) instructions. Although access to the EAR is privileged, the operating system can determine enables user-level applications to have access depending on the setting of EAR[E].

For example, if the external control facility supports a graphics adapter, the ecowx instruction could be used to send the translated physical address of a buffer containing graphics data to the graphics device. The ecowx instruction could be used to load status information from the graphics adapter.

The bits in the EAR are described in table 10.16; however, the specific interpretation of these bits depends on the device and the system.

Table 10.16 External Access Register (EAR) Bit		
Bit	**Name**	**Description**
0	E	Enable bit. If this bit is set, the eciwx and ecowx instructions can perform the specified external operation. If the bit is cleared, an eciwx or ecowx instruction causes a data access exception.
1-25	—	Reserved.
26-31	RID	Resource ID. Any bits defined for the RID field that are not used by a particular implementation are treated as reserved.

General SPRs (SPRG0-SPRG3). The SPRG0-SPRG3 registers (SPR272-SPR275) are provided for operating system use, typically for use as a scratch register or for holding addresses that point to memory space to be used by an exception handler. Because these registers are expected to hold addresses, these registers are 32 bits wide in 32-bit implementations and 64 bits wide in 64-bit implementations.

Table 10.17 provides a description of conventional uses of SPRG0 through SPRG3. Notice that although they are commonly used by exception handlers, the operating system is free to use these registers for other purposes.

Table 10.17 Conventional Uses of SPRG0-SPRG3	
Register	**Description**
SPRG0	Software may load a unique physical address in this register to identify an area of memory reserved for use by the first-level exception handler. This area must be unique for each processor in the system.
SPRG1	Scratch register used by the first-level exception handler to save the content of a GPR. That GPR can then be loaded from SPRG0 and used as a base register to save other GPRs to memory.
SPRG2	Determined by the operating system.
SPRG3	Determined by the operating system.

Implementation-Specific Registers (HID)

The PowerPC Architecture defines SPR register space for each processor to define registers for specific, implementation-specific purposes. For example, the 603 defines registers to support the power-saving modes. Notice that some of these registers are common among PowerPC processors even though they are not defined by the PowerPC Architecture.

Summary

In this chapter we have taken a look at the registers defined by the PowerPC Architecture, how they are used to support instruction processing, and features necessary for system management. This chapter also has given greater insight into the distinctions between the user level and the supervisor level.

As described in this chapter, registers are accessed either explicitly or implicitly, and most often as the result of the execution of an instruction. The next chapter describes the instructions defined by the PowerPC Architecture, describing in greater detail how registers are used for such things as arithmetic operations, loading and storing data, and the management of system resources.

Chapter 11

The PowerPC Instruction Set

The instruction set is the backbone of an architecture. The PowerPC Architecture adheres to the principles of RISC architecture in that it provides a separate set of load/store instructions to explicitly transfer data between physical memory (external memory or the cache) and the registers files—general-purpose registers (GPRs) and floating-point registers (FPRs).

There are essentially two types of load instructions. For integer operations, bytes, half words, words, and double words in 64-bit implementations can be transferred between memory and the GPRs. The GPRs are 32 bits wide in 32-bit processors and 64 bits wide in 64-bit processors.

Words (single-precision values) and double words (double-precision values) can be transferred between memory and a set of 32 floating-point registers (FPRs). The FPRs are 64 bits wide in all PowerPC implementations to accommodate double-precision operands.

Also typical of RISC architectures, all PowerPC instructions are of uniform length—32 bits, or one word. This uniform length simplifies the design of the processor and promotes easier implementation of more elaborate instruction processing.

In terms of the architectural definition, the instruction set can be broken into the three levels of the PowerPC Architecture—user instruction set architecture (UISA), virtual environment architecture (VEA), and operating environment architecture (OEA).

This chapter looks at the PowerPC instruction set, focusing in particular on the following:

- General characteristics about the instruction set

- Descriptions of each of the PowerPC instructions organized by user- and supervisor-level

- Examples showing the instruction syntax for each instruction

However, it is perhaps more useful to view the PowerPC instruction set from a programmer's perspective, that is, consisting of two major groups—user-level instructions (those that can be used by all software) and supervisor-level instructions (those that are available only to the operating system).

All supervisor-level instructions are defined by the OEA, in most cases to support operations necessary for system management, processor configuration, and exception handling.

The PowerPC instructions are grouped into the following functional categories:

- *Flow control instructions.* This category includes branch instructions, condition register logical instructions, trap instructions, and other instructions that determine the direction of the program flow.

- *Integer Register-to-Register Instructions.* This category includes integer arithmetic instructions, integer compare instructions, integer rotate and shift instructions, and integer logical instructions. Integer instructions use the GPRs for source and destination operands and also may pass results to the integer exception register (XER) and condition register (CR). Source operands can be specified as signed or unsigned.

- *Floating-point register-to-register instructions.* This category includes floating-point arithmetic instructions that perform single- or double-precision calculations, such as multiply, divide, and multiply-add, on data provided by the FPRs. These instructions then place the results in a destination FPR (frD). This category also includes instructions that affect the floating-point status and control register (FPSCR).

- *Load and store instructions.* Integer load and store instructions transfer data between the memory subsystem (caches or system memory) and the GPRs. Floating-point load and store instructions transfer data between the memory subsystem and FPRs. These registers are specified in the instruction encoding, along with the memory address (rA). Move instructions transfer data from one register to another.

- *Processor control instructions.* These instructions synchronize memory accesses and management of caches, TLBs, and the segment registers. Although these instructions are defined as user-level instructions, applications typically do not use these instructions.

- *Memory control instructions*. These instructions manage memory resources and ensure coherency among caches and look-aside buffers.

This chapter discusses each of these categories in detail.

Be aware that the PowerPC Architecture says nothing about how a particular processor handles execution for any instructions. Some PowerPC processors may use different algorithms for floating-point calculations. In fact, the architecture allows processors to implement some floating-point instructions in software, with the help of the floating-point assist exception.

> **Note**
>
> Processors can implement a separate load/store unit for load and store instructions. The 601 implements these instructions in its integer unit (although, of course, floating-point source and destination registers are defined as FPRs).

Although the PowerPC Architecture does not specify details of hardware implementations, each PowerPC processor must ensure that instructions record their results as though they were in strict program order. In the 601, for example, write-back can occur out of order; the processor monitors all data dependencies and guarantees that all of these dependencies are observed. The 603 has a completion buffer, however, that orders the write-back according to the program sequence.

Branch and Flow Control Instructions

Branch and flow control instructions determine the flow of instructions processing. Most of these instructions are branch-type instructions that can force instruction fetching to begin at a different portion of a program. Some branches are unconditional, that is, the branch is always taken; other branch instructions are conditional—whether the branch is taken depends on conditions, such as the value in a loop counter or on some type of logical comparison. Other instructions, such as the trap instruction and the system-call instruction, can redirect the program flow by deliberately causing an exception.

The PowerPC ISA is designed such that, conceptually, branch and flow control instructions are executed by the branch processing unit (BPU), which is integrated into the instruction unit. This is typically how BPUs are expected to be implemented, but this is not prescribed by the architecture.

Some branch instructions can redirect instruction execution conditionally, based on the value of bits in the CR. When a processor encounters one of these instructions, it can determine whether an outstanding instruction may affect the CR. If no instruction is outstanding, the BPU can determine whether the branch should be taken by checking the bit in the CR. The process described in the preceding sentences is called *branch resolution.*

When the BPU determines that an outstanding instruction will affect the CR, the direction of the branch is predicted. The encoding of the branch instruction includes a field with which the programmer can indicate whether the instruction is likely to be taken. The instruction fetcher can speculatively fetch instructions according to the prediction, and implementations can begin dispatching, decoding, and executing these instructions speculatively until the branch is resolved (as reflected by the state of the CR). If the prediction was correct, the fetched instructions can proceed through their respective pipelines and write back their results. If the branch is resolved and the branch is not taken, the instructions are flushed from the pipelines and instruction fetching can begin from the correct path.

Branch instructions compute the effective address (EA) of the next instruction address using the following addressing modes:

- Branch relative

- Branch conditional to relative address

- Branch to absolute address

- Branch conditional to absolute address

- Branch conditional to link register

- Branch conditional to count register

For branch conditional instructions, an operand in the instruction (the BO operand) specifies the conditions under which the branch is taken. The programmer can specify a value for BO that sets a five-bit field in the instruction machine-code that is decoded by the BPU. The first four bits of the BO field specify how the branch is affected by or affects the condition and count registers and whether the branch is to be taken when a condition is true or false.

The fifth bit can be used for branch prediction. That is, the programmer can set or clear this bit depending on whether or not the branch is likely to be taken. This method of branch prediction is called *static branch prediction*. Note that PowerPC implementations can implement more elaborate, dynamic branch prediction methods, some of which can make predictions based on previous branch resolutions.

The following sections describe the PowerPC branch instructions, showing the name, the operand syntax used for programming, and a brief description of the operations generated by the instruction.

Branch Unconditional Instructions

Table 11.1 lists the branch unconditional instructions. Notice that these instructions do not include the BO operand.

Static branch prediction
A method of branch prediction in which the likelihood of a branch being taken is predetermined. Either a fixed characteristic of the instruction, or a means for the programmer to make the prediction.

Table 11.1 Branch Unconditional Instructions		
Name	**Operand Syntax**	**Description**
Branch	b target_addr	Branch to the address computed as the sum of the immediate address and the address of the current instruction.
Branch Absolute	ba target_addr	Branch to the absolute address specified.
Branch then Link	bl target_addr	Branch to the address computed as the sum of the immediate address and the address of the current instruction. The instruction address following this instruction is placed into the LR.
Branch Absolute then Link	bla target_addr	Branch to the absolute address specified. The instruction address following this instruction is placed into the LR.

Branch Conditional Instructions

The branch conditional instructions, as shown in table 11.2, determine the program flow, based on conditions tracked by the condition register. The types of branch conditional instructions differ in how they determine the target address.

Table 11.2 Branch Conditional Instructions		
Name	**Operand Syntax**	**Description**
Branch Conditional	bc BO,BI,target_addr	Branch conditionally to the address computed as the sum of the immediate address and the address of the current instruction.
Branch Conditional Absolute	bca BO,BI,target_addr	Branch conditionally to the absolute address specified.
Branch Conditional then Link	bcl BO,BI,target_addr	Branch conditionally to the address computed as the sum of the immediate address and the address of the current instruction. The instruction address following this instruction is placed into the LR.
Branch Conditional Absolute then Link	bcla BO,BI,target_addr	Branch conditionally to the absolute address specified. The instruction address following this instruction is placed into the LR.

Branch Conditional to Link Register Instructions

Branch conditional to link instructions, described in table 11.3, are similar to the branch conditional instructions, in that the path is chosen according to bits in the CR and specified by the encoding of the BO and BI fields. In these instructions, the target is always the address in the LR.

Table 11.3 Branch Conditional to Link Register		
Name	**Operand Syntax**	**Description**
Branch Conditional to Link Register	bclr BO,BI	Branch conditionally to the address in the LR.
Branch Conditional to Link Register then Link	bclrl BO,BI	Branch conditionally to the address specified in the LR. The instruction address following this instruction is then placed into the LR.

Branch Conditional to Count Register

Branch conditional to count instructions are similar to the branch conditional to link instructions in how the path is chosen according to bits in the CR and specified by the encoding of the BO and BI fields. In these instructions, the target is always the address in the CTR.

Branch conditional to count instructions cannot specify that the CTR be decremented, as can the other branch conditional instructions. In this group of instructions, such encoding is considered invalid. Table 11.4 lists and describes these instructions.

Table 11.4 Branch Conditional to Count Register Instructions		
Name	**Operand Syntax**	**Description**
Branch Conditional to Count Register	bcctr BO,BI	Branch conditionally to the address specified in the count register.
Branch Conditional to Count Register then Link	bcctrl BO,BI	Branch conditionally to the address specified in the count register. The instruction address following this instruction is placed into the LR.

Condition Register Logical Instructions

Condition register logical instructions, shown in table 11.5, and the Move Condition Register Field (mcrf) instruction are defined as flow control instructions because they work in conjunction with the branch instructions to control the program flow. If the LR update option is enabled for any of these instructions, the PowerPC Architecture defines the instructions as invalid.

These instructions perform Boolean logical operations, such as AND, OR, XOR, and NAND, on specified bits in the condition register.

Table 11.5 Condition Register Logical Instructions		
Name	**Operand Syntax**	**Comments**
Condition Register AND	crand crbD,crbA,crbB	The CR bit specified by crbA is ANDed with the bit specified by crbB placed into the CR bit specified by crbD.

(continues)

Table 11.5 Continued		
Name	**Operand Syntax**	**Comments**
Condition Register OR	cror crbD,crbA,crbB	The CR bit specified by crbA is ORed with the bit specified by crbB placed into the CR bit specified by crbD.
Condition	crxor crbD,crbA,crbB	The CR bit specified by crbA is Register XOR XORed with the bit specified by crbB placed into the CR bit specified by crbD.
Condition Register NAND	crnand crbD,crbA,crbB	The CR bit specified by crbA is ANDed with the bit specified by crbB. The complemented result is placed into the CR bit specified by crbD.
Condition Register NOR	crnor crbD,crbA,crbB	The CR bit specified by crbA is ORed with the bit specified by crbB. The complemented result is placed into the CR bit specified by crbD.
Condition Register Equivalent	creqv crbD,crbA, crbB	The CR bit specified by crbA is XORed with the bit specified by crbB. The complemented result is placed into the CR bit specified by crbD.
Condition Register AND with Complement	crandc crbD,crbA,crbB	The CR bit specified by crbA is ANDed with the complement of the bit specified by crbB and the result is placed into the CR bit specified by crbD.
Condition Register OR with Complement	crorc crbD,crbA,crbB	The CR bit specified by crbA is ORed with the complement of the bit specified by crbB and the result is placed into the bit specified by crbD.
Move Condition	mcrf crfD,crfS	The contents of crfS are copied into crfD. No other condition register fields are changed.

Trap Instructions

The trap instructions, shown in table 11.6, test for a specified set of conditions. If any of those conditions are met, the system trap handler is invoked;

if the tested conditions are not met, instruction execution continues normally. If any bit in the TO operand is set and its corresponding condition is met by the result of a comparison, the trap exception is taken.

Table 11.6 Trap Instructions

Name	Operand Syntax	Description
Trap Double Word Immediate (64-bit only)	tdi TO,rA,SIMM	The contents of rA are compared with the sign-extended SIMM operand.
Trap Word Immediate	twi TO,rA,SIMM	The word in of rA is compared with the sign-extended SIMM operand.
Trap Double Word (64-bit only)	td TO,rA,rB	The contents of rA are compared with the contents of rB.
Trap Word	tw TO,rA,rB	The word in rA is compared with the word in rB.

System Linkage Instructions

The system linkage instructions, shown in table 11.7, provide an explicit way to enter and return from supervisor-mode.

Table 11.7 System Linkage Instructions

Name	Operand Syntax	Comments
System Call	sc	Generates a system call exception. This instruction is defined by the UISA and the OEA.
Return from Interrupt	rfi	Restores the state of the interrupted prcoess at the end of an exception handler. This instruction is defined by the OEA.

This section has described the PowerPC flow control instructions, which are typically executed by the BPU. The next section describes integer register-to-register instructions.

Integer Register-to-Register Instructions

The PowerPC integer register-to-register instructions consist of the following:

■ Integer arithmetic instructions

■ Integer compare instructions

■ Integer rotate and shift instructions

■ Integer logical instructions

Integer instructions use the GPRs for source and destination operands and may pass results to the integer exception register (XER) and condition register (CR). Source operands can be specified as signed or unsigned.

Most integer instructions are designed to execute in a single-cycle, although this may vary among the PowerPC processors.

Mnemonic
The shorthand name of the assembly language instruction.

Some integer instructions can be encoded to update the condition register by adding a period at the end of the *mnemonic*. Integer instructions update CR bits 0-3 (CR0). When the processor is configured in the default 64-bit mode, CR0 is set by a signed comparison of the 64-bit result to zero. In 32-bit mode (of 64-bit implementations), CR0 is set by a signed comparison of the low-order 32 bits of the result to zero. Note that instructions that affect the CR may cause delays to subsequent instructions.

The following sections provide descriptions of the integer register-to-register instructions. Unless otherwise noted in the tables, when CR0 and the XER are affected, they reflect the value placed in the target register.

Integer Arithmetic Instructions

The integer arithmetic instructions perform basic addition, subtraction, multiplication, and division. Some integer arithmetic instructions (addic, addic., subfic, addc, subfc, adde, subfe, addme, subfme, addze, and subfze) set the carry bit in integer exception register, XER[CA] to reflect the carry out of bit 0.

Overflow
The condition that occurs when the results of an operation exceed the maximum allowable value.

For most integer arithmetic instructions, if *overflow* is enabled (by specifying 'o' at the end of the mnemonic) the XER bits SO and OV to reflect overflow of the 64-bit result in 64-bit mode and 32-bit result in 32-bit mode. However, enabling overflow for the mulld and mullw instructions causes the SO and OV bits to reflect overflow of the 64-bit result (mulld) and overflow of the low-order 32-bit result (mullw).

Table 11.8 lists the integer arithmetic instructions for the PowerPC processors. Note that a period at the end of the mnemonic indicates that the instruction updates the condition register (CR).

Table 11.8 Integer Instructions

Name	Operand Syntax	Comments
Add Immediate	addi rD,rA,SIMM	(rA|0)+SIMM = rD.
Add Immediate Shifted	addis rD,rA,SIMM	(rA|0) + (SIMM || x'0000') = rD.
Add [1,2]	add rD,rA,rB	(rA) + (rB) = rD.
Subtract From [1,2]	subf rD,rA,rB	−(rA) + (rB) +1 = rD.
Add Immediate Carrying	addic rD,rA,SIMM	(rA) + SIMM = rD.
Add Immediate Carrying and Record	addic. rD,rA,SIMM	(rA) + SIMM = rD. The CR is updated.
Subtract from Immediate Carrying	subfic rD,rA,SIMM	−(rA) + SIMM + 1 =
Add Carrying [1,2]	addc rD,rA,rB	(rA) + (rB) = rD.
Subtract from Carrying [1,2]	subfc rD,rA,rB	−(rA) + (rB) + 1 = rD.
Add Extended [1,2]	adde rD,rA,rB	(rA) + (rB) + XER[CA] = rD.
Subtract from Extended [1,2]	subfe rD,rA,rB	−(rA) + (rB) + XER[CA] = rD.
Add to Minus One Extended [1,2]	addme rD,rA	(rA) + XER[CA] + x'FFFFFFFF' = rD.
Subtract from Minus One Extended [1,2]	subfme rD,rA	−(rA) + XER[CA] + x'FFFFFFFF' = rD.
Add to Zero Extended [1,2]	addze rD,rA	(rA) + XER[CA] = rD.
Subtract from Zero Extended [1,2]	subfze rD,rA	−(rA) + XER[CA] = rD.

(continues)

Table 11.8 Continued

Name	Operand Syntax	Comments
Negate [1,2]	neg rD,rA	−(rA) + 1 = rD.
Multiply Low Immediate	mulli rD,rA,SIMM	(rA) * SIMM = (rD). Operands are treated as signed integers; rD holds the low-order bits of the quad-word product.
Multiply Low Word [1,2]	mullw rD,rA,rB	(rA) * rB = (rD). Operands are treated as signed words.
Multiply Low Double Word [1,2] (64-bit only)	mulld rD,rA,rB	The low-order 64 bits of the 128-bit product are placed into rD. Operands are treated as signed integers.
Multiply High Word [1]	mulhw rD,rA,rB	Source operands are treated as 32-bit signed integers to form a 64-bit signed product.
Multiply High Double Word[1] (64-bit only)	mulhd rD,rA,rB	Source operands are treated as 64-bit signed integers to form a 128-bit signed product.
Multiply High Word Unsigned [1]	mulhwu rD,rA,rB	Source operands are treated as unsigned words to form an unsigned double-word product. If the CR update option is chosen, CR0[0_2] are cleared by signed comparison of the result.
Multiply High Double Word Unsigned[1] (64-bit only)	mulhdu rD,rA,rB	Source operands are treated as signed double words to form a 128-bit signed product of which the high-order 64 bits are placed into rD. If the CR update option is chosen, CR0[0_2] is cleared by signed comparison of the result.
Divide Word [1,2]	divw rD,rA,rB	The signed 32-bit dividend (rA) and divisor (rB) form a signed quotient. Source operands are sign-extended in 64-bit implementations; the high-order word is undefined.
Divide Double Word [1,2] (64-bit only)	divd rD,rA,rB	The signed 64-bit dividend (rA) and divisor (rB) form a 64-bit signed quotient.

Name	Operand Syntax	Comments
Divide Word Unsigned [1,2]	divwu rD,rA,rB	The unsigned 32-bit dividend (rA) and divisor (rB) form a signed quotient. Source operands are zero-extended in 64-bit implementations, but the high-order word is undefined.
Divide Double Word Unsigned [1,2] (64-bit only)	divdu rD,rA,rB	The unsigned 64-bit dividend (rA) and the unsigned 64-bit divisor (rB) form a 64-bit signed quotient.

[1]*The CR update option is indicated by appending a period '.' to the mnemonic.*
[2]*The record option is indicated by appending the letter 'o' to the mnemonic.*

Integer Compare Instructions

The integer compare instructions compare the contents of rA with the value in rB or with a signed or unsigned immediate value. The result of the comparison is recorded in CRn[0-2]. The CR field is indicated by crfD, although the operand can be omitted if the target field is CR0. If rA is less than the compared value, CRn[0] is set; if rA is greater than the compared value, CRn[1] is set; and if rA is equal to the compared value, CRn[2] is set. Only one of these bits can be set.

Table 11.9 summarizes the integer compare instructions.

For 64-bit implementations, if L is 1, the operand length is 64 bits; if it is 0, the operand length is 32 bits. The L bit should always be 0 for 32-bit implementations. In 64-bit implementations, when source operands are treated as 32-bit signed values, bit 32 is the sign bit.

Table 11.9 Integer Compare Instructions

Name	Operand Syntax	Comments
Compare Immediate	cmpi crfD,L,rA,SIMM	The signed integer in rA is compared with a signed immediate value (SIMM), treating the operands as signed integers.
Compare	cmp crfD,L,rA,rB	The signed integer in rA is compared with the signed integer in rB.

(continues)

Table 11.9 Continued		
Name	**Operand Syntax**	**Comments**
Compare Logical Immediate	cmpli crfD,L,rA,UIMM	The unsigned integer of rA is compared with the unsigned immediate value specified by the zero-extended value specified by UIMM,
Compare Logical	cmpl crfD,L,rA,rB	The unsigned integer in rA is compared with unsigned integer in rB.

Integer Logical Instructions

Integer logical instructions perform Boolean operations on integer operands. Logical instructions that update the condition register (indicated by a period at the end of the mnemonic). set CR0 to characterize the result of the logical operation. These fields are set as if the result were compared algebraically to zero.

Logical instructions do not generate overflows or carries, so they do not affect XER[SO], XER[OV], or XER[CA]. Table 11.10 describes these instructions.

Table 11.10 Integer Logical Instructions		
Name	**Operand Syntax**	**Comments**
AND Immediate	andi. rA,rS,UIMM	The value in rS is ANDed with the zero-extended unsigned immediate value and placed into rA.
AND Immediate Shifted	andis. rA,rS,UIMM	The value in rS is ANDed with the zero-extended unsigned immediate value shifted left 16 bits and placed into rA.
OR Immediate	ori rA,rS,UIMM	The value in rS is ORed with the zero-extended unsigned immediate value and placed into rA. The preferred no-op is ori 0,0,0.
OR Immediate	oris rA,rS,UIMM	The value in rS is ORed with the Shifted zero-extended unsigned immediate value shifted to the left by 16 bits and placed into rA.

Name	Operand Syntax	Comments
XOR Immediate	xori rA,rS,UIMM	The value in rS is XORed with the zero-extended unsigned immediate value and placed into rA.
XOR Immediate Shifted	xoris rA,rS,UIMM	The value in rS is XORed with the zero-extended unsigned immediate value shifted to the left by 16 bits and placed into rA.
AND [1]	and rA,rS,rB	The value in rS is ANDed with the value in rB and placed into rA.
OR [1]	or rA,rS,rB	The value in rS is ORed with the value in rB and placed into rA.
XOR [1]	xor rA,rS,rB	The value in rS is XORed with the value in rB and placed into rA.
NAND [1]	nand rA,rS,rB	The value in rS is ANDed with the value in rB. The one's complement of the result is placed into rA.
NOR [1]	nor rA,rS,rB	The value in rS is ORed with the value in rB. The one's complement of the result is placed into rA.
Equivalent [1]	eqv rA,rS,rB	The value in rS is XORed with the value in rB. The complemented result is placed into rA.
AND with Complement [1]	andc rA,rS,rB	The value in rS is ANDed with ANDed with the complement of the value in of rB and placed into rA.
OR with Complement [1]	orc rA,rS,rB	The value in rS is ORed with the complement of the value in rB and placed into rA.
Extend Sign Byte [1]	extsb rA,rS	The value in the low-order byte in rS is placed into the low-order byte in rA. The sign bit is extended.
Extend Sign Half Word [1]	extsh rA,rS	The low-order half word in rS is placed into the low-order byte in rA. The sign bit is extended.

(continues)

Table 11.10 Continued		
Name	**Operand Syntax**	**Comments**
Extend Sign Word [1](64-bit only)	extsw rA,rS	The low-order word in rS is placed into the low-order word in rA. The sign bit is extended.
Count Leading Zeros Word [1]	cntlzw rA,rS	The number of leading zero bits in the low-order word in rS is placed into rA. If CR update mode is chosen, CR0 reflects the result, and the LT field is cleared in CR0.
Count Leading Zeros Double Word [1] (64-bit only)	cntlzd rA,rS	The number of leading zero bits in the double word stored in rS is placed into rA. If CR update mode is chosen, CR0 reflects the result, and the LT field is cleared in CR0.

[1]*The CR update option is indicated by appending a period '.' to the mnemonic.*

Integer Rotate and Shift Instructions

The integer rotate and shift instructions manipulate bits in the GPRs. Table 11.11 describes these instructions. The SH operand indicates the number of bits the value in rS is to be shifted. The MB (mask begin) and ME (mask end) operands indicate the beginning and end (inclusive) of a bit mask. The mask is formed by setting all the bits between the bits in the range specified by the values in the MB and ME operands and clearing all of the rest, If only the ME operand is provided, all bits to the left (inclusive) are set and all bits to the right are cleared. If only the MB operand is provided, all bits to the left (exclusive) are cleared and all bits to the right (inclusive) are set.

In shift-right algebraic instructions, XER[CA] is set only when the appropriate word or double-word value in rS is negative and any "1" bits are shifted out of the least-significant bit position.

In shift-left instructions, bits shifted out of position 0 are lost. Zeros are supplied to the vacated positions on the right.

In shift-right algebraic instructions, the most-significant bit of the shifted memory unit is extended to the left; in regular shift-right instructions, zeros are shifted into the positions on the left and bits shifted out of the least-significant bit position are lost.

Table 11.11 Integer Rotate and Shift Instructions

Name	Operand Syntax	Comments
Rotate Left Double Word Immediate then Clear Left [1] (64-bit only)	rldicl rA,rS,SH,MB	The contents of rS are rotated left by the number of bits specified by SH, ANDed with the bit mask, and placed into rA.
Rotate Left Double Word Immediate then Clear Right [1] (64-bit only)	rldicr rA,rS,SH,ME	The contents of rS are rotated left by the number of bits specified by SH, ANDed with the bit mask, and placed into rA.
Rotate Left Double Word Immediate then Clear [1] (64-bit only)	rldic rA,rS,SH,MB	The contents of rS are rotated left by the number of bits specified by SH, ANDed with the bit mask, and placed into rA.
Rotate Left Word Immediate then AND with Mask	rlwinm rA,rS,SH,MB,ME	The contents of rS are rotated left by the number of bits specified by SH, ANDed with the bit mask, and placed into rA.
Rotate Left Double Word then Clear Left [1] (64-bit only)	rldcl rA,rS,rB,MB	The contents of rS are rotated left by the number of bits specified by the low-order six bits in rB, ANDed with the bit mask, and placed into rA.
Rotate Left Double Word then Clear Right [1] (64-bit only)	rldcr rA,rS,rB,ME	The contents of rS are rotated left by the number of bits specified by the low-order six bits in rB, ANDed with the bit mask, and placed into rA.
Rotate Left Word then AND with Mask[1]	rlwnm rA,rS,rB,MB,ME	The contents of rS are rotated left by the number of bits specified by the low-order six bits in rB, ANDed with the bit mask, and placed into rA.
Rotate Left Word Immediate then Mask Insert [1]	rlwimi rA,rS,SH,MB,ME	The contents of rS are rotated left by the number of bits specified by SH. The mask is shifted left by 32 bits. The rotated data is inserted into rA under control of the bit mask.
Rotate Left Double Word Immediate then Mask Insert [1] (64-bit only)	rldimi rA,rS,SH,MB	The contents of rS are rotated left by the number of bits specified by SH. A mask is generated from the bit specified by operand MB through 63 to

(continues)

Table 11.11 Continued

Name	Operand Syntax	Comments
		SH. The rotated data is inserted into rA under control of the bit mask.
Shift Left Double Word [1] (64-bit only)	sld rA,rS,rB	The contents of rS are shifted left the number of bits specified by the low-order seven bits in rB and placed into rA. Shift amounts from 64 to 127 give a zero result.
Shift Left Word [1]	slw rA,rS,rB	The low-order 32 bits of rS are shifted left the number of bits specified by the six low-order bits in rB and placed into rA. In 64-bit GPRs, the upper-order word in rA is cleared. Shift amounts from 32 to 63 give a zero result.
Shift Right Double Word [1] (64-bit only)	srd rA,rS,rB	The contents of rS are shifted right the number of bits specified by the seven low-order bits in rB and placed into rA. Shift amounts from 64 to 127 give a zero result.
Shift Right Word [1]	srw rA,rS,rB	The low-order 32 bits of rS are shifted right the number of bits specified by the six low-order bits in rB and are placed into rA. In 64-bit implementations, rA[0–31] is cleared. Shift amounts from 32–63 give a zero result.
Shift Right Algebraic Double Word Immediate [1] (64-bit only)	sradi rA,rS,SH	The contents of rS are shifted right the number of bits specified by SH. Bit 0 of rS is extended to the left and placed into rA. If SH is zero, rA is loaded with the contents of rS and XER[CA] is cleared.
Shift Right Algebraic Word Immediate [1]	srawi rA,rS,SH	The contents of the low-order 32 bits of rS are shifted right the number of bits specified by SH. Bit 32 of rS is extended to the left. The 32-bit result is sign extended and placed into rA. If SH is zero, rA is loaded with the low-order word in rS and XER[CA] is cleared.

Name	Operand Syntax	Comments
Shift Right Algebraic Double Word [1] (64-bit only)	srad rA,rS,rB	The contents of rS are shifted right the number of bits specified by the seven low-order bits in rB. Bit 0 of rS is extended to the left and placed into rA. If (rB) is zero, rA is loaded with the value in rS and XER[CA] is cleared. If the shift value is 64–127, rA holds 64 sign bits and XER[CA] holds the sign bit of rS.
Shift Right Algebraic Word [1]	sraw rA,rS,rB	The low-order word in rS is shifted right the number of bits specified by the six low-order bits in rB. Bit 32 of rS is extended to the left. The 32-bit result is placed into rA.

[1]*The CR update option is indicated by appending a period '.' to the mnemonic.*

Floating-Point Register-to-Register Instructions

This section describes the PowerPC floating-point instructions that are used for performing register-to-register operations. These include the following:

- Floating-point arithmetic instructions

- Floating-point multiply-add instructions

- Floating-point rounding and conversion instructions

- Floating-point compare instructions

- Floating-point status and control register instructions

For information about floating-point load and store instructions, see "Load, Store, and Move Instructions" later in this chapter.

Floating-Point Arithmetic Instructions

For all but three types of floating-point arithmetic instructions, if the most significant bit of the resultant significand is not a one, the result is normalized. The result is rounded to the target precision determined by the setting of FPSCR[RN] and placed into frD. The three exceptions to this rule are the optional Floating-Point Reciprocal Estimate (fres), Floating-Point Reciprocal Square-Root Estimate (frsqrte) and Floating-Point Select (fsel) instructions.

In floating-point addition, the exponents of the two operands are compared. The significand for the smaller exponent is shifted right, and its exponent is incremented for each bit shifted until the two exponents are equal. The two significands are then added algebraically to form an intermediate sum. All significands and all three guard bits (G, R, and X) enter into the computation. If a carry occurs, the sum's significand shifts right one place, and the exponent is incremented. FPSCR[FPRF] is set to the class and sign of the result, except for invalid operation exceptions when FPSCR[VE] = 1.

Floating-point subtraction is identical to floating-point addition, except that the contents of frB participate in the operation with its sign bit (bit 0) inverted. FPSCR[FPRF] is set to the class and sign of the result, except for invalid operation exceptions when FPSCR[VE] = 1.

Floating-point multiplication and division are based on exponent addition and subtraction respectively. The respective multiplication and division of the significands. FPSCR[FPRF] is set to the class and sign of the result, except for invalid operation exceptions when FPSCR[VE] = 1 and zero divide exceptions when FPSCR[ZE] = 1.

Table 11.12 summarizes the floating-point arithmetic instructions.

Table 11.12 Floating-Point Arithmetic Instructions		
Name	**Operand Syntax**	**Comments**
Floating-Point Add (Double-Precision)[1]	fadd frD,frA,frB	The value in frA is added to the value in frB.
Floating-Point Add Single-Precision [1]	fadds frD,frA,frB	The value in frA is added to the value in frB.
Floating-Point Subtract (Double-Precision)[1]	fsub frD,frA,frB	The value in frB is subtracted from the value in frA.
Floating-Point Subtract Single-Precision[1]	fsubs frD,frA,frB	The value in frB is subtracted from the value in frA.
Floating-Point Multiply (Double-Precision)[1]	fmul frD,frA,frC	The value in frA is multiplied by the value in frC.

Name	Operand Syntax	Comments
Floating-Point Multiply Single-Precision[1]	fmuls frD,frA,frC	The value in frA is multiplied by the value in frC.
Floating-Point Divide (Double-Precision)[1]	fdiv frD,frA,frB	The value in frA is divided by the value in frB. No remainder is preserved.
Floating-Point Divide Single-Precision[1]	fdivs frD,frA,frB	The value in frA is divided by the value in frB. No remainder is preserved.
Floating-Point Square Root (Double-Precision)[1]	fsqrt frD,frB	The square root of the value in frB is placed into frD. FPSCR[FPRF] reflects the class and sign of the result except for invalid operation exceptions when FPSCR[VE] = 1. This instruction is optional.
Floating-Point Square Root Single-Precision[1]	fsqrts frD,frB	The square root of the value in frB is placed into frD. FPSCR[FPRF] reflects the class and sign of the result except for invalid operation exceptions when FPSCR[VE] = 1. This instruction is optional.
Floating-Point Reciprocal Estimate Single-Precision [1]	fres frD,frB	A single-precision estimate of the reciprocal of the value in frB is placed into frD. The estimate placed into frD is correct to a precision of one part in 256 of the reciprocal of frB. FPSCR[FPRF] reflects the class and sign of the result except for invalid operation exceptions when FPSCR[VE] = 1 and zero divide exceptions when FPSCR[ZE] = 1. This instruction is optional.
Floating-Point Reciprocal Square Root Estimate [1]	frsqrte frD,frB	A double-precision estimate of the reciprocal of the square root of the value in frB is placed into frD. The result is correct to a precision of one part in 32 of the reciprocal of the square root of frB. FPSCR[FPRF] is set to the class and sign of the result, except for invalid operation exceptions when FPSCR[VE] = 1 and zero divide exceptions when FPSCR[ZE] = 1. This instruction is optional.

(continues)

Table 11.12 Continued		
Name	**Operand Syntax**	**Comments**
Floating-Point Select	fsel frD,frA,frC,frB	The value in frA is compared to the value zero. If the operand is greater than or equal to zero, frD is set to the contents of frC. If the operand is less than zero or is a NaN, frD is set to the contents of frB. The comparison ignores the sign of zero (that is, regards +0 as equal to _0). This instruction is optional.

[1]*The CR update option is indicated by appending a period '.' to the mnemonic.*

Floating-Point Multiply-Add Instructions

One of the distinguishing features of the PowerPC instruction set is the inclusion of a set of four single-precision and four double-precision instructions that perform multiplication and either addition or subtraction.

At first glance, these instructions may appear to violate the basic principles of RISC architecture (which favor an orthogonal instruction set). These instructions are useful, however, because in most implementations they can be performed in the same amount of time that it takes to perform an individual multiply, add, or subtract operation. Further, because rounding only occurs once, at the end of the operation, these instructions produce more accurate results than do a series of individual operations. These factors make these instructions particularly useful for vector arithmetic.

If the most significant bit of the resultant significand is not a one, the result is rounded to the target precision as determined by the setting of FPSCR[RN]. FPSCR[FPRF] is set to the class and sign of the result, except for invalid operation exceptions when FPSCR[VE] = 1.

The floating-point multiply-add instructions are described in table 11.13.

Table 11.13 Floating-Point Multiply-Add Instructions		
Name	**Operand Syntax**	**Comments**
Floating-Point Multiply-Add (Double-Precision) [1]	fmadd frD,frA,frC,frB	The value in frA is multiplied by the value in frC. The value in frB is added to this intermediate result.

Name	Operand Syntax	Comments
Floating-Point Multiply-Add Single-Precision [1]	fmadds frD,frA,frC,frB	The value in frA is multiplied by the value in frC. The value in frB is added to this intermediate result.
Floating-Point Multiply-Subtract (Double-Precision)[1]	fmsub frD,frA,frC,frB	The value in frA is multiplied by the value in frC. The value in frB is subtracted from this intermediate result.
Floating-Point Multiply-Subtract Single-Precision[1]	fmsubs frD,frA,frC,frB	The value in frA is multiplied by the value in frC. The value in frB is subtracted from this intermediate result.
Floating-Point Negative Multiply-Add (Double-Precision)[1]	fnmadd frD,frA,frC,frB	The value in frA is multiplied by the value in frC. The value in frB is added to this intermediate result.
Floating-Point Negative Multiply-Add Single-Precision [1]	fnmadds frD,frA,frC,frB	The value in frA is multiplied by the value in frC. The value in frB is added to this intermediate result.
Floating-Point Negative Multiply-Subtract (Double-Precision)[1]	fnmsub frD,frA,frC,frB	The value in frA is multiplied by the value in frC. The value in frB is subtracted from this intermediate result.
Floating-Point Negative Multiply-Subtract Single-Precision[1]	fnmsubs frD,frA,frC,frB	The value in frA is multiplied by the value in frC. The value in frB is subtracted from this intermediate result.

[1]*The CR update option is indicated by appending a period '.' to the mnemonic.*

Floating-Point Rounding and Conversion Instructions

The floating-point rounding instruction (frsp) is used to truncate a 64-bit, double-precision number to a 32-bit, single-precision, floating-point number. The floating-point convert instructions convert a 64-bit, double-precision, floating point number to a 32-bit, signed, integer number.

The PowerPC Architecture defines bits 0-31 of floating-point register frD as undefined when executing the Floating-Point Convert to Integer Word (fctiw) and Floating-Point Convert to Integer Word with Round toward Zero (fctiwz) instructions. The floating-point rounding instructions are shown in table 11.14.

For all rounding, the rounding mode is determined by the setting of FPSCR[RN].

FPSCR[FPRF] is set to the class and sign of the result, except for invalid operation exceptions when FPSCR[VE] = 1.

If a floating-point value cannot be rounded to form an integer value, convert-to-integer instructions may generate default values. If the value in frB exceeds the value that can be expressed as an integer, frD is set to x'7FF...FFF'. If the operand in frB is less than what can be expressed as a negative integer, frD is set to x'800...000'.

In 64-bit implementations in which the results are words, bits 0-32 are undefined.

Table 11.14 Floating-Point Rounding and Conversion Instructions

Name	Operand Syntax	Comments
Floating-Point Round to Single-Precision [1]	frsp frD,frB	A double-precision value in frB is rounded to single-. precision
Floating-Point Convert from Integer Double Word (64-bit only)[1]	fcfid frD,frB	The 64-bit signed integer operand in frB is converted to an infinitely precise floating-point integer.
Floating-Point Convert to Integer Double Word (64-bit only)[1]	fctid frD,frB	The value in frB is converted to a 64-bit signed integer.
Floating-Point Convert to Integer Double Word with (64-bit only)[1]	fctidz frD,frB	The value in frB is converted to a 64-bit signed integer, placed in frD.
Floating-Point Convert to Integer Word [1]	fctiw frD,frB	The value in frB is converted to a 32-bit signed integer, using the rounding mode specified by FPSCR[RN], and placed in frD.
Floating-Point Convert to Integer Word with Round toward Zero	fctiwz frD,frB	The value in frB is converted to a 32-bit signed integer, rounded toward zero, and placed in frD.

[1]*The CR update option is indicated by appending a period '.' to the mnemonic.*

Floating-Point Compare Instructions

Floating-point compare instructions compare the contents of two FPRs. The results of this comparison are recorded in the CR field specified by crfD and in the identical four-bit field, FPSCR[FPCC]. Only one of these bits can be set. These bits are described in table 11.15.

Table 11.15 CR Bit Settings		
Bit	**Name**	**Description**
0	FL	(frA) < (frB)
1	FG	(frA) > (frB)
2	FE	(frA) = (frB)
3	FU	(frA) ? (frB) (unordered)

[1]*If an operand is a NaN, either quiet or signaling, crfD and the FPCC are set to reflect unordered.*

The floating-point compare instructions are described in table 11.16.

Table 11.16 Floating-Point Compare Instructions		
Name	**Operand Syntax**	**Comments**
Floating-Point Compare Unordered	fcmpu crfD,frA,frB	The value in frA is compared to the value in frB. If an operand is a signaling NaN, VXSNAN is set.
Floating-Point Compare Ordered	fcmpo crfD,frA,frB	The value in frA is compared to the value in frB. If an operand is a signaling NaN, VXSNAN is set, and if invalid operation is disabled (VE = 0) VXVC is set. If an operand is a Quiet NaN, VXVC is set.

Floating-Point Status and Control Register Instructions

The PowerPC Architecture defines a set of instructions for transferring data between the FPSCR and either the CR or a specified FPRs. These instructions ensure that all previous floating-point instructions (and any exceptions they may cause) appear to have completed before the FPSCR instruction is initiated and that no subsequent floating-point instructions appear to be dispatched until the FPSCR instruction has completed.

Floating-point memory access instructions are not affected by the execution of the floating-point status and control register instructions.

The FPSCR instructions are described in table 11.17.

Table 11.17 Floating-Point Status and Control Register Instructions

Name	Operand Syntax	Comments
Move from FPSCR[1]	mffs frD	The contents of the FPSCR are placed into frD. Bits 0_31 are undefined.
Move to Condition Register from FPSCR	mcrfs crfD,crfS	The contents of the FPSCR field specified by crfS are copied to the CR field specified by crfD. All exception bits copied(except FEX and VX bits) are cleared in the FPSCR.
Move to FPSCR Field Immediate [1]	mtfsfi crfD,IMM	The immediate value specified by IMM is placed into the FPSCR field specified by crfD. The value of FPSCR[FX] is altered only if crfD = 0. When FPSCR[0_3] is specified, bits 0 (FX) and 3 (OX) are set explicitly to the values IMM[0] and IMM[3]. FEX and VX are not set explicitly.
Move to FPSCR Fields [1]	mtfsf FM,frB	Bits 32–63 of frB are placed into the FPSCR under control of the field mask, FM, which identifies the four-bit fields affected. When FPSCR[0–3] is specified, bits 0 (FX) and 3 (OX) are explicitly set to the values of frB[32] and frB[35]. FEX and VX cannot be altered explicitly by this operation.
Move to FPSCR Bit 0 [1]	mtfsb0 crbD	The FPSCR bit specified by crbD is cleared. FEX and VX cannot be explicitly cleared.
Move to FPSCR Bit 1 [1]	mtfsb1 crbD	The FPSCR bit specified by crbD is set. FEX and VX cannot be explicitly set.

[1]*The CR update option is indicated by appending a period '.' to the mnemonic.*

The following section describes the load and store instructions, which are used to read data from memory into either the GPRs or FPRs, and to store results of integer and floating-point operations to memory.

Load and Store Instructions

This section describes the PowerPC load and store instructions, which are grouped into the following types:

- Integer Load Instructions
- Integer Store Instructions
- Integer Load and Store with Byte Reversal Instructions
- Integer Load and Store Multiple Instructions
- Integer Move String Instructions
- Floating-Point Load Instructions
- Floating-Point Store Instructions
- Floating-Point Move Instructions
- Floating-Point Load Instructions
- Floating-Point Store Instructions

All of these instructions, except for the floating-point move instructions, access the GPRs to calculate an effective address. The floating-point move instructions, which transfer data from one FPR to another, do not require an effective address.

Integer Load Instructions

Integer load instructions are used to load the byte, half word, word, (or double word in 64-bit implementations) addressed by the EA into the GPR specified by rD.

If the address update mode is used, the EA is placed into rA and the memory element (byte, half word, word, or double word) addressed by EA is loaded into rD (assuming rA - 0 and rA - rD).

Except for algebraic instructions, if the value loaded into rD does not fill the GPR, the remaining bits are cleared, For algebraic instructions the remaining bits replicate the highest-order bit of the loaded value. The PowerPC Architecture defines as invalid forms all load with update instructions with operand rA = 0 or rA = rD. Results are right-justified in rD.

Table 11.18 describes the load instructions.

Table 11.18 Integer Load Instructions		
Name	**Operand Syntax**	**Comments**
Load Byte and Zero	lbz rD,d(rA)	The byte addressed by the EA, (rA) + d, is loaded into rD.
Load Byte and Zero Indexed	lbzx rD,rA,rB	The byte addressed by the EA, (rA|0) + (rB), is loaded into rD.
Load Byte and Zero with Update	lbzu rD,d(rA)	The byte addressed by the EA, (rA) + d, is loaded into rD.
Load Byte and Zero with Update Indexed	lbzux rD,rA,rB	The byte addressed by the EA, (rA) + (rB), is loaded into rD.
Load Half Word and Zero	lhz rD,d(rA)	The half word addressed by the EA, (rA|0) + d, is loaded into rD.
Load Half Word and Zero Indexed	lhzx rD,rA,rB	The half word addressed by the EA, (rA|0) + (rB), is loaded into rD.
Load Half Word and Zero with Update	lhzu rD,d(rA)	The half word addressed by the EA, (rA) + d, is loaded into rD.
Load Half Word and Zero with Update Indexed	lhzux rD,rA,rB	The half word addressed by the EA, (rA) + (rB), is loaded into rD.
Load Half Word Algebraic	lha rD,d(rA)	The half word addressed by the EA, (rA|0) + d, is loaded into rD.
Load Half Word Algebraic Indexed	lhax rD,rA,rB	The half word addressed by the EA, (rA|0) + (rB), is loaded into rD.
Load Half Word Algebraic with Update	lhau rD,d(rA)	The half word addressed by the EA, (rA) + d, is loaded into rD.
Load Half Word Algebraic with Update Indexed	lhaux rD,rA,rB	The half word addressed by the EA, (rA) + (rB), is loaded into rD.

Name	Operand Syntax	Comments
Load Word and Zero	lwz rD,d(rA)	The word addressed by the EA, (rA|0) + d, is loaded into rD.
Load Word and Zero Indexed	lwzx rD,rA,rB	The word addressed by the EA, (rA|0) + (rB), is loaded into rD.
Load Word and Zero with Update	lwzu rD,d(rA)	The word addressed by the EA, (rA) + d, is loaded into rD.
Load Word and Zero with Update Indexed	lwzux rD,rA,rB	The word addressed by the EA, (rA) + (rB), is loaded into rD.
Load Word Algebraic (64-bit only)	lwa rD,ds(rA)	The word addressed by the EA, (rA|0) + (ds‖b'00'), is loaded into rD.
Load Word Algebraic Indexed (64-bit only)	lwax rD,rA,rB	The word addressed by the EA, (rA|0) + (rB), is loaded into rD.
Load Word Algebraic with Update Indexed (64-bit only)	lwaux rD,rA,rB	The word addressed by the EA, (rA) + (rB), is loaded into rD.
Load Double Word (64-bit only)	ld rD,ds(rA)	The double word addressed by the EA, (rA|0) + (ds‖b'00'), is loaded into rD.
Load Double Word Indexed (64-bit only)	ldx rD,rA,rB	The double word addressed by the EA,(rA|0) + (rB), is loaded into rD.
Load Double Word with Update (64-bit only)	ldu rD,ds(rA)	The double word addressed by the EA, (rA) + (ds‖b'00'), is loaded into rD.
Load Double Word with Update Indexed (64-bit only)	ldux rD,rA,rB	The double word addressed by the EA, (rA) + (rB), is loaded into rD.

Integer Store Instructions

Integer store instructions store the value in rS into the byte, half word, word, or double word addressed by EA. If the address update mode is selected, the rA is updated with the effective address. If rA - 0, the effective address is placed into rA (otherwise, the instruction is invalid). If rS = rA, the contents of rS are copied to the target memory element, then the generated EA is placed into rA (rS). The PowerPC Architecture defines store with update instructions with operand rA = 0 as invalid forms.

Table 11.19 provides a summary of the integer store instructions.

Table 11.19 Integer Store Instructions		
Name	**Operand Syntax**	**Comments**
Store Byte	stb rS,d(rA)	The low-order byte in rS is stored into the byte addressed by the EA, (rA|0) + d.
Store Byte Indexed	stbx rS,rA,rB	The low-order byte rS is stored into the byte addressed by the EA, (rA|0) + (rB).
Store Byte with Update	stbu rS,d(rA)	The low-order byte in rS is stored into the byte addressed by the EA, (rA) + d.
Store Byte with Update Indexed	stbux rS,rA,rB	The low-order byte in rS is stored into the byte addressed by the EA (rA) + (rB)).
Store Half Word	sth rS,d(rA)	The low-order half word in rS is stored into the half word addressed by the EA, (rA|0) + d.
Store Half Word Indexed	sthx rS,rA,rB	The low-order half word in rS is stored into the half word addressed by the EA, (rA|0)+(rB).
Store Half Word with Update	sthu rS,d(rA)	The low-order half word in rS is stored into the half word addressed by the EA, (rA) + d.
Store Half Word with Update Indexed	sthux rS,rA,rB	The low-order half word in rS is stored into the half word addressed by the EA, (rA) + (rB).
Store Word	stw rS,d(rA)	The word in rS is stored into the word addressed by the EA, (rA|0) + d.
Store Word Indexed	stwx rS,rA,rB	The word in rS is stored into the word addressed by the EA, (rA|0) + (rB).
Store Word with Update	stwu rS,d(rA)	The word in rS is stored into the word addressed by the EA, (rA) + d.
Store Word with Update Indexed	stwux rS,rA,rB	The word in rS is stored into the word addressed by the EA, (rA) + (rB).
Store Double Word (64-bit only)	std rS,ds(rA)	The value in rS is stored into the double word addressed by the EA, (rA|0) + (ds||b'00').

Name	Operand Syntax	Comments
Store Double Word Indexed(64-bit only)	stdx rS,rA,rB	The value in rS is stored into the double word addressed by the EA, (rA) + (rB).
Store Double Word with Update (64-bit only)	stdu rS,ds(rA)	The value in rS is stored into the double word addressed by the EA, (rA) + (ds‖b'00').
Store Double Word with Update Indexed (64-bit only)	stdux rS,rA,rB	The value in rS is stored into the double word addressed by the EA, (rA) + (rB).

Integer Load and Store with Byte Reversal Instructions

Table 11.20 describes integer load and store with byte reversal instructions. Note that in some PowerPC implementations, load byte-reverse instructions may have greater latency than other load instructions.

When used in a PowerPC system operating with the default big-endian byte order, these instructions have the effect of loading and storing data in little-endian order. Similarly, when used in a PowerPC system operating with little-endian byte order, these instructions have the effect of loading and storing data in big-endian order.

Table 11.20 Integer Load and Store with Byte Reversal Instructions

Name	Operand Syntax	Comments
Load Half Word Byte-Reverse Indexed	lhbrx rD,rA,rB	The two bytes in the half word addressed by the EA, (rA|0) + (rB), are swapped and placed into rD.
Load Word Byte-Reverse Indexed	lwbrx rD,rA,rB	Bytes 1 and 4 are swapped and bytes 2 and 3 are swapped in the word addressed by the EA, (rA|0) + (rB) and places into rD
Store Half Word Byte-Reverse Indexed	sthbrx rS,rA,rB	The two bytes in the half word in rS are in the half word addressed by the EA, (rA|0) + (rB).
Store Word Byte-Reverse Indexed	stwbrx rS,rA,rB	Bytes 1 and 4 are swapped and bytes 2 and 3 are swapped in the word in rS and are stored into bits 0_7 of the word addressed by EA, (rA|0) + (rB).

Integer Load and Store Multiple Instructions

The load/store multiple instructions are used to move blocks of data to and from the GPRs. These compound instructions are not typical of RISC; they are used for saving and restoring registers for process switching. In the load/store multiple instructions, the combination of the EA and rD (rS) is such that the low-order byte of GPR31 is loaded from or stored into the last byte of an aligned quad word in memory. If the effective address is not correctly aligned, the instruction may take significantly longer to execute.

If a load multiple and store multiple instruction requires memory accesses crossing a 4-KB page boundary, a data access exception may occur with the address translation of the second page. If the EA is not a multiple of four, the alignment exception handler is invoked, or the results are boundedly undefined.

In some PowerPC implementations operating with little-endian byte order, execution of an lmw or stmw instruction causes a system alignment error exception condition. Table 11.21 describes the load/store multiple instructions.

Table 11.21 Integer Load and Store Multiple Instructions		
Name	**Operand Syntax**	**Comments**
Load Multiple Word	lmw rD,d(rA)	The instruction loads all GPRs between the GPR specified by rD and GPR31 with the succession of words addressed by EA, (rA|0) + d. If rA is in the range of registers to be loaded, the instruction form is invalid.
Store Multiple Word	stmw rS,d(rA)	The instruction stores words of data into successive memory locations specified by EA, (rA|0) + d. The range of registers between the GPR specified by rS and GPR31 hold the data stored to memory.

Integer Move String Instructions

The integer move string instructions move portions of data between memory and registers without being affected by alignment.

These instructions can be used for a short move between memory locations or to initiate a long move between misaligned memory fields. In some implementations, these instructions may take longer to execute than a sequence of individual load or store instructions.

Load and store string instructions execute more efficiently when rD or rS = GPR5 and the last register loaded or stored is less than or equal to GPR12. Table 11.22 describes the integer move string instructions.

Table 11.22 Integer Move String Instructions		
Name	**Operand Syntax**	**Comments**
Load String Word Immediate	lswi rD,rA,NB	The EA is (rA|0). Data is loaded into the low-order four bytes of each specified GPR; the high-order four bytes are cleared. Bytes are loaded left to right in each register. The sequence of registers wraps around to r0 if required. If the low-order four bytes of rD + nr _ 1 are only partially filled, the unfilled low-order byte(s) of that register are cleared. If rA is in the range of registers specified to be loaded, the instruction form is invalid.
Load String Word Indexed	lswx rD,rA,rB	The value in XER[25_31] specifies the number of bytes to load from the EA, (rA|0) + (rB). Data is loaded into the low-order four bytes of each GPR; the high-order four bytes are cleared .
Store String Word Immediate	stswi rS,rA,NB	The EA is (rA|0). Data is loaded into the low-order four bytes of each GPR; the high-order four bytes are cleared . Bytes are stored left to right from each register. The sequence of registers wraps around through GPR0 if required.
Store String Word Indexed	stswx rS,rA,rB	The EA is the sum (rA|0) +(rB). The number of bytes to store is specified by XER[25_31]. Consecutive bytes starting at the EA are stored beginning with the GPR specified in rS.

(continues)

Table 11.22 Continued		
Name	**Operand Syntax**	**Comments**
		Data is loaded into the low-order four bytes of each GPR; the high-order four bytes are cleared . Bytes are stored left to right from each register. The sequence of registers wraps around through GPR0 if required.

A non-word-aligned string operation that crosses a 4-KB boundary or a word-aligned string operation that crosses a 256-MB boundary causes an alignment exception. A non-word-aligned string operation that crosses a double-word boundary is slower than a word-aligned string operation.

Floating-Point Load Instructions

Floating-point load instructions are defined for single-precision (32-bit) and double-precision (64-bit) values. FPRs are 64-bits wide, and all floating-point values are put in double-precision format, regardless of precision, before being placed in an FPR. The PowerPC Architecture defines load with update instructions with rA = 0 as an invalid form.

Table 11.23 describes the floating-point load instructions.

Table 11.23 Floating-Point Load Instructions		
Name	**Operand Syntax**	**Comments**
Load Floating-Point Single-Precision	lfs frD,d(rA)	The word addressed by the EA, (rA|0) + d, is placed into frD.
Load Floating-Point Single-Precision Indexed	lfsx frD,rA,rB	The word addressed by the EA, (rA|0) + (rB), is placed into frD.
Load Floating-Point Single-Precision with Update	lfsu frD,d(rA)	The word addressed by the EA, (rA) + d, is placed into frD.
Load Floating-Point Single-Precision with Update Indexed	lfsux frD,rA,rB	The word addressed by the EA, (rA) + (rB), is placed into frD.

Name	Operand Syntax	Comments
Load Floating-Point Double-Precision	lfd frD,d(rA)	The double word addressed by the EA, (rA|0) + d, is placed into frD.
Load Floating-Point Double-Precision Indexed	lfdx frD,rA,rB	The double word addressed by the EA, (rA|0) + (rB), is placed into frD.
Load Floating-Point Double-Precision with Update	lfdu frD,d(rA)	The double word addressed by the EA, (rA) + d, is placed into frD.
Load Floating-Point Double-Precision with Update Indexed	lfdux frD,rA,rB	The double word addressed by the EA, (rA) + (rB), is placed into frD.

Floating-Point Store Instructions

This section describes floating-point store instructions. The store instructions take three basic forms: single-precision, double-precision, and integer. The integer form is supported by the optional stfiwx instruction. Because the FPRs support only floating-point, double-precision format for floating-point data, single-precision floating-point store instructions convert double-precision data to single-precision format before storing the operands. The PowerPC Architecture defines load with update instructions with rA = 0 as an invalid form.

Table 11.24 describes the floating-point store instructions.

Table 11.24 Floating-Point Store Instructions		
Name	**Operand Syntax**	**Comments**
Store Floating-Point Single-Precision	stfs frS,d(rA)	The contents of frS are converted to single-precision and stored into the word addressed by the EA, (rA|0) + d.
Store Floating-Point Single-Precision Indexed	stfsx frS,rA,rB	The contents of frS are converted to single-precision and stored into the word addressed by the EA, (rA|0) + (rB).

(continues)

Table 11.24 Continued

Name	Operand Syntax	Comments
Store Floating-Point Single-Precision with Update	stfsu frS,d(rA)	The contents of frS are converted to single-precision and stored into the word addressed by the EA, (rA) + d.
Store Floating-Point Single-Precision with Update Indexed	stfsux frS,rA,rB	The contents of frS are converted to single-precision and stored into the word addressed by the EA, (rA) + (rB).
Store Floating-Point Double-Precision	stfd frS,d(rA)	The contents of frS stored into the double word addressed by the EA, (rA|0) + d.
Store Floating-Point Double-Precision Indexed	stfdx frS,rA,rB	The contents of frS are stored into the double word addressed by the EA,(rA|0) + (rB).
Store Floating-Point Double-Precision with Update	stfdu frS,d(rA)	The contents of frS are stored into the double word addressed by the EA, (rA) + d.
Store Floating-Point Double-Precision with Update Indexed	stfdux frS,rA,rB	The contents of frS are stored into the double word addressed by EA, (rA) + (rB).
Store Floating-Point as Integer Word Indexed	stfiwx frS,rA,rB	The contents of the low order low-order 32 bits of frS are stored, without conversion, into the word addressed by EA, (rA|0) + (rB). If the precision of frS were determined by an lfs instruction, single-precision arithmetic instruction, or frsp, the value is stored in undefined. This instruction is optional.

Floating-Point Move Instructions

Floating-point move instructions copy data from one FPR register to another. The fneg, fabs, and fnabs instructions may alter the sign bit of a NaN. These instructions do not modify the FPSCR. The CR update option in these instructions controls the placing of result status into CR1. If the CR update option is enabled, CR1 is set; otherwise, CR1 is unchanged. Table 11.25 describes the floating-point move instructions.

Table 11.25 Floating-Point Move Instructions

Name	Operand Syntax	Comments
Floating-Point Move Register [1]	fmr rD,frB	The value of frB is placed into frD.
Floating-Point Negate [1]	fneg frD,frB	The value of frB with bit 0 inverted is placed into frD.
Floating-Point Absolute Value [1]	fabs frD,frB	The value of frB with bit 0 cleared is placed into frD.
Floating-Point Negative Absolute Value [1]	fnabs frD,frB	The value of frB with bit 0 set is placed into frD.

[1]*CR update option is indicated by appending a period '.' to the mnemonic.*

The next section describes instructions that enforce strict ordering for memory accesses.

Memory Synchronization Instructions

Memory synchronization instructions, defined by the UISA and the VEA levels of the PowerPC architecture, can be used to enforce strict order for memory operations. Table 11.26 describes memory synchronization instructions. For load word instructions in 64-bit implementations, register rD[0-31] bits are cleared. These instructions are particularly useful in multiprocessor implementations.

The UISA defines the load/store with reservation instructions and the Synchronize instruction.

The load/store with reservation instructions can be used to ensure that an attempt to atomically update an aligned word or double word was successful. The load with reservation instructions place a reservation on a particular word or double word. The corresponding store conditional instructions look for that reservation. It should be noted that this instruction pair does not guarantee that an *atomic memory access* will occur, because they do not provide a mechanism to prevent another operation to store to the specified address, which explains why the store instruction is conditional. The conditional part of the instruction name refers to whether the reservation still exists. If the reservation still exists, the word or double word is stored, the

Atomic memory access
One in which two load and store operations to a location have occurred without an intervening store. The term comes from the Greek word for atom, meaning not broken.

reservation is cleared, and the access is guaranteed to be atomic. If the reservation has been cleared (as the result of a previous store to that address or another load with reservation or store conditional instruction to an address) the store operation is not performed. So, not only does an atomic access not occur, the store conditional instruction does not access memory at all.

Although these instructions are defined by the UISA and are user-level instructions, these instructions are not typically used explicitly by a user-level application. They are intended for use in system programs, where they are programmed to perform various synchronization functions, which are accessible to user-level applications.

When a load with reservation instruction is executed the word or double word in memory is loaded into rD. This instruction creates a reservation for use by an stwcx. or stdcx. instruction, respectively. An address computed from the EA is associated with the reservation and replaces any address previously associated with the reservation.

When a store indexed instruction is executed and a reservation exists, the value in rS is stored into the word or double word addressed by the EA, the reservation is cleared, and CR0[EQ] is set; otherwise the instruction completes without altering memory or the contents of the cache.

The VEA defines memory synchronization instructions that control the order in which memory operations are completed with respect to asynchronous events, and the order in which memory operations are seen by other devices that share the physical memory space.

The Instruction Synchronize (isync) instruction causes the processor to discard all prefetched instructions, wait for any preceding instructions to complete, and then branch to the next sequential instruction Executing the isync instruction has the effect of clearing the pipeline behind the isync instruction.

Table 11.26 Memory Synchronization Instructions

Name	Operand Syntax	Comments
Load Double Word and Reserve Indexed (64-bit only)	ldarx rD,rA,rB	If the EA is not a multiple of 8, an alignment exception occurs or the results are boundedly undefined.

Name	Operand Syntax	Comments
Load Word and Reserve Indexed	lwarx rD,rA,rB	If the EA is not a multiple of 4, an alignment exception occurs or the results are boundedly undefined.
Store Double Word Conditional Indexed (64-bit only)	stdcx. rS,rA,rB	If the EA, (rA|0) + (rB), is not a multiple of 8, an alignment exception occurs or the results are boundedly undefined.
Store Word Conditional Indexed	stwcx. rS,rA,rB	If the EA is not a multiple of 4, an alignment exception occurs, or the results are boundedly undefined.
Synchronize	sync	All previously initiated instructions appear to complete (with respect to all resources) before subsequent instructions are initiated by the given processor.
Enforce In-Order Execution of I/O	eieio	Ensures that all previously initiated memory accesses initiated by the processor are complete with respect to main memory before allowing any memory accesses subsequently initiated by the processor to access main memory.
Instruction Synchronize	isync	This instruction waits for all previous instructions to complete, and then discards any fetched instructions, causing subsequent instructions to be fetched (or refetched) from memory and to execute in the context established by the previous instructions. This instruction has no effect on other processors or on their caches.

Processor Control Instructions

Processor control instructions are used to read from and write to the CR, MSR, and SPRs. Table 11.27 describes the instructions for reading from or writing to the condition register.

Table 11.27 Processor Control Instructions-User Level

Name	Operand Syntax	Comments
Move to Condition Register Fields	mtcrf CRM,rS	The word in rS is placed into the CR under control of the field mask specified by operand CRM.
Move to Condition Register from XER	mcrxr crfD	The contents of XER[0–3] are copied into the CR field designated by crfD. No other CR fields are affected. The contents of XER[0–3] are cleared.
Move from Condition Register	mfcr rD	The contents of the CR are placed into rD. The contents of rD[0–31] are cleared.
Move from Time Base	mftb rD, TBR	The TBR field denotes either the time base lower or time base upper.
Move to Special Purpose Register	mtspr SPR,rS	The contents of rS are placed into the designated SPR. This instruction is considered user-level when used to access a supervisor-level SPR.
Move from Special Purpose Register	mfspr rD,SPR	The contents of the designated SPR are placed into rD. This instruction is considered user-level when used to access a supervisor-level SPR.

Processor Control Instructions— Supervisor Level

Table 11.28 describes the processor control instructions that are used to read from and write to the MSR and to SPRs. These instructions are used for system configuration and memory management.

Table 11.28 Processor Control Instructions-Supervisor Level

Name	Operand Syntax	Comments
Move to Machine State Register	mtmsr rS	The contents of rS are placed into the MSR.

Name	Operand Syntax	Comments
Move from Machine State Register	mfmsr rD	The contents of the MSR are Placed into rD. This is a supervisor-level instruction.
Move to Special Purpose Register	mtspr SPR, rS	The contents of rS are placed into the designated SPR. This instruction is considered supervisor-level when used to access a supervisor-level SPR.
Move from Special Purpose Register	mfspr rD, SPR	The contents of the designated SPR are placed into rD. This instruction is considered supervisor-level when used to access a supervisor-level SPR.

Memory Control Instructions— User Level

Memory control instructions include the following types of instructions:

- Cache management instructions (user-level and supervisor-level)

- Segment register manipulation instructions

- Translation look-aside buffer management instructions

- User-Level Cache Instructions

This section describes the user-level cache management instructions. These instructions provide user-level programs the ability to manage on-chip caches.

As with other memory-related instructions, the effect of the cache management instructions on memory are weakly ordered. If the programmer needs to ensure that cache or other instructions have been performed with respect to all other processors and mechanisms, a sync instruction must be placed in the program following those instructions.

When data address translation is disabled (MSR[DT] = 0), the Data Cache Block Set to Zero (dcbz) instruction allocates a cache block and may not verify that the physical address is valid. If a cache block is created for an invalid physical address, a machine check condition may result when an attempt is made to write that cache block back to memory.

Any cache control instruction that generates an effective address that falls within an I/O controller interface segment (SR[T] = 1) behaves as a no-op.

Table 11.29 summarizes the cache instructions that are accessible to user-level programs.

Table 11.29 User-Level Cache Instructions		
Name	**Operand Syntax**	**Comments**
Data Cache Block Touch	dcbt rA,rB	This instruction provides a method for improving performance through the use of software-initiated fetch hints, loading data from the EA, (rA|0) + (rB). This instruction allows the program to request a cache block fetch before it is needed. The program can later perform loads to put data into registers. However, the processor is not obliged to load the addressed cache block into the data cache.
Data Cache Block Touch for Store	dcbtst rA,rB	This instruction provides a method for improving performance through the use of software-initiated fetch hints by loading data from the EA, (rA|0) + (rB). This instruction allows the program to request a cache block fetch before it is needed by the program. The program can later store data to memory, but the processor need not load the addressed cache block into the data cache.
Data Cache Block Set to Zero	dcbz rA,rB	This instruction is used to clear the cache block containing byte addressed by the EA, (rA|0) + (rB). Behavior of this instruction depends on the memory configuration.
Data Cache Block Store	dcbst rA,rB	The EA is the sum(rA|0) + (rB). This instruction causes the data in the cache block referenced by EA to be stored to external memory. Behavior of this instruction depends on the memory configuration.

Name	Operand Syntax	Comments
Data Cache Block Flush	dcbf rA,rB	Flushes a cache block in the data cache(s) associated with the EA, (rA|0) + (rB). Specific details depend on the memory configuration.
Instruction Cache Block Invalidate	icbi rA,rB	Invalidates (removes) a cache block in the instruction cache(s) associated with the EA, (rA|0) + (rB). Specific details depend on the memory configuration.

Memory Control Instructions-OEA

The OEA defines one memory control instruction—Data cache Block Invalidate (dcbi), which is described in table 11.30. If the effective address lies within an I/O controller interface segment, the instruction behaves as a no-op.

Table 11.30 Cache Management Supervisor-Level Instruction		
Name	**Operand Syntax**	**Comments**
Data Cache Block Invalidate	dcbi rA,rB	The EA is the sum (rA|0) + (rB). Invalidates the addressed cache block and possibly cache blocks on other processors depending on the memory configuration.

Segment Register Manipulation Instructions

The operating system uses the supervisor-level instructions described in table 11.31 to access to the segment registers. These register are used for memory management. These instructions execute regardless of whether logical-to-physical translation is enabled.

Table 11.31 Segment Register Manipulation Instructions

Name	Operand Syntax	Comments
Move to Segment Register (32-bit only)	mtsr SR,rS	The contents of rS are placed into the specified SR.
Move to Segment Register Indirect (32-bit only)	mtsrin rS,rB	The contents of rS are copied to the SR selected by bits 0–3 of rB.
Move from Segment Register (32-bit only)	mfsr rD,SR	The contents of the SR specified by operand SR are placed into rD.
Move from Segment Register (32-bit only)	mfsrin rD,rB	The contents of the SR selected by bits 0–3 of rB are copied into rD.

Segment/Translation Look-Aside Buffer Management Instructions— Supervisor Level

Implementations may use translation look-aside buffers (TLBs) and segment look-aside buffers (SLBs) to store recently used translation information. These are implemented much like a small cache. The OEA provides instructions to selectively invalidate these resources; because the resources are optional, the instructions are optional. If an implementation does not implement SLBs or TLBs, the instructions are treated as no-ops or as illegal instructions.

The invalidation operations initiated by instructions listed in table 11.32 occur regardless of whether address translation is disabled.

Table 11.32 Translation Look-Aside Buffer Management Instruction

Name	Operand Syntax	Comments
SLB Invalidate Entry (64-bit only)	slbie rB	If an SLB entry corresponds to the EA, (rB), it is invalidated.
SLB Invalidate All (64-bit only)	slbia	All SLB entries are invalidated.
Translation Lookaside Buffer Invalidate Entry	tlbie rB	If a TLB entry corresponds to the EA, (rB), it is invalidated.

Name	Operand Syntax	Comments
TLB Invalidate All	tlbia	All TLB entries are invalidated.
TLB Synchronize	tlbsync	Synchronizes TLB control instructions. This instruction is implemented if a TLB invalidation instruction that signals the invalidation in hardware or the eciwx or ecowx instructions are implemented.

External Control Instructions-Optional

The OEA defines two optional external control instructions that allow a user-level program to communicate with a special-purpose device. Table 11.33 summarizes the external control instructions.

Table 11.33 External Control Instructions		
Name	**Operand Syntax**	**Comments**
External Control Input Word Indexed	eciwx rD,rA,rB	If EAR[E] is set, a load request for the physical address corresponding to the EA, (rA|0) + (rB), is sent to the device identified by the EAR[RID]. The value in rD[0_31] is cleared. The word returned by the device is placed in rD.
External Control Output Word Indexed	ecowx rS,rA,rB	If EAR[E] is cleared, a request is made to the physical address corresponding to the EA, (rA|0) + (rB), and the word in rS is sent to the device identified by EAR[RID].

Summary

This chapter has summarized the PowerPC instructions identifying those user-level instructions that are associated with applications and compilers and the supervisor-level instructions that are used by the operating system.

Typically, the processor enters supervisor level when an exception is taken. The next chapter discusses the exceptions defined by the PowerPC Architecture.

Chapter 12

PowerPC Memory Conventions

There are many considerations that an architecture must address. The most visible and distinctive of these concern the type of instructions, the register set, and the mechanisms employed for defining memory—those characteristics that distinguish one architecture from another. However, there are basic, and somewhat mundane, conventions that must be decided for how data is stored in registers and in memory.

The existence of conflicting systems for the storage and retrieval of data actually predates the computer era. The recording industry presents examples that date back into the previous century. While Thomas Edison was convinced that cylinders made the best media and that the best method for recording was to impress the vibrations in the bottom of the groove, other manufacturers favored flat discs with the data in the sides of the groove. A few manufacturers designed their records to be played starting at the center and moving to the outside. Over the years compatibility issues moved to record speeds, and to various tape formats.

For an architecture design, most of the decisions about data representation in memory boil down to choosing between existing conventions, some of which are defined quite formally and some of which are not. For example, the Institute of Electrical and Electronics Engineers (IEEE) has defined a standard (IEEE 754) for floating-point operations that, among other things, specifies how floating-point data is represented. The PowerPC Architecture adheres to this definition.

In this chapter, you learn the following:

■ How single- and double-precision floating-point values are represented in physical memory and in the FPRs

■ Details regarding how data should be aligned and how PowerPC processors handle misaligned data

■ Information about how PowerPC processors can be configured to support either big- or little-endian byte addressing modes

Other conventions are less clearly defined. In particular, there is no single industry standard for how bytes are to be ordered within bytes of memory. Some designs place the most significant byte of a multiple-byte data type in the addressed byte, while other designs place the least-significant in the addressed byte. These approaches are referred to respectively as big- and little-endian.

Floating-Point Operand Representation

Floating-point values can be represented in two formats, single-precision, which is represented in 32 bits, and double-precision, which is represented in 64 bits.

The formats for these two representations are shown in Figure 12.1 and Figure 12.2.

Figure 12.1
Single-Precision Data Representation.

Figure 12.2
Double-Precision Data Representation.

Sign bit
Indicates whether a value is negative or positive. Sign bits can be explicit or implicit.

Values in floating-point format consist of the following three fields:

S (*sign bit*)

EXP (biased exponent)

FRACTION (fraction)

The true value of the exponent can be determined by subtracting 127 for single-precision numbers and 1,023 for double-precision numbers. The exponent uses excess $(2m-1)+1$ notation. The actual value is represented by adding that value to $(2m-1)-1$ where m is the number of bits in the exponent. For single-precision values, there are eight bits, so m = 8. The value stored in the exponent field then is $(28-1)-1$ $(27)-1$ or 127 bits greater than the actual exponent. For double-precision values, the exponent is expressed in 11 bits. So the actual value of the exponent can be determined by subtracting $(2^{10})-1$, or 1,023, from the biased exponent.

Using excess 127 allows a contiguous range of positive and negative exponents from –128 to +127 for single-precision numbers, and excess 1,023 data representation can be used for values from –1,022 to +1,023. This method of value representation also makes the most-significant bit an implicit sign bit. If the first bit is a one, the exponent is positive; otherwise, the exponent is negative or zero.

> ### Note
>
> The PowerPC Architecture follows the IEEE-754 standard for 32- and 64-bit floating-point arithmetic. For single-precision arithmetic, all operands and results must be single-precision. Double-precision arithmetic may be performed using either single- or double-precision operands, but always produce double-precision results.

Data in the 64-bit FPRs can only be represented as double-precision numbers, but data in memory can be represented in either form. Data used in single-precision arithmetic operations must be converted from double-precision when it is retrieved from the FPRs as source operands and converted back to double-precision when results are stored in the target FPR. When a single-precision value is represented in double-precision format in an FPR, the low-order 29 fraction bits are zero.

Value Representation

Single- and double-precision formats provide a range of discreet values that can be used to approximate real numbers. Clearly, more real numbers can be represented with 64 bits than with 32 bits, both in terms of larger and smaller values and in terms of how precisely a value can be represented (that is, a smaller rounding error).

However, calculations can generate results that fall outside the range of a particular format, or paradoxical numbers, such as those that occur when attempting to divide a number by zero. The single- and double-precision formats reserve bit combinations to represent these results. These non-numerical values include the positive and negative infinities and the NaNs ('not a number's).

Table 12.1 shows the relationships used by both single- and double-precision formats to represent numerical and nonnumerical values.

Table 12.1 Representable Floating-Point Values				
Sign Bit	**Biased Exponent**	**Leading Bit**	**Fraction**	**Value**
0	Maximum	x	Nonzero	NaN
0	Maximum	x	Zero	+Infinity
0	0 < Exp < Maximum	1	Nonzero	+Normalized
0	0	0	Nonzero	+Denormalized
0	0	0	Zero	+0
1	0	0	Zero	–0
1	0	0	Nonzero	–Denormalized
1	0 < Exp < Maximum	1	Nonzero	–Normalized
1	Maximum	x	Zero	–Infinity
1	Maximum	x	Nonzero	NaN

The various representable values are described as follows:

- Normalized numbers are those numbers that can be represented in the format in which they can be used as operands. For these values, the sign bit always indicates whether it is a positive or a negative number, the exponent falls between the reserved values of all zeros and all ones, the leading-bit is always one and therefore the fraction is always a nonzero.

- Infinities are used to represent the values that exceed the range of normalized numbers. The sign bit indicates whether this is a positive or negative infinity, the leading bit is ignored, and the fraction consists of binary zeros.

- Zeros are represented with zeros in all fields, except possibly the sign bit. If the sign bit is one and all other bits are zero, the value is considered a positive zero. If the sign bit is a zero, the value is considered a negative zero. These numbers are numerically equivalent.

- Denormalized numbers are those positive and negative numbers that lie between zero and the range of normalized numbers. Some of those denormalized values are representable by the bits provided in the single- and double-precision formats. These numbers are indicated with a zero leading bit and a non-zero fraction. The sign bit indicates whether the number is positive or negative.

- Not-a-Numbers are used to convey diagnostic information such as the representation of uninitialized variables. The representation of NaNs is distinguished from that of infinities in that the fraction can be a non-zero value.

Figure 12.3 shows how these values (except NaNs) can be mapped to a number line.

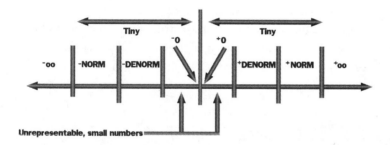

Figure 12.3
Approximation to Real Numbers.

Normalization and Denormalization

When a floating-point instruction executes, it produces a number that is considered infinitely precise, and in order for that number to be stored to an FPR, it must be converted to double-precision format (and perhaps to a single-precision value represented in double-precision format).

If after normalization or denormalization, the infinitely precise result cannot be represented in the precision required by the instruction, it must be rounded. There are four rounding modes that can be selected by the two-bit FPSCR[RN] field, as shown in table 12.2.

Table 12.2 Rounding Modes	
RN Setting	**Rounding Mode**
00	Round to nearest
01	Round toward zero
10	Round toward +infinity
11	Round toward –infinity

Data Organization in Memory and Data Transfers

Bytes in memory are numbered consecutively starting with 0. Each number is the address of the corresponding byte.

Memory operands may be bytes, half words, words, or double words, or, for the load/store multiple and move assist instructions, a sequence of bytes or words. The address of a memory operand is the address of its first byte (that is, of its lowest-numbered byte). Operand length is implicit for each instruction.

Data Alignment

In single-register load and store instructions, operands are aligned according to their length. In other words, the address of an aligned operand is an integral multiple of the operand length. The alignment of larger units of data can be described in terms of the units of which an address is a multiple. That is, if the starting address is divisible by eight, the data is said to be double-word-aligned; if it's divisible by four (as in the case of instructions), it is said to be word-aligned.

Effect of Operand Placement on Performance

The location and alignment of an operand in memory can affect the performance of memory accesses. The best performance is guaranteed if memory operands are aligned. In other words, they are placed in memory at an address that is divisible by the size of the data type—half words should be half word aligned, words should be word-aligned, double words should be double-word aligned, and quad words should be quad-word aligned.

The performance of accesses may vary depending on the size and alignment of an operand, whether the processor is configured big-endian or little-endian mode, and whether the access crosses a cache block boundary, a page boundary, a BAT boundary, or a segment boundary.

Representation of Data in Memory— Big- and Little-Endian Byte Ordering

There are different kinds of formats for storing data in memory—the single- and double-precision formats described above provide a way to represent numerical values to various degrees of precision in 32 and 64 bits, respectively. Likewise, integer values are represented in a more straightforward manner, and characters can be stored according to the conventions of ASCII or EBCDIC encodings.

These conventions, however, do not address a more basic question of how these representations are to be physically stored in memory. Should the most significant data unit be on the left or on the right?

The ordering of bits within a byte is essentially trivial—it doesn't matter which end of the byte has the most- or the least-significant byte. And typically, the smallest addressable unit is the byte, as is the case with the PowerPC Architecture.

However, the ordering of bytes within larger units becomes more of a problem. In an addressing scheme in which four-byte words are accessed in memory by addressing the lowest byte, the question remains whether the addressed byte in the lowest of the four positions is the most-significant byte or the least-significant byte. The decision is trivial if compatibility is not an issue—one choice is as good as the other, but the decision has to be made before the memory system can be designed. But when compatibility is an issue, the difference becomes significant.

This described a basic characteristic that defines different computer systems. Systems that place the most-significant byte of a four-byte word in the addressed byte are referred to as big-endian, and systems that place the least significant byte in the addressed byte are called little-endian systems.

The terms come from a tale in Jonathan Swift's *Gulliver's Travels* which tells of war erupting because of a dispute over whether eggs should be broken at the big or little end. Because it makes the most sense to break the egg at the big end, the PowerPC Architecture is big-endian, by default.

Other big-endian machines include Motorola's 680x0 chips and IBM's 360. Little-endian machines include Intel's x86 chips, DEC VAX, and DEC RISC.

In systems in which bytes are the smallest addressable unit, store byte instruction can specify precisely the byte in memory where it should be stored. If a byte is stored at address x'FFF0', only the addressed byte is affected.

However, if a store half word instruction is used to store a four-digit hexadecimal value x'12AB', the bytes in which x'12' and x'AB' would be stored would depend on whether the system is big- or little-endian. In a big-endian system x'12' would be stored at x'FFF0' and x'AB' would be stored at x'FFF1'. In little-endian systems this would be reversed.

Tables 12.3 and 12.4 show the same collection of data as they would appear in big- and little-endian systems, respectively. This data is as follows:

- A string of bytes representing the characters A through H stored in consecutive bytes x'00' through x'07'

- A single-precision floating-point value (word) stored at address x'08'

- An integer half-word value stored at address x'0E'

- A double-precision floating-point value (double word) stored at address x'10'

Table 12.3 Big-Endian Data Representation

00	A 00	B 01	C 02	D 03	E 04	F 05	G 06	H 07
08	sin 08	gle 09	preci OA	sion OB	 OC	 OD	half OE	word OF
12	do 10	ub 11	le 12	pr 13	ec 14	is 15	io 16	n 17

As shown in tables 12.3 and 12.4, when this data is represented in either a big- or little-endian system, the string of byte-length characters is represented in consecutive bytes. The characters are assigned to the same byte addresses in both systems (that is, A is at x'00', B is at x'01', and so forth).

In the big-endian system, the single-precision value is stored in bytes x'08' through x'0B' with the most-significant byte in the addressed byte, x'08'. In the little-endian system, the single-precision value is also stored in bytes x'08' through x'0B', but with the most significant value stored in byte x'0B'.

The half-word integer occupies bytes x'0E' and x'0F' in both big- and little-endian systems. However, the most-significant byte in the big-endian system is stored at address x'0E'; whereas, in the little-endian system the most-significant byte is stored at byte address x'0F'.

Lastly, the double-precision value occupies the double word at address x'10', and once again, the most-significant byte of that value is stored at address x'10' in the big-endian system and at address x'17' in the little-endian system.

Table 14.4 Little-Endian Data Representation

H 07	G 06	F 05	E 04	D 03	C 02	B 01	A 00	00
half 0F	word 0E	0D	0C	sin 0B	gle 0A	preci 09	sion 08	08
do 17	ub 16	le 15	pr 14	ec 13	is 12	io 11	n 10	10

Obviously, if a big-endian system using a single-precision operand were expecting the first bit at the address to be the sign bit but instead got a bit that fell somewhere in the fraction, progress would be hopeless.

Larger data units become more complex. The PowerPC Architecture can specify that values be quad-word aligned in memory and memory can be populated with variable-sized data units. For example, single- and double-precision values are represented in fields that are indifferent to internal byte ordering. Likewise, if the instruction fetcher accesses instructions (each a word long) from memory that is organized in the other endian mode, some assembly would be required for the instruction to be recognizable to the processor.

Although, the PowerPC Architecture is big-endian by default, it can be configured to operate in either big- or little-endian byte ordering. The MSR includes two bits that control the byte ordering. If MSR[LE] is set, the processor is configured to run in little-endian mode; otherwise, it runs in big-endian mode. The MSR[ILE] bit determines which mode should be used when an exception is taken. When an exception occurs, this bit is copied directly into the MSR[LE] bit to establish the machine state in the exception handler. Again, if the bit is clear, the processor handles exceptions in big-endian mode, and if it is set, exceptions are handled in little-endian mode.

Summary

This chapter has looked at how PowerPC processors represent data in memory and in registers and has taken a brief look at how to configure a PowerPC processor to operate in either big- or little-endian mode.

The next chapter provides an overview of the PowerPC memory management model, which governs how memory is subdivided into segments, blocks, and pages, and how effective addresses generated by software are translated to the physical addresses required for accessing memory, and how memory can be protected.

Chapter 13

PowerPC Memory Management Model

The PowerPC Architecture (OEA) provides a model for memory management in PowerPC processors. This definition takes into account the necessary differences between implementing 64- and 32-bit address space, and provides a smooth transition to 64-bit devices to ensure software compatibility.

This chapter also focuses on addresses translation—the mechanism(s) by which logical (effective) addresses generated by a program can be translated to the physical addresses necessary to access the caches (which are physically addressed) and external memory. In addition, the mechanisms by which these translations, or portions of them, can be saved and retrieved by subsequent accesses, also is discussed.

In this chapter, you learn the following:

- The PowerPC Architecture definition of memory management resources

- The partitioning of the logical and physical memory space

- Memory protection

How the Logical and Physical Memory Space Is Partitioned

The logical address space can be divided into 256MB *segments* or into variable-sized blocks, which can range from 128KB to 256MB. If the segments are memory mapped, they can be subdivided into 4KB *pages*. These blocks and pages define the memory units for which regions of memory can be characterized (for example, whether it is write-back or write-through, whether logical-to-physical translation is enabled or disabled, and whether access is provided at user or supervisor level).

Segment
A 256MB memory region.

Page
A 4KB memory region, as defined in the OEA portion of the PowerPC Architecture.

How Memory Can Be Accessed and Protected

Page table entry
A record, set up by the operating system, which defines characteristics of a page in memory.

Physical memory space
The actual memory space in which data and instructions reside.

For each of the pages and blocks, the operating system generates an address descriptor—a *page table entry* (PTE) for each page and a BAT array entry for each block.

The *physical memory space* typically is occupied with areas of memory that are accessed to provide the instructions and data for both user- and supervisor-level programs, as well as memory-mapped I/O devices. Care must be taken that access to such regions of memory be controlled, as a matter of protecting the integrity of data within a region.

Table 13.1 Page Access Protection Options				
Option	**User Read**	**User Write**	**Supervisor Read**	**Supervisor Write**
Supervisor-only	Not allowed	Not allowed	Allowed	Allowed
Supervisor write-only	Allowed	Not allowed	Allowed	Allowed
Both user/ supervisor	Allowed	Allowed	Allowed	Allowed
Both read-only	Allowed	Not allowed	Allowed	Not allowed

The page access options are described as follows:

- *Supervisor only*. These pages can be read and written by supervisor-level software only. They cannot be read or written by user-level software.

- *Supervisor write-only*. These pages can be read and written by supervisor-level software. They can be read but cannot be written by user-level software.

- *User level (Unprotected)*. These pages can be written or read by either supervisor- or user-level software.

- *Both read-only*. These pages can be read by user- or supervisor-level software, but can be written to by neither.

> **Note**
>
> Notice that no pages can be configured to allow user-level access without also permitting supervisor-level access. The access privileges are determined by the MSR[PR] bit. For user-level applications, the PR bit is set; and for operating system operations (such as exception handling), the PR bit is cleared. If a user-level program attempts to access a page that is available only to supervisor-level software, an exception is taken.

Block protection allows individual blocks to be independently defined as accessible by user- and supervisor-level software. Blocks can be configured so an attempt to access a supervisor-level block by user software is ignored, allowing supervisor and user programs to use the same logical address space that maps to unique physical addresses without causing exceptions.

In a 32-bit implementation, when a segment is defined as an I/O controller interface region (by setting SR[T]), instructions cannot be fetched from that segment. An attempt to do so causes an exception. Similarly, any memory segment can be specifically defined to prevent instruction access by setting the SR[N] bit. This feature is provided to designate segments as supporting data access only. An attempt to fetch an instruction from this segment causes an instruction access exception.

How Addresses Are Translated

The PowerPC Architecture defines four types of address translation:

- *Block address translation*. Translates the block number for 128KB to 256MB blocks.

- *Page address translation*. Translates the page frame address for a 4KB page. Page translations are controlled by the segment registers.

- *I/O controller interface address translation*. Used to generate I/O controller interface accesses on the external bus; not optimized for performance— present for compatibility only. I/O controller interface address translations are controlled by the segment registers in 32-bit implementations and or STES in 64-bit implementations.

- *No translation*. Address translation is disabled separately for instructions and for data. If MSR[IT] = 0 or MSR[DT] = 0, the effective (logical) address is the same as physical address.

These four translation methods are shown in Figure 13.1.

Figure 13.1
Address Transla-
tion Types.

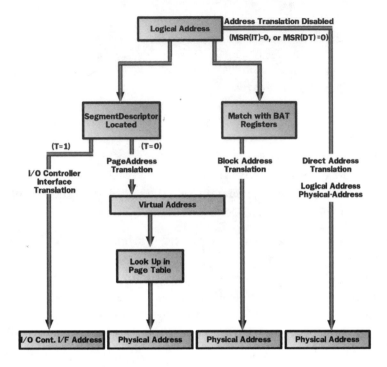

Block Address Translation

The BAT registers (four IBATs and four DBATs, each implemented as two SPRs) are provided for translating instruction and data addresses and can be treated as an eight-entry, fully-associative BAT array. The effective address is compared to the block logical page index field (BLPI) in all of the BATs, and if there is a match, the BAT register is used to generate the physical address, even when a match is simultaneously found in the segment descriptor.

This process is shown in Figure 13.2.

As well as providing an index for logical addresses, the BAT registers define the size of the block and an index to the corresponding physical block (PBN).

Page Address Translation

Page table
A table in memory that holds recently used logical-to-physical address translations for pages in memory.

Page address translation differs from block address translation in that it involves an intermediate virtual address (this is a 52-bit address in 32-bit implementations and an 80-bit address in 64-bit implementations). The virtual address is then used to locate the translation information that is stored in tables, called *page tables*, in memory.

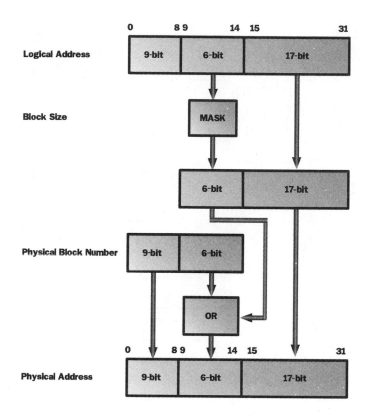

Figure 13.2
Block Address
Translation Flow
Diagram.

These tables may be in external memory, in a cache, or in a *translation look-aside buffer*, which stores the most recently used PTEs. These TLBs are defined, but not required, by the PowerPC Architecture. The search, called a table search or a table walk, is performed with information in the table search description register (SDR1). This search is performed within memory structures, called page table entry groups, or PTEGs.

When a table search operation begins, the virtual address is altered through the use of a primary hashing function. The results are concatenated with bits from SDR1 to create the physical address of the primary PTEG. If the PTE is not in the primary PTEG, a new physical address is generated for the PTEG by using a secondary hashing function. The resulting secondary PTEG address is used to search for the PTE.

If the PTE is not found, a page fault occurs and a data or instructions access exception is taken.

Figure 13.3 provides an overview of how logical-to-virtual address translation is performed.

Translation look-aside buffer (TLB)
A memory resource on the processor used to hold recently used instruction or data address translations. TLBs are optional in the PowerPC Architecture.

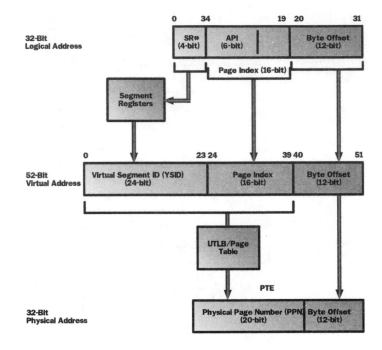

Figure 13.3
Page Address
Translation Flow
Diagram.

Notice that both page and block address translation occur simultaneously, but if the translation is found in the BAT, it is used even if the page table is found. Notice that information regarding the translation requires access to segment descriptors (in 64-bit implementations this information is accessed indirectly though the Address Space Register, or ASR). The T bit must be cleared to use the segment register for regular memory accesses. If T = 1, the access is to I/O controller interface areas, which is described in the next section.

I/O Controller Interface Translation

I/O controller interface address translation is used when block translation fails and the SR[T] bit is set. If T = 1, the remaining segment information and logical address bits are used to generate the packets used in an I/O controller interface access on the external interface.

Notice that this translation occurs simultaneously with a BAT translation. If there is a hit in the BATs, the I/O controller interface translation is ignored.

No Translation Mode

Translation can be disabled by setting bits in the MSR. IF MSR[IT] = 0, instruction address translation is disabled; if MSR[DT] = 0, data address translation is disabled.

Summary

This chapter has provided a general overview of the PowerPC memory management model, describing the features provided by the PowerPC Architecture for defining memory regions, protecting areas of memory, and translating the effective addresses generated by software to the physical addresses used by memory devices to store data and instructions.

Closely related to the memory management model is the cache model, which is described in the next chapter.

Chapter 14

PowerPC Cache Implementation Model

The memory system remains the critical bottleneck that restricts performance in any computer system—regardless of whether it is based on RISC or CISC architecture, and many millions of research and development dollars have been spent on reducing the effect that memory access has on overall performance. This chapter looks in general at various mechanisms used to reduce the effect of memory latency, and in particular at the PowerPC Architectural definition of the cache model.

Typically, the system bus is much slower than the processor, sometimes three or four times slower, so processors adapt various strategies to minimize the effect that such accesses have on overall performance. Put simply, the goals are to avoid memory accesses, make them as fast as possible, get as much useful data as possible when memory is accessed, and make the mechanism used to access the bus as flexible as possible to enable it to prioritize and schedule bus activities accordingly.

Implementing some of these tactics can become quite elaborate and all are subject to the price versus performance tradeoffs.

The system bus is only one bottleneck in the memory system, but it is one in which the processor has the most control. Taking the most general overview of memory systems, it is possible to identify several levels of memory from the perspective of the processor. Typically, memory resources that can be accessed more quickly are the most expensive—1MB of memory space gets progressively more expensive as you go from floppy and hard disks to DRAM chips to caches.

In this chapter you learn the following:

- A general overview of how caches function with respect to other memory devices

- Special concerns for cache implementations in multi-processor systems

- The relationship between the memory management model and the cache model regarding cache attributes

- Instructions for controlling caches both in single and multiprocessing environments

- A common mechanism used for ensuring cache coherency (MESI protocol)

This chapter provides an overview of the effect that memory accesses have on performance, addressing, in particular, ways in which the PowerPC Architecture addresses those concerns and how certain PowerPC processors adopt specific methods to reduce the effect of memory latency. This chapter progresses by looking at memory from the outside in. Such an approach illustrates the flexible nature of the PowerPC Architecture definition. In particular, the PowerPC Architecture prescribes very little about the hardware aspect of the processor's design. Therefore, chip designers can choose the solutions most appropriate for the price and performance requirements of an implementation.

Slow and Inexpensive Memory Resources

The slowest and least expensive storage mechanism are disk and hard drives, which are used for long-term storage of data and programs. Here, memory space is relatively inexpensive, but memory latency can be considerable because of the access time required to read the data. Such resources are far removed from the jurisdiction of the architectural definition itself. However, the PowerPC Architecture defines memory-mapped I/O as an efficient way of accessing I/O devices (as well as the I/O controller interface provided for compatibility with existing I/O devices used in some PowerPC systems).

On-Board Memory

Accessing external memory space in a RAM device is faster than accessing a magnetic storage device, but it also is considerably more expensive. These devices hold as much data and application program code as possible. The smaller this resource is, the more often the storage devices must be accessed. The processor, and possibly other devices in the system, access the system memory through the system bus.

Accesses to system memory are time-consuming for several reasons:

- The speed at which data can be transferred is limited by the bus frequency, which may be much slower than the processor frequency.

- The amount of data transferred per bus clock is limited by the width of the data bus.

■ Bus protocol is required to access memory, so only a portion of the time spent reading or writing from memory actually is spent in transferring data. The address must be transmitted first, and both the address and data transactions require a certain number of cycles for directing bus traffic, so bus mastership must be granted to a processor, transfers must be acknowledged, and both data and addresses must be checked for parity.

■ In a system where external memory can be accessed, multiple devices such as another processor or a DMA device (direct-memory access device), additional logic and bus cycles must be spent to ensure that memory is accessed in an orderly manner. Each device must arbitrate for access to the bus, which further reduces the amount of time that the busses can be used for transferring addresses or data.

Although details about the hardware used to provide access to the bus are left largely up to the individual implementations, the PowerPC Architecture defines several mechanisms that optimize bus activity. The most important is a concept that is central to the RISC philosophy. That is, arithmetic calculations are isolated as much as possible from memory accesses through the definition of a set of load and store instructions that access memory explicitly. Arithmetic instructions use memory resources (register files) built into the processor itself.

The PowerPC Architecture also assumes the processor's ability to perform memory accesses out of order, so a memory read generated by the instruction unit can be given priority over a memory write generated by a store instruction. This is called a weakly ordered memory model.

The use of a weakly ordered memory model allows the PowerPC Architecture to perform speculative loading; that is, the instruction set includes two so-called "touch" instructions (Data Cache Block Touch, or dcbt; and Data Cache Block Touch for Store, or dcbtst; instructions), which can be used by a compiler to schedule memory accesses before they are needed. These are considered low-priority bus operations that are performed only if they do not interfere with other transactions on the bus. That is, they take place only if the bus isn't busy doing anything else. Otherwise, the memory access takes place when it would normally have taken place—explicitly generated by the load or store instruction. So nothing is lost, and there is the potential of performing the bus operation in such a way that the memory latency incurred by negotiating for bus access and transferring data has little or no effect on overall performance.

Bus pipelining
The ability to begin a second address transaction on the bus before the first data tenure is begun.

Also, the PowerPC Architecture supports the implementation of busses in which the address transactions are decoupled from the data transactions. This allows a second address to be broadcast on the bus before the first data transaction has begun. This is called *bus pipelining*, and it can be implemented at various "depths." For example, the 601 allows a second address tenure to begin, but it would take considerable additional logic to keep track of a third address transaction. This is called 1-level pipelining. Some PowerPC implementations may have no restriction on the number of nested bus transactions that may occur; this is called n-level bus pipelining.

The PowerPC Architecture also supports the ability to pipeline separate address and bus transactions from multiple processors onto the same bus. This type of bus implementation is called a split-transaction bus.

The Advantages of Caches

Despite the various means by which PowerPC processors optimize memory accesses, such accesses are still best avoided. Caches may reside on the processor's side of the memory bus. These devices allow the most recently used data and instructions (which is typically also the most often used data and instructions) to be stored closer to the processor where it can be accessed without having to deal with the memory bus. The PowerPC Architecture allows memory to be defined as either caching-inhibited or caching-enabled.

Write-back
A cache behavior in which data can be modified in the cache without updating external memory.

Write-through
A cache behavior in which updates to the cache also update external memory.

There are many types of cache configurations and implementations, and the PowerPC Architecture supports, or at least does not preclude, the use of a variety of implementations. The PowerPC Architecture does specify that the cache implementation be physically addressed; that is, it is addressed by using the same address that is used to access system memory.

Caches may be implemented on or off of the processor chip, and some systems may support both on-chip caches and an additional (and usually larger) secondary, or level 2 (L2), cache. The relationship between the cache and system memory can be described as either *write-back* or *write-through*. In a write-through configuration, data written to the cache must also be written through to system memory. In a write-back configuration, the cache is allowed to contain data that is more current than the data in system memory.

In this case, the memory representation in cache is said to be modified, or dirty. This eliminates much bus activity. The PowerPC Architecture allows ranges of memory to be defined as either write-back or write-through.

On-chip caches can be more tightly integrated into the processor design, providing faster and more flexible access methods to the various units on the processor that require cache access, such as the following:

- Instruction units fetch instructions from the cache.

- Execution units that execute load and store instructions must be able to access the caches.

- MMUs must be able to access the cache to store and retrieve data and instruction address translations. Instruction fetches, load and store operations (and in the PowerPC Architecture, additional address-only operations, such as the cache control instructions), generate effective addresses. Typically the processor is configured in such a way that these effective (or logical) addresses must be translated to a physical address in order to access the memory location in the cache or in the external memory. Translations for these accesses are themselves saved in system memory, so to access memory, an additional memory access may be generated to locate the translation.

- Access also must be provided between the cache and the bus interface to allow caches to be loaded from system memory and to allow cached data to be written back to memory (which may occur for a variety of reasons).

- In systems where multiple caching devices can share the memory bus, cache accesses may be generated for handling the *snooping* that may occur to ensure data coherency among all of the caches. This is the case with the 603.

Snooping
A mechanism used to ensure cache coherency in a multiprocessing environment.

Systems that employ multiple caching devices must ensure that each cache provides the device it serves with an accurate view of memory. This is called memory coherency.

The PowerPC Architecture also requires that coherency be maintained among the caches. That is, if the most current data for a memory location is in one cache it can be accessed by other devices that have access to system memory.

Therefore, the cache with the modified data should be able to check all of the addresses that are broadcast onto the address bus to ensure that no other device is requesting its modified data. This is called snooping, and it too requires access between the cache (tags) and the bus.

The 601, which is optimized for multiprocessing implementations, provides a separate port to each of the cache blocks, so snooping does not require an additional bus cycle.

Although the 603 is not intended for multiprocessing systems, it may share external memory with other devices. Unlike the 601, the data cache tags are single-ported, so snooping must occur before memory can read or be written to. Unless there is a snoop hit, the load or store operations are deferred to the next clock cycle. If a snoop hit occurs, actions must be taken to ensure coherency.

The 601 and 603 cache implementations are discussed in further detail in Chapters 16 and 18.

The PowerPC Architecture allows memory to be defined as either coherency enforced or not enforced. For example, the PowerPC Architecture supports memory-mapped I/O. Memory spaces defined for I/O accesses do not need to be kept coherent. Likewise, because instructions are typically not modified, program space may be configured to not enforce coherency.

Separate cache resources may be provided to hold instructions and data. This is called Harvard architecture, named after Harvard University where the Mark-I through Mark-IV computers were developed by Howard Aiken in the 1940s. These computers maintained separate memory resources for data and memory. There are many advantages to this type of cache design. The primary advantage is that both caches can be accessed simultaneously, so there is less opportunity for a bottleneck to occur. Typically, instructions cannot be modified. The PowerPC Architecture does not support self-modifying code; therefore, coherency need not be enforced in instructon caches.

The PowerPC Architecture also supports the use of separate instruction and data caches, and defines a set of instructions for controlling caches by generating operations that may invalidate the data in a cache block, force modified data to be written to system memory, or clear the contents of a cache block.

Register Files

Additional memory resources that are distinct from the physical memory system (caches and internal memory) can be integrated into the processor. This is another concept essential to the PowerPC Architecture and to the RISC philosophy in general; it is often called a register-to-register architecture because arithmetic instructions use registers instead of system memory for source and destination operands. These registers provide dedicated memory resources that can very quickly be accessed by the processor.

The registers defined by the PowerPC Architecture are described in Chapter 11, "The PowerPC Instruction Set," but the most important of these are the two register files—the 32 general-purpose registers (GPRs) and the 32 floating-point registers (FPRs).

Translation Look-Aside Buffers (TLB)

The PowerPC Architecture defines (but does not require) special-purpose caches that are used to save the most recently used page address translations. These translations are incorporated into the MMU, and like the caches, may be implemented in layers. For example, separate data and instruction TLBs can be maintained and a larger unified TLB may be implemented for when a translation is not found in one of those (a TLB miss). A TLB miss might generate an access to the traditional cache implementation, which may cause additional latency due to access time and contention for the cache.

Cache Implementations in PowerPC Processors

The VEA portion of the PowerPC Architecture defines aspects of the cache implementations for PowerPC processors, although it does not require caches to be present. The definition of the cache model is closely tied to the memory management model, because it is the memory management model that defines cache-related attributes of blocks or pages in memory.

Additionally, the architecture defines the behavior of the cache in a multiprocessing environment, and in particular defines aspects of *cache coherency* and

Cache coherency
Achieved by providing each device in a multiprocessing environment with an accurate view of memory.

a set of instructions that can generate address-only operations on a processor's external bus that can control memory in another cache in the system on a cache block basis.

Cache Coherency

The primary objective of a coherent memory system is to provide the same image of memory to all devices using the system. Coherency allows synchronization, cooperative use of shared resources, and task migration among the processors. Otherwise, multiple copies of a memory location, some containing stale values, could exist in a system, resulting in errors when the stale values are used. Each potential bus master must follow rules for managing the state of its cache. For example, a device must broadcast its intention to read a sector that is not currently in the cache. It also must broadcast the intention to write into a sector that is currently not owned exclusively. Other devices respond to these broadcasts by snooping their caches for the broadcast addresses and reporting status back to the originating device.

The status returned includes a shared indicator (another device has a copy of the addressed sector) and a retry indicator (another device either has a modified copy of the addressed cache block that it needs to push out of the chip, or another device had a problem that prevented appropriate snooping).

For faster performance, the 601 has a second path into the cache directory, so snooping and mainstream instruction processing occur concurrently. Instruction processing is interrupted only when the snoop control logic detects a state change, or that a snoop push of modified data is required to maintain memory coherency.

> **Note**
>
> To maintain coherency, secondary caches must forward all relevant system bus traffic onto the 601 bus, which takes the appropriate actions to maintain the MESI protocol.

Support for lwarx and stwcx. instructions on non-cacheable pages may be somewhat more complicated for a secondary cache than normal cacheable memory accesses. This is because the secondary cache may not normally forward writes to non-cacheable pages in the processor. However, to maintain the reservation coherency bit, the secondary cache must forward all writes that hit against the address of a reservation set by a lwarx instruction until the reservation is cleared.

Memory Management Access Mode Bits—W, I, M, and G

Some memory characteristics can be set on either a block or page basis by using the W, I, M, and G bits (The first three are referred to collectively as the WIM bits). These four bits are provided in the BAT registers (which the operating system can access through the mtspr/mfspr instructions) or page table entries (PTEs) (which are accessed indirectly through the segment descriptors during memory configuration) respectively.

The WIM bits control the following functionality:

■ *Write-through (W bit)*. If this bit is set, the block or page is defined as write-through. That is, a write to the cache is always echoed to external memory. The processor can still take advantage of reading the most recently used data directly from the cache without having to use the system bus, but the cache cannot be modified without generating bus traffic. In terms of MESI protocol, the cache block can be characterized as exclusive, shared, or invalid. One advantage of this configuration is seen in a system in which many devices may require access to system memory. Because the processor always modifies system memory automatically, there is no wait for modified data to be written to memory when that data is needed by another processor.

If the W bit is cleared, the block or page is configured as write-back. That is, write operations are allowed to modify the cache block without being echoed back to system memory. This makes data available where it can be most easily accessed and reduces bus activity.

■ *Caching-inhibited (I bit)*. When the I bit is set, the block or page is caching-inhibited. Read and write operations to this memory area always generate bus transactions. This is most typically the configuration for I/O accesses. When caching is inhibited, the W and M bits become don't cares.

When the I bit is cleared, caching is enforced for the block or page, and the caching characteristics are further defined by the W and M bits.

■ *Memory coherency (M bit).* If the M bit is set, the processor enforces memory coherency for the page or block, and does not enforce coherency when the bit is cleared. There are certain regions of memory (such as those associated with read-only memory devices or instructions) for which coherency need not be enforced. By eliminating coherency-checking where it is not necessary, processor performance may be improved. For example, if coherency is not required, there is no need to snoop addresses, and snooping can be time-consuming.

If the M bit is cleared, coherency is not enforced for this block or page.

■ *Memory guarded or not guarded.* If the G bit is set, the block or page is guarded, and data or instructions cannot be fetched for speculative operations. If the G bit is celared, there is no such restriction on memory accesses.

MESI Protocol

MESI protocol provides a model that describes how memory coherency can be maintained in a multiple-cache system. Although the PowerPC Architecture makes no mention of MESI protocol, it is easy to describe the coherency mechanisms of the 601 and 603 processors in terms of a MESI coherency model. The four MESI states are described as follows:

■ *Modified (M).* The addressed block is not valid in external memory, but is valid only in one cache. That is, the cache block is modified with respect to system memory. This is often referred to as dirty. If another device requests data from this cache block, it must be provided from the modified block. In the 601, this requires first writing the block back to external memory.

■ *Exclusive (E).* The addressed block is valid in system memory and is valid in only one cache. If another device needs to load this data, the state must change. In the 601, the state changes to shared. If another device writes to this data in the 601, this cache block is invalidated.

- *Shared (S)*. The addressed block is valid in the cache and in at least one other cache. Generally speaking, there are two types of shared states—shared exclusive, in which case shared data is consistent with external memory; and shared modified, in which case two caches may have identical copies of modified data that have not been written back to external memory. In the 601, the shared state is always shared exclusive.

- *Invalid (I)*. The data in a cache block that is marked invalid is not usable.

MESI protocol can be maintained in several ways. Typically, a state diagram defines how states should change based on various criteria. That is, how coherency is maintained is generally affected by the memory configuration (most importantly in the 601, whether the cache block is configured to be write-back or write-through) and the transitions that should occur for various cache transactions, primarily reads or writes.

For example, in the 601 whether a cache block is loaded (allocated) from external memory on a write miss depends on whether the cache block is configured as write-back or write-through. If the cache block is configured as write-back, the block is allocated and the write occurs in the cache and the cache block is marked as modified. The bus operation is called a read-with-intent-to-modify operation.

If the cache block is configured as write-through, the write operation goes directly out to external memory and the results are not allocated to the cache.

In other words, the 601 does not "write allocate" in write-through mode, but does write allocate in write-back mode.

Given the same configuration as above, if the cache block were marked exclusive before the write occurred, a write-through configuration would allow the data to be updated both in the cache and in external memory. Although the cache contents would change (as would memory), the state would remain exclusive because a write-through configuration does not permit modified state. If the cache block were configured as write-back, a write to an exclusive block would not be passed on to external memory, and the state would change from exclusive to modified.

In a write-through case, if the cache block had been shared, the write operation would not automatically update the other cache. So after the write, the initiating processor's cache block would be exclusive and the other processor's cache block would go from being marked shared to being invalid. Similarly, in a write-back configuration, the other cache block must be invalidated. The 601 performs this invalidation by automatically generating address-only operations on the external bus that are similar to those generated explicitly by the cache control instructions.

The state diagram that describes the MESI coherency for the 601, assuming that caching is permitted (I = 0), write-back mode (W = 0), and coherency enforced (M = 1) is shown in Figure 14.1.

Figure 14.1
601 MESI State Diagram (WIM = 001).

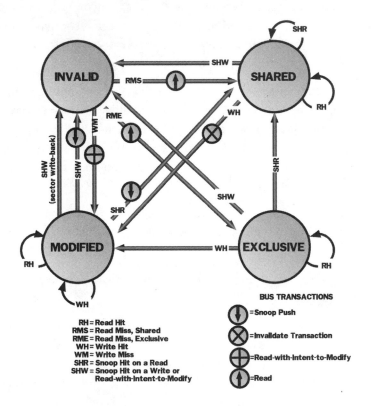

Cache Control Instructions

The PowerPC Architecture defines a set of cache-control instructions, most of which generate address-only bus transactions that affect caches in other processors that share the system bus. Most of these instructions are defined by the virtual environment architecture (VEA) and are provided with user-level access, even though they typically would not be used by application programs. Compilers can make use of these instructions to optimize bus activity. One instruction (Data Cache Block Invalidate, dcbi) is defined by the operating environment architecture (OEA) which can be accessed only by supervisor-level program software (typically the operating system) to invalidate cache blocks in other caching devices.

Table 14.1 summarizes the cache instructions that are accessible to user-level programs.

Table 14.1 User-Level Cache Instructions		
Name	**Operand Syntax**	**Comments**
Data Cache Block Touch	dcbt rA,rB	This instruction provides a method for improving performance through the use of software-initiated fetch hints, loading data from the EA, (rA|0) + (rB). This instruction allows the program to request a cache block fetch before it is needed. The program can later perform loads to put data into registers. However, the processor is not obliged to load the addressed cache block into the data cache.
Data Cache Block	dcbtst rA,rB	This instruction provides a Touch for Store method for improving performance through the use of software-initiated fetch hints by loading data from the EA, (rA|0) + (rB). This instruction allows the program to request a cache block fetch before it is needed by the program. The program can later store data to memory, but the processor need not load the addressed cache block into the data cache.
Data Cache Block Set to Zero	dcbz rA,rB	This instruction is used to clear the cache block containing byte addressed by the EA, (rA|0) + (rB). Behavior of this instruction depends on the memory configuration.

(continues)

Table 14.1 Continued

Name	Operand Syntax	Comments
Data Cache Block Store	dcbst rA,rB	The EA is the sum of (rAl0) + (rB). This instruction causes the data in the cache block referenced by EA to be stored to external memory. Behavior of this instruction depends on the memory configuration
Data Cache Block Flush	dcbf rA,rB	Flushes a cache block in the data cache(s) associated with the EA, (rAl0) + (rB). Specific details depend on the memory configuration.
Instruction Cache Block Invalidate	icbi rA,rB	Invalidates (removes) a cache block in the instruction cache(s) associated with the EA, (rAl0) + (rB). Specific details depend on the memory configuration.

Table 14.2 describes the only supervisor-level cache control instruction.

Table 14.2 Cache Management Supervisor-Level Instruction

Name	Operand Syntax	Comments
Data Cache Block	dcbi rA,rB	The EA is the sum.
Invalidate	(rAl0) + (rB).	Invalidates the addressed cache block and possibly cache blocks on other processors depending on the memory configuration.

Summary

This chapter has provided a brief overview in the PowerPC cache model, describing the flexibility of the options for chip designers. In particular, this chapter described aspects of cache coherency, details regarding unified and Harvard architecture cache implementations, and cache control instructions.

The next chapter describes the exception model defined by the PowerPC Architecture.

Chapter 15

PowerPC Exception Model

The OEA portion of the PowerPC Architecture defines the PowerPC exception mechanism. The operating system uses the exceptions defined by the architecture to manage the processor operations, and it is via the exception mechanism that the processor moves to and from supervisor level.

Exceptions are provided to handle a variety of special situations, some of which are routine circumstances that a certain processor may handle in software, while others can be relatively catastrophic, such as when a serious system error occurs and processing cannot continue. More specifically, exceptions are defined to handle situations such as the following:

- When an instruction attempts to do something that is not supported in hardware. For example, lower-cost PowerPC processors may perform some or all floating-point operations in software. Floating-point instructions that are not supported in hardware cause the processor to take an exception an exception handler provides software routines that complete the required operations.

- When an instruction attempts to perform an illegal operation, such as access a protected memory region.

- When an illegal instruction is encountered—either an instruction that is not defined by the PowerPC Architecture or when a user-level program attempts to execute a supervisor-level instruction.

- When a predefined signal is asserted, such as when an input-output device requires attention (an external *interrupt*) or a serious hardware problem occurs (such as an error on the system bus).

In this chapter, you learn the following:

- The types of exceptions— precise and imprecise, synchronous and asynchronous, and maskable and nonmaskable

- The exceptions that are defined by the PowerPC Architecture

- The conditions that can cause each of the exceptions

- The flexibility of the PowerPC Architecture with regard to how an individual implements exceptions

Interrupts
Refers to a specific type of exception, namely those that are triggered by the assertion of an external signal.

Exceptions
Refers to all instances where an event causes the processor to save its state and transfer control to a predefined software program.

■ When the processor encounters a predefined instruction or data, This type of *exception* is used for debugging software.

As noted in the preceding list, exceptions can occur for various reasons, either in the regular course of operations or when a problem is encountered. As an example of the former, a decrementer exception occurs when the value in the decrementer register passes through zero. The operating system may depend on the decrementer exception handler to allow the system to swap between multiple processes. A machine check exception is an example of the latter. This exception is usually taken as the result of a very serious hardware problem, such as a data parity error, and the processor may not be able to continue processing.

> **Note**
>
> For flexibility, the PowerPC Architecture defines a five-digit vector offset rather than a specific vector address to point to where the exception handler software resides. The actual vector address is determined by the setting of the exception prefix bit (MSR[EP]). If the bit is set, the five-digit, hexadecimal exception vector offset, *nnnnn,* is appended to all F's (x'FFF*n_nnnn*' in 32-bit implementations and x'FFFF_FFFF_FFF*n_nnnn*' in 64-bit implementations). If MSR[EP] is zero, the vector offset is appended to all zeros.

When exceptions occur, information about the state of the processor is saved to SRR0 and SRR1, the processor begins to operate in supervisor mode to execute the exception handler software that resides at the unique address, or exception vector, specified for the exception. In some cases additional information about the exception is saved in exception-related registers (such as the DSISR or the DAR) which the exception handler uses to determine the source of the exception. When the exception handler completes its operation, the bits in SRR0 and SRR1 are used to restore the machine state of the interrupted process and to fetch the next exception to be executed.

The PowerPC Architecture defines a precise exception model, that its instruction-caused exceptions are taken in program order so the processor can resume execution with the next instruction when exception handling is complete. The architecture does allow the optional implementation of two floating-point imprecise modes (recoverable and nonrecoverable). Any incomplete instructions ahead of the excepting instruction (in program order) are allowed to complete execution and present their results, which may mean updating memory, or GPRs or FPRs, and handling any exception associated with those instructions.

In a superscalar implementation, this requires sufficient logic to be able to restore program order even though instructions execute in separate pipelines. The architecture does not prescribe the mechanism that restores program order.

Only one exception can be handled at a time, although additional exceptions may occur while the processor is handling an exception. If a single instruction causes multiple exceptions, those exceptions are handled sequentially.

The OEA architecture supports four types of exceptions depending on whether they are synchronous (caused by instructions) or asynchronous (initiated by signals). Synchronous exceptions can be either precise or imprecise (that is whether execution resumes without the loss of any instruction results or processor state). Some asynchronous exceptions can be masked, such that the exception is not taken when the exception condition occurs. Nonmaskable exceptions cannot be delayed or ignored.

The different types of exceptions are described as follows:

- *Synchronous, precise exceptions*. All instruction-caused exceptions are handled precisely; that is, the machine state at the time the exception occurs is known and can be restored after the exception handler issues the rfi instruction. When these exceptions are taken, the address of the next instruction to be fetched is saved in SRR0. For most exceptions, this is the instruction that caused the exception. This ensures that no execution results are lost. Trap and system call exceptions save the address of next instruction in the instruction flow.

- *Synchronous, imprecise exceptions*. The PowerPC Architecture defines two optional imprecise floating-point exception modes, recoverable and nonrecoverable. These modes can be selected through setting MSR[FE0] and MSR[FE1].

- *Asynchronous, maskable exceptions*. The external interrupt and decrementer exceptions are maskable asynchronous exceptions that are handled precisely. These exceptions provide a mechanism for handling system resources. When these exceptions occur, their handling is post-poned until all instructions, and any exceptions associated with those instructions, complete execution. These exceptions can be masked by setting the MSR[EE] bit.

■ *Asynchronous, nonmaskable exceptions.* The nonmaskable asynchronous exceptions, system reset, and machine check exceptions are initiated by signals, and although these exceptions may not be fully recoverable, implementations may provide a limited degree of recoverability to allow diagnostic operations.

Additional exceptions can be defined for each processor. For example, the 603 implements the hardware interrupt exception, an additional maskable, asynchronous exception that functions like the external interrupt exception. The hardware interrupt exception is provided to support power management.

PowerPC Exception Definitions

The following sections describe the exceptions defined by the PowerPC Architecture. Notice that some of these exceptions are optional.

System Reset Exception (x'00100')

The system reset exception is a nonmaskable, asynchronous exception signaled to the processor either through the assertion of system-defined signals. Table 15.1 shows how the state of the interrupted process is saved when the exception is taken. Exception handlers should restore the machine state when exception handling completes.

Table 15.1 System Reset Exception—Register Settings	
Register	**Contents**
SRR0	Holds the effective address of the next instruction in the interrupted process.
SRR1	All bits except 1-6 and 42-47 (33-36 and 10-15 in 64-bit implementations) are cleared. All other bits are loaded by equivalent bits from the MSR.
MSR	ELE, ME, and EP are not altered, SF is set, and all other bits are cleared.

Notice that some processors may implement multiple versions of this exception, corresponding to power-on reset and other types of system resets (such as soft and hard resets).

Machine Check Exception (x'00200')

The machine check exception is usually taken when a serious error occurs, such as a bus parity error or an uncorrectable memory ECC error, that would prevent execution from continuing correctly. However, the conditions that may cause this exception are implementation-dependent.

This exception can be disabled, by setting the MSR[ME] bit. This is not masking in the usual sense, because execution will not continue unaffected; instead, the processor enters the checkstop state, which is provided for debugging. When the processor is in checkstop state, instruction processing is suspended, and usually the processor must be restarted. When a machine check exception is taken, registers are updated as shown in table 15.2.

Table 15.2 Machine Check Exception—Register Settings	
Register	**Contents**
SRR0	May hold any instruction from the interrupted process when the exception was taken. Implementation-dependent.
SRR1	The state of the error recoverable bit (MSR[RE]) is stored in the equivalent position in SRR1, indicating whether execution can resume when exception handling is complete. The setting of all other SRR1 bits is implementation-dependent.
MSR	ELE, ME, and EP are not altered, SF is set, and all other bits are cleared.

Typically, execution cannot resume in the same context that existed before the machine check exception.

Data Access Exception (x'00300') and Instruction Access Exception (x'00400')

The data and instruction access exceptions are used by the memory management unit (MMU) to help find address translations and to ensure memory integrity. Data access exceptions can be generated by load/store instructions, cache control instructions (dcbi, dcbz, dcbst, and dcbf), or the eciwx/ecowx instructions when the translation information cannot be found for this data access (that is, a page fault occurs) or when the access would violate memory protection (for example, if an attempt to fetch data from a protected memory region). Some implementations may take this exception if an stwcx./stdcx. instruction has an EA for which a normal store operation would cause a data access exception but the processor does not have the reservation from a lwarx/ldarx instruction.

Load/store multiple/string instructions may be partially executed when they cause a data access exception; however, partial execution is not allowed for other operations. Instructions that update the condition register do not perform the update operation.

Table 15.3 shows how the state of the interrupted process is saved when the exception is taken. Exception handlers should restore the machine state when exception handling completes.

Table 15.3 Data Access Exception—Register Settings	
Register	**Contents**
SRR0	Holds the effective address of the next instruction in the interrupted process.
SRR1	All bits except 1-6 and 42-47 (33-36 and 10-15 in 64-bit implementations) are cleared. All other bits are loaded by equivalent bits from the MSR.
MSR	ELE, ME, and EP are not altered, SF is set, and all other bits are cleared.
DSISR	Provides information to help determine the exception condition.
DAR	Provides information to help determine the exception condition.

An instruction access exception occurs when an attempt to fetch the next instruction fails because the translation information cannot be found for this instruction access; that is, a page fault occurs. The exception is also taken when an attempted instruction access would violate memory protection, for example on an attempt to fetch an instruction from a region of memory specified as I/O space.

Register settings for instruction access exceptions are shown in Table 15.4.

Table 15.4 Instruction Access Exception—Register Settings

Register	Setting
SRR0	Holds the effective address of the next instruction in the interrupted process.
SRR1	Holds bits from the MSR from the interrupted process and provides additional information about the exception.
MSR	ELE, ME, and EP are not altered, SF is set, and all other bits are cleared.

External Interrupt (x'00500')

The PowerPC Architecture defines an external interrupt to handle hardware-related exception conditions. The exception is signaled by the assertion of a signal or signals determined uniquely for each implementation. The external interrupt can be masked by clearing the MSR[EE] bit. Clearing this bit also masks the decrementer exception.

The register settings for the external interrupt exception are shown in table 15.5.

Table 15.5 External Interrupt—Register Settings

Register	Contents
SRR0	Holds the effective address of the next instruction in the interrupted process.
SRR1	All bits except 1-6 and 42-47 (33-36 and 10-15 in 64-bit implementations) are cleared. All other bits are loaded by equivalent bits from the MSR.
MSR	ELE, ME, and EP are not altered, SF is set, and all other bits are cleared.

Alignment Exception (x'00600')

Performance is optimized when accesses are aligned to the memory units defined by the architecture. For example, the architecture defines the 32-bit word as the basic unit and buffers and cache blocks are designed according to that specification and hardware is optimized with that assumption. Operands in memory are allowed to be misaligned, but handling such accesses incurs either additional hardware expenses or the latency required to handle the misalignment by invoking the alignment exception.

Alignment exceptions may be taken due to the following conditions:

- The operand of a floating-point or an integer double-word load or store is not word-aligned.

- The operand of a floating-point load or store operation is in an I/O controller interface segment (SR[T]=1).

- The operand of an lmw, stmw, lwarx, stwcx., eciwx, or ecowx instruction is not word-aligned, or the operand of ldarx or stdcx. is not double-word aligned.

- The operand of a lmw or stmw instruction crosses a segment or BAT boundary.

- The operand of a load (including string load) instruction crosses a protection boundary.

- The operand of a Data Cache Block Set to Zero (dcbz) instruction is in a page specified as write-through or cache-inhibited for a page-address translation access.

- The operand of a single-register load or store is not aligned.

The following operations may cause boundedly-undefined results in some implementations:

- When the operand of an lmw or an stmw instruction is not aligned in big-endian mode.

- When an operand of a lwarx, stwcx., ldarx, stdcx., eciwx, or ecowx is not aligned in either endian mode. Note that for eciwx and ecowx instructions when EAR[E] = 0, an implementation may choose to generate a data access exception.

The term protection boundary refers to the boundary between protection domains. A protection domain is an I/O controller interface segment, a block of memory defined by a BAT entry, or a 4KB block of memory defined by a page table entry.

The register settings for alignment exceptions are shown in Table 15.6.

Table 15.6 Alignment Exception—Register Settings	
Register	**Contents**
SRR0	Holds the effective address of the next instruction in the interrupted process.
SRR1	All bits except 1-6 and 42-47 (33-36 and 10-15 in 64-bit implementations) are cleared. All other bits are loaded by equivalent bits from the MSR.
MSR	ELE, ME, and EP are not altered, SF is set, and all other bits are cleared.
DSISR	Identifies the excepting instruction.
DAR	Set to the EA of the data access as computed by the instruction causing the alignment exception.

The architecture does not support the use of an misaligned EA by load/store with reservation instructions or by the eciwx and ecowx instructions. If one of these instructions specifies an misaligned EA, the exception handler should not emulate the instruction, but should treat the occurrence as a programming error.

Integer Alignment Exceptions

Operations that are not naturally aligned may suffer performance degradation, depending on the processor design, the type of operation, the boundaries crossed, and the mode that the processor is in during execution. More specifically, these operations may either cause an alignment exception or they may cause the processor to break the memory access into multiple, smaller accesses with respect to the cache and the memory subsystem.

A 32-bit processor can initiate an alignment exception for direct translation accesses (MSR[DT] = 0 and SR[T] = 0), page address translations (MSR[DT] = 1 and SR[T] = 0) and I/O controller interface accesses (SR[T] = 1). The 64-bit implementations use a different mechanism to access the T bit.

Whether an exception will be taken is determined before the instruction begins execution, so if an alignment exception is taken, no portion of the instruction will have been executed.

Program Exception (x'00700')

A program exception occurs when no higher priority exception exists and one or more of the following exception conditions, which correspond to bit settings in SRR1, occur during execution of an instruction:

- *System floating-point enabled exception.* A system floating-point enabled exception is generated when FPSCR[FEX] is set and either (or both) of the MSR[FE0] or MSR[FE1] bits is set.

  FPSCR[FEX] is set by the execution of a floating-point instruction that causes an enabled exception or by the execution of a "move to FPSCR" type instruction that sets an exception bit when its corresponding enable bit is set. In the processor, all floating-point enabled exceptions are handled in a precise manner. As a result, all program exceptions taken on behalf of a floating-point enabled exception clear SRR1[15] to indicate that the address in SRR0 points to the instruction that caused the exception.

- *Illegal instruction.* An illegal instruction program exception is generated when execution of an instruction is attempted with an illegal opcode or illegal combination of opcode and extended opcode fields (these include PowerPC instructions not implemented in the processor), or when execution of an optional or a reserved instruction not provided in the processor is attempted.

  Individual implementations can determine whether the following instructions cause an illegal instruction program exception:

  When the instruction is an invalid class, the results may be boundedly undefined.

  An lswx instruction for which rA or rB is in the range of registers to be loaded may cause results that are boundedly undefined.

  A move to/from SPR instruction with an SPR field that does contain one of the defined values.

  ```
  MSR[PR] = 1 and SPR[0] = 1. This causes a privileged instruction
  program exception.
  MSR[PR] = 0 or SPR[0] = 0. This causes boundedly undefined results.
  ```

An unimplemented floating-point instruction that is not optional causes a floating-point assist exception.

■ *Privileged instruction.* A privileged instruction type program exception is generated when the execution of a privileged instruction is attempted and the processor is operating in user mode (MSR[PR] is set). Some implementations may generate this exception for mtspr or mfspr with an invalid SPR field if SPR[0]=1 and MSR[PR]=1. An illegal instruction program exception may instead occur if a specified SPR field (for a move to/from SPR instruction) is not defined for a particular implementation.

■ *Trap.* A trap program exception is generated when any of the conditions specified in a trap instruction is met. Trap instructions are described in Chapter 11, "The PowerPC Instruction Set."

The register settings when a program exception is taken are shown in table 15.7.

Table 15.7 Program Exception—Register Settings	
Register	**Contents**
SRR0	Holds the address of the next instruction to be executed when control is returned to the excepting program. If floating-point exceptions are imprecise MSR[FF0] - MSR[FE1], this may be the excepting instruction or a subsequent instruction. For sync or isync instructions, the address will not be more than four bytes beyond the sync or isync instruction.
SRR1	0-32 Loaded with equivalent bits from the MSR 33-36 Cleared. 37-41 Loaded with equivalent bits from the MSR 42 Cleared. 43 Set for a floating-point enabled program exception; otherwise cleared. 44 Set for an illegal instruction program exception; otherwise cleared. 45 Set for a privileged instruction program exception; otherwise cleared. 46 Set for a trap program exception; otherwise cleared. 47 Cleared if SRR0 contains the address of the instruction causing the exception, and set if SRR0 contains the address of a subsequent instruction. Note that only one of bits 43-47 of SRR1 can be set. 48-63 Loaded with equivalent bits from the MSR
MSR	ELE, ME, and EP are not altered, SF is set, and all other bits are cleared.

■ *Floating-Point Enabled Program Exceptions.* These exceptions are signaled by condition bits set in the floating-point status and control register (FPSCR). These conditions can also be selectively disabled by setting bits in the FPSCR. These bit settings are described in Chapter 10, "The PowerPC Register Set."

Handling of these exceptions can be precise or imprecise (or disabled entirely) according to the settings of MSR[FE0] and MSR[FE1] as described in Chapter 11, "The PowerPC Instruction Set."

If exceptions are disabled, an FPSCR instruction can be used to force any exception conditions, due to instructions initiated before the FPSCR instruction, to be recorded in the FPSCR. A sync instruction can also be used to force exceptions, but is likely to degrade performance more than an FPSCR instruction.

Floating-Point Unavailable Exception (x'00800')

Floating-point unavailable exceptions are taken when the floating-point available bit in the MSR is disabled, (MSR[FP]=0) and an attempt is made to execute a floating-point instruction. The register settings for floating-point unavailable exceptions are shown in Table 15.8.

Table 15.8 Floating-Point Unavailable Exception—Register Settings	
Register	**Contents**
SRR0	Set to the effective address of the instruction that caused the exception.
SRR1	All bits except 1-6 and 42-47 (33-36 and 10-15 in 64-bit implementations) are cleared. All other bits are loaded by equivalent bits from the MSR.
MSR	ELE, ME, and EP are not altered, SF is set, and all other bits are cleared.

Decrementer Exception (x'00900')

A decrementer exception occurs when the decrementer register contents go from all zeroes to all ones. The decrementer and the external interrupt exception can be masked by clearing MSR[EE]. The decrementer exception request is canceled when the exception is handled.

The decrementer can be accessed by using the mtspr/mfspr instructions, which can be used by supervisor-level instructions. The decrementer register, which is described in Chapter 11, "The PowerPC Instruction Set," is decremented at the same frequency as the time base, taken from the processor clock. The register settings for the decrementer exception are shown in table 15.9.

Table 15.9 Decrementer Exception—Register Settings

Register	Contents
SRR0	Holds the effective address of the next instruction in the interrupted process.
SRR1	All bits except 1-6 and 42-47 (33-36 and 10-15 in 64-bit implementations) are cleared. All other bits are loaded by equivalent bits from the MSR.
MSR	ELE, ME, and EP are not altered, SF is set, and all other bits are cleared.

System Call Exception (x'00C00')

The UISA level of the architecture defines a user-level instruction, System Call (sc), which can be used to force an exception. The system call exception causes the next instruction to be fetched from offset x'00C00'. Like other precise exceptions, all previously dispatched instructions are allowed to complete execution before the exception is taken. Register settings are shown in table 15.10.

Table 15.10 System Call Exception—Register Settings

Register	Contents
SRR0	Holds the effective address of the instruction following the System Call instruction
SRR1	All bits except 1-6 and 42-47 (33-36 and 10-15 in 64-bit implementations) are cleared. All other bits are loaded by equivalent bits from the MSR.
MSR	ELE, ME, and EP are not altered, SF is set, and all other bits are cleared.

Trace Exception (x'00D00')

The trace exception is used to force an exception. This exception, which is useful for software debugging, is enabled when the MSR[SE] bit is set. When the trace exception is enabled, the exception is taken after the successful execution of each instruction. This continues until an rfi instruction is encountered or an instruction causes another exception. MSR[SE] is cleared when the trace exception is taken. In the normal use of this function, MSR[SE] is restored when the exception handler returns to the interrupted program using an rfi instruction.

The trace exception also is taken when the branch enable bit in the MSR is set and a branch instruction completes execution. Register settings for the trace mode are described in table 15.11.

Table 15.11 Trace Exception—Register Settings	
Register	**Setting**
SRR0	Holds the address of the next instruction to be executed in the program for which the trace exception was generated.
SRR1	All bits except 1-6 and 42-47 (33-36 and 10-15 in 64-bit implementations) are cleared. All other bits are loaded by equivalent bits from the MSR.
MSR	ELE, ME, and EP are not altered, SF is set, and all other bits are cleared.

Floating-Point Assist Exception (x'00E00')

The optional floating-point assist exception can be used to provide software support for PowerPC implementations for which hardware support is not provided for all floating-point operations, such as denormalization, require to make floating-point values conform to operand conventions necessary for performing calculations. This exception can also be used to emulate floating-point instructions that are not optional that are not implemented in hardware. Register settings for the floating-point assist exceptions are described in table 15.12.

Table 15.12 Floating-Point Assist Exception—Register Settings	
Register	**Setting**
SRR0	Holds the effective address of the next instruction in the interrupted process.
SRR1	All bits except 1-6 and 42-47 (33-36 and 10-15 in 64-bit implementations) are cleared. All other bits are loaded by equivalent bits from the MSR.
MSR	ELE, ME, and EP are not altered, SF is set, and all other bits are cleared.

Summary

This chapter has described how operating systems designed for PowerPC processors use exceptions to handle special situations, and took a brief look at how each of those exceptions are defined.

This chapter and the previous chapters have presented a close-up look at the PowerPC Architecture, describing the instructions, registers, memory characteristics, and exceptions that all PowerPC processors have in common. The most important recurring themes in these chapters are compatibility and flexibility. That is, this architectural definition provides a way to ensure compatibility among all PowerPC processors, yet provides chip designers with a great deal of flexibility to allow a wide range of possible processor designs.

The remaining chapters looks closely at the first two PowerPC processors, the 601, which is designed for desktop and workstation systems, and the 603, which is intended for low-powered very portable personal computers and other devices.

Chapter 16

The PowerPC 601 RISC Processor

The 601 is the first processor based on the PowerPC Architecture. It is designed for low- to medium-cost workstations and desktop systems. The 601 also includes multiprocessor features that make it suitable for high-end systems.

The 601 uses an advanced, four-level, 0.6 micron, 3.6V CMOS process technology and maintains full compatibility with TTL devices. The 601 processor was initially made available with processor speeds of 50- and 66MHz. Subsequently, 80MHz parts have been made available, and faster 601's are expected in the future. At the 1993 Fall Comdex, Motorola demonstrated an IBM RS/6000 system with a 601 running at 95MHz.

The 601 consists of 2.8 million transistors on a 11 x 11 mm die.

The 601 employs the PowerPC 32-bit instruction set, register set, precise exception model, cache implementation, and memory management. The 601 takes advantage of the PowerPC Architecture's application of RISC design principles to create a high-performance, single-chip processor that allows a high-degree of pipelining and out-of-order, superscalar dispatch to the three execution units—the branch processing unit (BPU), integer unit (IU), and floating-point unit (FPU).

The 601 has a 64-bit data bus and a 32-bit address bus modeled closely on the Motorola 88110 processor's system bus.

The 601 has more in common with IBM's POWER architecture and with the RS/6000 processor than other chips in the PowerPC family. While the 601

In this chapter, you learn the following:

- How the 601 implements the PowerPC Architecture workstation systems

- Specific details about hardware characteristics

- Details about special features of the 601 processor

- Information about the internal operation of the 601 processor

implements the PowerPC Architecture and is compatible with other PowerPC processors, it is also compatible with the POWER architecture instruction set architecture (ISA), which allows it to run the large base of RS/6000 AIX applications in addition to the applications created especially for PowerPC processors.

Many instructions are defined by both the PowerPC and POWER instruction set architectures; however, the 601 implements additional POWER instructions not defined for the PowerPC Architecture. These instructions are guaranteed to trap on other PowerPC processors and ensure compatibility with IBM's AIX-based applications. The 601 also implements the MQ and RTC registers defined by the POWER architecture, which are used for POWER compatibility but are avoided for PowerPC compatibility. The decrementer register (DEC) is defined slightly differently in the two architectures—it can be read by user-level software in the POWER architecture while the PowerPC Architecture specifies that it can only be read by supervisor-level software.

> **Note**
>
> Chapter 9, "The RS/6000 POWER Connection," provides more details about the relationship between the PowerPC Architecture and the IBM POWER architecture.

This chapter touches briefly on 601 instruction timing, which is described in greater detail in the following chapter.

PowerPC 601 Microprocessor Overview

The 601 implements the 32-bit portion of the PowerPC Architecture, which provides 32-bit effective (logical) addresses, integer data types of 8, 16, and 32 bits, and floating-point data types of 32 and 64 bits. Instructions that require 64-bit addressing are guaranteed to trap on the 601 (and on all 32-bit PowerPC processors).

The 601 is a superscalar processor. It can dispatch instructions out-of-order, one to each of three execution units—a branch processing unit (BPU), an integer unit (IU), and a floating-point unit (FPU)—that operate in parallel.

The three execution units are fully pipelined. For most instructions, the IU can complete one instruction per clock cycle while the FPU can complete one single-precision instruction per clock cycle, and one double-precision instruction every two clock cycles. The ability to execute instructions in parallel and the pipelined execution units yield high performance.

The 601 allows instructions to complete out-of-order; however, the 601 makes execution appear sequential. In other words, the 601 checks for any data dependencies that would be violated if results are written back and forces those instructions to write back in order. If there is no dependency, the instruction is allowed to write back its results.

The 601 incorporates a physically-addressed unified cache, and logical-to-physical address translation is performed by a single MMU, which supports demand-paged virtual memory address translation and variable-sized block translation. As part of defining memory as pages or blocks, the MMU also determines whether these blocks can be accessed by user- or supervisor-level software, and whether the accesses are cacheable and, if so, whether data written to the cache must be kept coherent with that in other caching devices that access system memory. The MMU also specifies whether data write operations to a particular block or page are written both to the cache and to system memory (write-through mode) or whether valid data may remain in the cache without being written to memory (write-back mode).

The 601 system interface includes a 32-bit address bus and a 64-bit data bus. The interface allows address and data transactions to be pipelined—that is, the address and data tenures of the bus transaction are decoupled so that two consecutive address tenures may occur before the data tenure tied to the first address tenure occurs. This independence is particularly useful in multiprocessor implementations—if two processors are competing for system memory, the address and data tenures of processor A may not occur consecutively; an address and/or data tenure for processor B may occur in between.

> **Note**
>
> The 601 supports single-beat and burst data transfers for memory accesses; it also supports both memory-mapped I/O and I/O controller interface addressing.

In multiprocessor systems, an external arbiter is required for directing bus traffic generated by each of the processors or other devices that must access system memory. The device that controls the bus is called the bus master. The bus interface allows a wide range of arbiter designs.

To maintain coherency among caching devices that access system memory, the 601 provides separate ports for snooping address transactions. When an address that is being broadcast on the bus matches one in a cache (that is, a snoop hit), the 601 takes the appropriate steps to ensure that each processor's has an accurate view of memory.

Figure 16.1

The 601 Block Diagram.

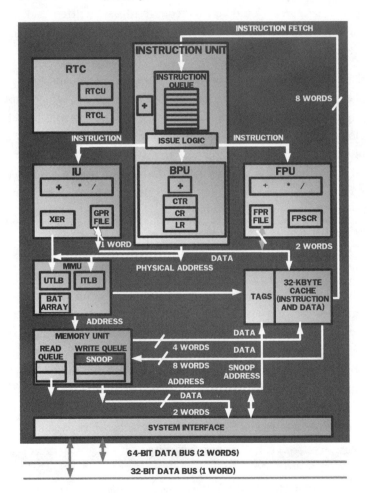

The block diagram shows the flow of instructions and data through the 601. Instructions are fetched from the 601's unified cache, saved in the instruction queue, from which they are dispatched to the three execution units—IU,

FPU, and BPU—which operate independently and in parallel. The block diagram also shows the relationship between the instruction units and the GPRs and FPRs and the memory resources (the cache and system memory).

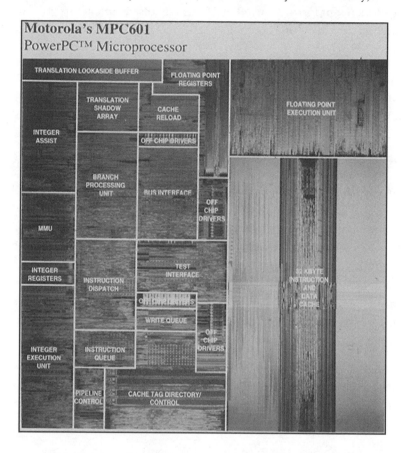

Figure 16.2
PowerPC 601 Microprocessor Block Diagram.

The 601 Instruction Unit and Branch Processing Unit

The instruction unit determines which instruction should be fetched next, updating the instruction queue continually so no opportunities to dispatch instructions are missed. The 601 instruction unit contains the eight-entry instruction queue and the BPU. In some respects, the BPU can be considered a separate execution unit, like the IU and the FPU; however, it is seen as part of the instruction unit because of the critical role branching plays in determining the instruction flow. This relationship between the BPU and the instruction unit is defined by the PowerPC Architecture.

The instruction queue (IQ) holds as many as eight instructions and can be filled from the cache during a single processor clock cycle. The ability to fetch eight instructions is tuned to the cache implementation—it is the length of a cache block (eight instructions) that offsets any disadvantages to the fetching mechanism caused by the fact that the 601 does not have a separate instruction cache.

Floating-point and branch instructions can be dispatched from any of the bottom four positions in the IQ. Integer instructions are dispatched from IQ0, from which most integer instructions are decoded.

The instruction unit clearly demonstrates the advantages of one of the basic tenets of RISC design—simple, uniform-length instructions.

Because all instructions are the same length, each of the elements in the IQ need only be 32 bits wide. More importantly, instruction fetching is greatly simplified because no preliminary decoding is necessary to identify instructions of different lengths, and because the IQ is eight words long, it can be updated with an entire cache block of instructions with no risk that an instruction may span cache blocks. Updating the queue is simplified because indexing the cache block is simple—for example, if there is room in the queue for three instructions, the fetcher can easily use this information to determine how many instructions to fetch from the cache block.

Also, the large instruction queue makes up for advantage lost from not implementing separate instruction and data caches—cache accesses are prioritized, and instruction fetching has a low priority, but because so many instructions can be fetched at a time, the instruction queue is rarely empty.

Perhaps most importantly, fixed-length instructions, and the ability to queue a large number of instructions in the instruction queue makes it easy to identify branch instructions, predict whether they will be taken or not taken, fetch instructions according to that prediction, speculatively execute those instructions, and recover if the prediction was incorrect.

The instruction fetching logic, the BPU, and the 601's exception mechanism determine the next instruction to be fetched.

The priority is as follows:

1. If an exception occurs, the processor changes states and instructions are fetched from the exception vector address.

2. If a previous branch had been predicted incorrectly, the BPU provides the address of the correct instruction. This is called the "mispredict recovery" address.

3. If a branch is encountered in the IQ, the BPU predicts whether the branch will be taken, based on the setting of a bit in the instruction encoding. This kind of branch prediction is called static branch prediction.

4. If neither an exception has occurred nor a branch instruction has been encountered, instruction fetching continues at the next sequential address. This means continuing to fetch instructions from the current cache block or from another block in the cache. If the address generated is not in the cache, the fetch is sent to system memory over the system bus.

To determine the next sequential address, a dedicated adder in the instruction unit computes its effective address based on the address of the last fetch and indexed by the number of instructions (each a single word in length) accepted into the queue. As stated above, this ability to calculate sequential instruction addresses is an important advantage of RISC instruction sets. The BPU also contains an adder for computing branch target addresses.

The BPU also contains three registers closely tied to branch operations—the link register (LR), the count register (CTR), and the condition register (CR). Using separate registers for such operations, and reserving the GPRs and FPRs for use by the IU and FPU, reduces the likelihood of contention for register resources and allows the three execution units to operate independently.

Note

Branch instructions can be dispatched from the four lowest positions in the IQ (IQ0-IQ3). The BPU uses the static branch prediction mechanism defined by the PowerPC Architecture for conditional branch instructions. That is, the programmer can predict whether the branch will be taken or not taken by setting a bit in the BO encoding. Notice, however, that other PowerPC processors may implement more elaborate dynamic branch-prediction schemes.

Execution for most branch instructions consists of determining the direction of the program flow; however, some branch instructions update register resources, such as the LR or CTR. These instructions typically have a write-back stage. Unless the branch instruction has a dependency for which a branch write-back stage is required, most branch instructions can be removed from the instruction flow. This is called branch folding. Unconditional branch instructions are always folded.

Notice that in the 601, when a branch is predicted, instructions from the target stream are allowed to execute speculatively even though these instructions cannot write back their results until it is certain that the prediction is determined to be either correct or incorrect (otherwise the branch is resolved). If the branch was predicted incorrectly, the instructions are flushed from the various stages (the instruction queue, the dispatch stage, and any of the various execution stages) and instruction fetching begins at the mispredict recovery address.

The 601 Integer Unit (IU)

Integer instructions are dispatched from the lowest position in the IQ (IQ0), in which position they are also usually decoded.

The IU contains the arithmetic logic unit (ALU), multiplier, and divider for performing arithmetic operations. Adhering to the PowerPC Architecture model it also contains register resources—the integer exception register (XER), and the 32 32-bit GPRs. The IU executes all integer arithmetic and logical instructions and both integer and floating-point load and store operations, taking advantage of the adder provided in the IU to calculate effective addresses. Effective addresses are calculated using values in the GPR and immediate operands. Because the IU calculates effective addresses, all instructions for which effective addresses must be calculated are executed in the IU, such as the cache control instructions.

The IU also executes move to/from SPR instructions.

The IU is fully pipelined, and for most instructions the IU executes one instruction per clock cycle. Integer divide instructions, instructions with data dependencies, load/store string/multiple instructions, and certain mfspr and mtspr instructions typically encounter longer latencies.

As is typical of RISC implementations, and as is specified by the PowerPC Architecture, all integer computations are performed with source and destination operands provided by the GPRs. Additionally, the GPRs are used for source and target registers for integer load and store operations. Floating-point load and store instructions, which are executed in the IU, access the FPRs, which reside in the FPU.

Load and store instructions take advantage of the connection between the cache and the MMU. Load and store instructions are executed in program order; however, the memory unit can reorder memory accesses (weak-ordering) unless synchronizing instructions are used to ensure strict ordering.

Typically, once the effective address is calculated, the load/store instructions no longer place demands on the integer pipeline, even though the actual cache or memory access may occur many clock cycles later. Therefore, a series of load and store instructions can complete one instruction per clock cycle, assuming that the address translation is readily available— either in the unified TLB (UTLB) or in the BAT array—and the access is aligned. The TLB and BAT mechanisms are described in Chapter 13, "PowerPC Memory Management Model."

> **Note**
>
> Another feature of the IU that is specific to the 601 is the tagging mechanism used to synchronize certain operations among three execution units, such as updating the CR, CTR, and LR. This mechanism also ensures a precise exception model—that is, after an exception is handled, operation will resume with the next sequential instruction in the correct context.

The 601 Floating-Point Unit

FPU instructions can be dispatched from IQ0-IQ3 either to the floating-point decode stage or to a buffer stage if the floating-point decode stage is full.

The FPU executes all floating-point computational instructions; floating-point load and store operations are executed in the integer unit, although source and destination registers for load and store operation are provided by the thirty-two 64-bit FPRs, which are contained within the FPU. For floating-point calculations, the FPU implements a multiply-add array for multiply, add, divide, and multiply-add instructions.

The FPU unit is pipelined—a series of single-precision instructions (including a floating-point multiply-add) can execute at a rate of one instruction per clock cycle (for most instructions and assuming no data dependencies). A series of double-precision instructions can typically be executed at a rate of one instruction every other clock cycle. There are three stages in the floating-point pipeline which can perform a floating-point multiply-add operation (Ax + B) in a single pass. Notice that although this instruction seems atypical of RISC instructions, it can be executed at no extra expense—that is a series of single-precision operations (fmadds) has a throughput of one instruction per cycle and a series of double-precision operations (fmadd) has a throughput of one instruction per two cycles. Many other floating-point operations can be thought of as multiply-add instructions with certain values held constant. For example, a multiply operation is expressed as Ax + B, where B is zero, and an add operation is expressed as Ax + B, where A is 1.

Notice that the throughput for floating-point instructions is reduced when there are data dependencies, when the CR must be updated (indicated by adding a period to the end of some mnemonics), or when the processor is configured with precise mode enabled (by setting either or both of the MSR[FE0] and MSR[FE1] bits).

The FPU also contains the floating-point status and control register (FPSCR) which indicate the sources of floating-point exceptions, provide bits to enable and disable certain floating-point exceptions, and the method of rounding to be implemented (round to nearest, round to zero, round to +infinity, and round to -infinity). The 601 supports all IEEE 754 floating-point data types (normalized, denormalized, NaN, zero, and infinity) in hardware. Note that the PowerPC Architecture allows processors to perform these operations in software by taking exceptions.

601 Memory Management Unit (MMU) and Cache Implementation

The memory management and cache implementations control address translation, memory protection, and memory coherency for the memory system used by the 601 processor or processors and other devices that access memory.

The register set includes several register resources, such as the BATs, table search descriptor register (SDR1), and segment registers to support memory translation and protection.

The exception model includes the data access and instruction access exceptions used to access address translations when the addresses are not resident in the memory resources. This condition is referred to as a page fault.

Memory can be accessed by instruction fetches and by a number of different kinds of instructions. In addition to the extensive set of load and store instructions, the memory also can be accessed by cache control instructions and certain memory synchronization instructions, each of which generate effective (logical) addresses that must be mapped to the physical address locations in external memory or in the physically-addressed on-chip unified cache. I/O devices can be accessed by accessing memory, and memory-mapped I/O is the preferred method of I/O handling. The 601 also supports the I/O controller interface accesses defined by the PowerPC Architecture, although these accesses are typically less efficient.

The 601 implements a unified cache, which affects many aspects of the memory management and cache implementation. One memory management unit is implemented to support both data and instruction access. The 601 does, however, maintain a separate four-entry instruction TLB (ITLB) to support the instruction unit.

As a 32-bit PowerPC implementation, the 601 provides 4GB of logical address space with a 4KB pages and 256MB segments. Blocks range from 128KB to 8MB. Although the 601 varies somewhat in the specifics of the memory management implementation, it essentially follows the memory translation and protection schemes defined by the PowerPC Architecture—using a 52-bit virtual address and hashed page tables of the logical-to-physical address translation.

The 601 implements translation look-aside buffers (TLBs) which are defined by the PowerPC Architecture, although not required by it. A 256-entry, two-way set-associative unified TLB (UTLB) caches the most recently used page table entries and can be accessed in parallel with the access to the on-chip cache.

If the translation is not present in the ITLB or UTLB, a table search begins. This is implemented in hardware in the 601. Other processors, such as the 603, require software support for this operation.

The 601 uses a four-entry ITLB, which contains the most recently used instruction address translations on a page or block basis. If the instruction address translation for the page or block in which the next instruction fetch occurs is present, addresses generated for address fetching can be quickly translated. If it is not present in the ITLB, it is next searched for in the UTLB and BAT arrays.

> **Note**
>
> In the 601, the block address translation (BAT) array is implemented as four pairs of SPRs. However, the PowerPC Architecture defines two sets of four pairs of BATs, one each for instructions and for data. The 601 implements those defined as IBAT0U-IBAT3U and IBAT0L-IBAT3L (SPR528-SPR535). BAT registers maintain recently used address translations for memory blocks.

To support the table-search operations, the 601 uses a hashed page table as specified by the PowerPC Architecture. This is the table that defines the mapping between virtual and physical page numbers. The page table contains a number of 64-byte PTEGs comprised of eight eight-byte page table entries (PTEs).

The 601 Cache Implementation

The 601 has a 32KB, eight-way set-associative unified (instruction and data) cache. The cache is physically-addressed, which simplifies the snooping of address bus activity on the bus, since external memory is also, by definition, physically addressed. Memory can be defined as write-back or write-through, caching enforced or caching inhibited, and coherencies enforced or not enforced on a page or block basis. Typically, memory that is defined as I/O space does not permit caching.

The cache is organized into eight sets of 64 lines that consist of 16 contiguous words in memory and are aligned along 16-word boundaries; therefore, cache lines can never cross page boundaries. Each line consists of two eight-word sectors. The sector is the coherency unit, or cache block, for the 601. This means that only one sector may be loaded into the cache for a given line, and the adjacent sector may have different MESI states—for example, one sector can be modified while the other is invalid.

Each sector also contains address tags and two state bits that indicate the MESI state of the sector. The sector also contains several replacement control bits.

Cache sectors can be stored to or loaded from memory by four-beat burst transactions. Cache load operations allow the four words that contain the requested data (called the critical quad-word) to be loaded as soon as the second beat of the four-beat transaction arrives. The memory unit contains a 16-byte buffer that allows the quad-word to be loaded in a single clock cycle. The cache is free to allow other accesses (such as instruction fetches, and data reads and writes) while the remaining data is being loaded into the 16-byte buffer. As the critical quad-word is loaded into the cache, the requested data is simultaneously forwarded to the appropriate GPR, FPR, or to the instruction unit. This is one of several feedforwarding mechanisms implemented on the 601 to reduce stalls in the instruction pipeline.

After the requested sector is loaded, the adjacent sector may (or may not) be updated. This low-priority operation can be disabled by the system software.

Because it is optimized for multiprocessor implementations, the 601 employs MESI cache coherency protocol in hardware. Each block in the cache is characterized as either modified (valid in the cache but nowhere else, including system memory), exclusive (valid both in the cache and in system memory, but not in another cache), shared (valid in the cache, system memory, and in at least one other cache), or invalid (the data in the cache is not valid). Valid data for this memory location may be either in system memory, in another cache, or both.

If the address associated with a memory access is configured to be cache-coherent among all caching devices, addresses passed to the system interface are snooped by those other devices. If a device recognizes an address as one that it has in its cache (that is, a snoop hit occurs) certain operations are initiated depending on whether the data associated with that address is modified, shared, or exclusive. These actions may be simply a matter of invalidating the cache block, or if the data is modified, the processor may be required to write this data back to memory as well as changing the MESI state.

Another aspect of the 601's emphasis on multiprocessing can be seen in the hardware snooping mechanism. The 601 provides a port to the cache tag directory dedicated to snooping (rather than forcing snooping to share the port with regular memory accesses, as in the 603). Therefore, snooping does not require additional clock cycles. Of course, snoop hits can delay the address transaction that generated the snoop hit while the cache status is updated. Load and store operations can occur on a byte, half word, or word basis, and on double words for floating-point loads and stores.

Pages or blocks of memory can be designated as write-back or write-through, caching-enforced or caching-inhibited, and coherency-enforced or not enforced though the WIM bit settings. These bits are set by the operating system as part of the memory configuration.

The cache is accessed by the instruction fetch unit and the integer execution unit (for load and store instructions). The 32-byte (eight-word) data bus between the cache and the instruction unit allows an entire cache block of instructions to be loaded into the eight-word instruction queue.

The 601 Memory Unit

The memory unit provides a buffer between the processor core and the external memory bus. It is comprised of read and write queues that buffer data, addresses, and control information for read and write operations. The 601 can generate bus transactions under several circumstances:

- Instruction fetches that miss in the cache.

- Load and store operations that miss in the cache or are designated to memory space as cache inhibited.

- Operations required for maintaining cache coherency (such as cache reloads, snoop copy-back operations, optional reloads of the adjacent cache sector, cast-outs of the least-recently-used cache block, and read-with-intent-to-modify operations).

- Table search operations for page table address translations.

- Address-only operations (explicitly the result of cache and TLB control instructions, and implicitly caused by certain other transactions).

- I/O controller interface operations.

As shown in Figure 16.3, each of the three elements of the write queue can hold a cache block of data, which is posted here to be written back to memory in a four-beat burst transaction. Notice that sometimes the write queue may contain modified data that is no longer in the cache (for example, when the least-recently-used cache block is cast out when the cache is updated). This does not cause a coherency problem, because these locations and each cache block in the write queue maintain MESI state information and snoop addresses that are broadcast on the address bus.

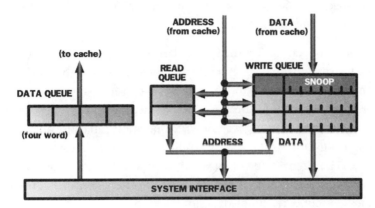

Figure 16.3
The 601 Memory Unit.

When a snoop hit occurs and the cache block is in the modified state, the requesting device that initiated the address transaction on the bus is forced to retry the operation because the modified data must be first written back to external memory before it can be retrieved by the requesting device. The requesting device is detained by the assertion of the address retry (ARTRY—) signal while the modified cache block can be written back to memory. The requesting device then accesses the block from system memory.

The processor can be configured in such a way that this write-back of requested data becomes the highest priority bus operation. When this is done, the requested data is buffered in a dedicated element of the write queue, marked snoop in Figure 16.3. If the processor is not configured for these high-priority operations, this element behaves like the other write queue elements.

> **Note**
>
> Single-beat write operations are not snooped in the write queue, and the cache-control mechanism uses other means to ensure coherency (typically address-only bus transactions that invalidate the block in other caches when system memory is updated).

Because modified data can be in the write queue, the write queue also must participate in snooping when addresses are broadcast on the address bus to ensure coherency. However, if a store instruction or other operation generates a memory-write access that does not cause the entire cache block to be written back to memory, the write data (which is handled with a single-beat write operation) in the write queue is not snooped; coherency is ensured through the use of special cache operations that are broadcast on the bus along with the single-beat write transaction.

Read and write operations on the bus are largely independent from the load and store instructions that generate them. From the perspective of the instruction pipeline, a load or store instruction is considered complete when the address is translated. At this point no instruction-related exceptions can occur. However, the resulting read or write operation can cause an external exception. For example, a bus parity error will cause the Transfer Error Acknowledge (TEA) signal to be asserted, which in turn causes a machine check exception (or it causes the processor to enter the checkstop state if the machine check exception is disabled: MSR[ME] = 0).

Also, although load and store instructions are always issued and translated in program order, an access that hits in the cache can complete ahead of one that misses. Memory accesses on the 601 are weakly-ordered, as is assumed by the PowerPC Architecture—loads and stores that miss the cache can be reordered as they arbitrate for the system bus. However, load and store operations can be forced to execute in strict program order.

The 601 Register Set

The 601 closely adheres to the PowerPC Architecture definition for 32-bit implementations. However, there are some additional registers not defined by the architecture, and some registers have additional functionality not defined by the PowerPC Architecture. These are as follows:

- *Real-time clock (RTC) registers.* RTCU and RTCL (RTC upper and RTC lower). These registers are used in the 601 in place of the time base registers. The registers can be read from by user-level software, but can be written to only by supervisor-level software. The RTC and decrementer are updated at a frequency of 7.8125 MHz. This difference is invisible to the instruction set. The mftb instruction, which is designed to read the time base defined by the PowerPC Architecture, can be used for the same purpose on the 601 because it is guaranteed to trap as an illegal instruction. The time-base access can be emulated in the exception handler using the RTC registers and instructions to access them instead.

■ *MQ register (MQ).* The 32-bit MQ register is not defined by the PowerPC Architecture. It is used to accommodate the product for the multiply instructions and the dividend for the divide instructions. It is also used as an operand of long rotate and shift instructions. This register and the instructions that require it are provided for compatibility with POWER architecture.

■ *Block-address translation (BAT) registers.* The 601 includes eight block-address translation registers (BATs), consisting of four pairs of BATs (BAT0U-BAT3U and BAT0L-BAT3L). The PowerPC defines two sets of BATs, one each for instructions and data, but since the 601 has a unified cache and MMUs, it implements only the BAT registers defined by the PowerPC Architecture as instruction BATs, and uses them for both instructions and data.

■ *Hardware implementation registers (HID0-HID2, HID5, and HID15).* The PowerPC Architecture provides space in the SPR definition for implementation-specific HID registers for special operations. Most of the HID registers in the 601 are used as debugging tools. Notice that while it is not guaranteed that the implementation of HID registers is consistent among PowerPC processors, other processors use similar or identical HID registers.

■ *HID0 (also called the Checkstop Sources and Enables Register).* The processor can be put into checkstop state as the result of a number of different, usually catastrophic, events such as cache or bus parity errors or multiple hits in a cache or TLB. When the processor is in checkstop state, all instruction processing stops and the contents of the latches are frozen, within a couple of cycles of the time that the checkstop condition occurs. Typically, the processor cannot resume processing without being reset—special hardware debugging utilities (such as the ESP interface) can be used to identify design problems. The source bits identify the condition that caused a checkstop, and the enable bits allow a designer to prevent those conditions from causing the checkstop.

- *HID1 (also called the Debug Modes Register).* HID1 is used for debugging software and is used in connection with the run mode exception, which also is 601-specific and not defined by the PowerPC Architecture.

- *HID2 (also called the Instruction Address Breakpoint Register, or IABR).* The IABR can hold the effective address that is compared against instructions as they are decoded. When the instructions match, the action that occurs is determined by the debug mode selected by the bit settings in HID1.

- *HID5 (also called the Data Address Breakpoint Register, or DABR).* This register can hold the effective address specified by a load or store instruction. A match can cause a data access exception, and subsequent actions are determined by the setting of HID1. The least significant bits (DABR[1,2]) can selectively enable or disable breakpoints for loads or stores.

- *HID15 (also called the Processor Identification Register, or PIR).* This register holds a four-bit processor identification tag, or PID, used to identify the processor, for example, for I/O controller interface operations.

> **Note**
>
> The 601 includes the optional external access register (EAR), along with the optional External Control Input/Output Word Indexed instructions (eciwx and ecowx), which support the use of special input/output operations.

601 Instruction Set

The 601 implements the instruction set defined for 32-bit PowerPC processors, with the following variations and options:

The 601 supports the optional External Control Input Word Indexed (eciwx) and External Control Output Word Indexed (ecowx) instructions. These are the only optional PowerPC instructions that are supported by the 601. The other optional PowerPC instructions can be trapped and emulated in software.

The PowerPC Architecture defines a number of instructions specific to controlling data and instruction caches. Because the 601 implements a unified cache, several of these cache control instructions may provide a subset of the functions of the instruction. The Instruction Cache Block Invalidate instruction (icbi) behaves like a no-op (although it should not be used as a no-op for compatibility with other PowerPC implementations).

The Move From Time Base instruction, mftb, which is defined by the PowerPC Architecture, is not implemented in the 601. However, because it is guaranteed to trap on this instruction, it should be used in place of the mfspr instruction for reading the real-time clock registers. This guarantees software compatibility across processors that implement the time base, which is the time-of-day resource defined by the architecture.

The 601 also supports a number of POWER instructions that are otherwise not implemented in the PowerPC Architecture.

The 601 Exception Model

The 601 implements the exception model defined by the PowerPC Architecture, with some variations that are allowed by the architecture. Table 16.1 shows how the exceptions defined by the PowerPC Architecture are implemented on the 601, as well as the exceptions that are unique to the 601.

Table 16.1 Exceptions and Conditions

Exception	Conditions
System reset	The 601 implements two types of system resets—hard reset, which is triggered by the HRESET- signal, and soft reset, which is triggered by the SRESET- signal. When the exception is taken, processing resumes at vector offset x'00100'.
Machine check	On the 601, a machine check is caused by the assertion of the TEA- signal during a data bus transaction. Notice that the TEA- signal is not defined by the PowerPC Architecture. Other processors can define other conditions to cause the machine check exception. When the exception is taken, processing resumes at vector offset x'00200'.
Data access	The cause of a data access exception can be determined by the bit settings in the DSISR. When the exception is taken, processing resumes at vector offset x'00300'.
Instruction access	An instruction access exception is caused when an instruction fetch cannot be performed for any of the reasons defined by the PowerPC Architecture. When the exception is taken, processing resumes at vector offset x'00400'.

(continues)

Table 16.1 Continued

Exception	Conditions
External interrupt	In the 601, the external interrupt occurs when the INT-signal is asserted. Notice that the PowerPC Architecture does not define signals. When the exception is taken, processing resumes at vector offset x'00500'.
Alignment	An alignment exception is caused when the 601 cannot perform a memory access for any of several reasons, such as when the operand of a floating-point load or store operation is in an I/O controller interface segment (SR[T] = 1) or when a load/store operand crosses a page boundary. When the exception is taken, processing resumes at vector offset x'00600'.
Program	A program exception is caused by one of the following exception conditions, which correspond to bit settings in SRR1 and arise during execution of an instruction:
	An illegal instruction program exception is generated when the processor encounters an instruction whose primary and/or secondary opcodes are not supported. These include instructions that are not supported by the PowerPC Architecture, optional instructions supported by the PowerPC Architecture not implemented in the 601, or 64-bit instructions not included in the 32-bit instruction set.
	A privileged instruction program exception occurs when the processor is operating in user-mode and an attempt is made to execute a supervisor-level instruction.
	A floating-point enabled exception condition is generated when FPSCR[FEX] is 1 and the MSR is configured for either floating-point precise or imprecise modes. FPSCR[FEX] is set when a floating-point instruction incurs an exception condition or a Move to FPSCR instruction sets both an exception condition bit and its corresponding enable bit in the FPSCR.
	A trap exception is generated when any of the conditions specified in a trap instruction is met. When the exception is taken, processing resumes at vector offset x'00700'.
Floating-point unavailable	A floating-point unavailable exception occurs when the floating-point available bit is disabled, and the processor encounters floating-point arithmetic, load, store, or move instructions. When the exception is taken, processing resumes at vector offset x'00800'.
Decrementer	The decrementer exception occurs when the most significant bit of the decrementer register transitions from 0 to 1. This exception can be disabled with the MSR[EE] bit. When the exception is taken, processing resumes at Exception Conditionsvector offset x'00900'.

Exception	Conditions
I/O controller interface error	An I/O controller interface error exception is taken when an I/O controller interface segment access fails, indicated by a particular bus reply packet. This exception is 601-specific. When the exception is taken, processing resumes at vector offset x'00A00'.
System call	A system call exception occurs when a System Call (sc) instruction is executed. When the exception is taken, processing resumes at vector offset x'00C00'.
Run mode/ trace exception	This exception is provided for software debugging. The type of run mode exception taken is determined by settings of the HID1 register: *Normal run mode.* No address breakpoints are specified and the 601 executes from zero to three instructions per cycle. *Single instruction step mode.* One instruction is processed at a time. The appropriate break action is taken after an instruction is executed and the processor quiesces. *Limited instruction address compare.* The 601 runs at full speed (in parallel) until the EA of the instruction being decoded matches the EA contained in HID2. Addresses for branch instructions and floating-point instructions may never be detected. *Full instruction address compare.* Processing proceeds out of IQ0. When the EA in HID2 matches the EA of the instruction in IQ0, the appropriate break action is performed. Unlike the limited instruction address compare mode, all instructions pass through the IQ0 in this mode. That is, instructions cannot be folded out of the instruction stream. The *trace mode* is taken when the MSR[SE] bit is set. When the trace mode is enabled, an exception is taken after each instruction that does not cause an additional exception, or the Return from Interrupt instruction (rfi) is encountered. The PowerPC Architecture defines this as a separate exception assigned to vector offset x'00D00'. In the 601, the vector offset is x'02000'.

The 601 System Interface

The 601 system interface consists of a 32-bit address bus and a 64-bit data bus. The interface is synchronous, with timing derived from the rising-edge impulse of the bus clock cycle. The system interface allows separate address and bus transactions, as well as address-only bus transactions such as those generated by the cache control and synchronization instructions and those that are automatically generated to ensure cache coherency. Data can be transferred in single-beat reads and writes (1-8 bytes) or four-beat burst

(32 bytes) transactions. Burst transactions that update or transfer the contents of an entire cache block are the most common data transactions.

The address and data buses are independent and support one-level pipelining (that is, a second address tenure can begin before the data transaction associated with the first address transaction completes).

The 601 provides limited support for out-of-order split-bus transactions; that is, the address and data bus are allowed to have different bus masters in multiprocessing environments. The system bus can be used by other processors or other memory devices (such as DMA devices), and access (mastership) to the bus is determined by a separate bus arbiter.

The PowerPC Architecture does not address how a given processor should implement its bus interface; however, there are certain aspects of the architectural specification that determine the nature of the bus interface. For example, the architecture is optimized for a weakly-ordered memory system (that is, one in which loads and stores may occur out of order). Each processor is free to realize this specification in the manner that is most appropriate for the price/performance trade-offs that govern the design. Because the 601 is intended for multiprocessing implementations, its interface is designed to share a memory bus with other devices. For example, it implements a signal (global or GBL-) that when asserted indicates that a particular bus operation should be snooped by other devices.

Also, the interface includes separate ports to the cache tags so snooping does not interfere with other address bus transactions. Additional signals are provided to expedite certain bus activity useful in a multiprocessor implementation, such as the bus grant input signal (BG-), which when asserted permits the processor to have access to the address bus. This signal, which is typically granted by an external arbiter, can be disabled in a single-processor environment. Signals can be implemented in such a way that when a snoop hit occurs, the requested data can be passed to external memory as a high-priority operation, cutting ahead of any other operations that may be queued in the memory unit. This functionality can be disabled and the buffer can be configured to behave like the other two elements in the write queue.

The 601 has a 32-bit address bus and a 64-bit data bus. The 601 includes additional control and information signals that do the following:

- Conduct the bus protocol required to transfer the addresses and data.

- Indicate the configuration of the processor.

- Provide information about the type of transfers that are taking place.

- Provide indications when an action has been successful or unsuccessful.

- Define the clocking scheme for the bus interface. Because the bus may not operate at as fast a frequency as the processor, the clocking signals provide a way for the bus to operate at one-half, one-third, one-fourth (and so forth), of the processor clock frequency.

Test Signals Are Provided for Hardware Debugging

The 601 signals are grouped as follows:

- *Address arbitration signals.* These signals are used when the processor needs to be granted access to the address bus.

- *Address transfer start signals.* After address bus mastership has been granted, these signals indicate that the address bus transaction has begun.

- *Address transfer signals.* These signals, which consist of the address bus, address parity, and address parity error signals, transfer the address over the address bus and ensure the integrity (parity) of the transfer.

- *Transfer attribute signals.* These signals indicate the type of data transaction (whether it is a four-beat burst transaction and how much data is to be transferred if it is a single-beat transfer). The transfer is also characterized by whether it is write-through, coherency enforced, or cache-inhibited. The global signal indicates whether the access is to a portion of memory that should permit snooping.

- *Address transfer termination signals.* These signals acknowledge (address acknowledge, AACK-) the end of the address phase of the transaction. If the address tenure needs to be repeated (such as when the address is snooped and hit by another caching device), the address tenure must be retried to allow the modified data to be written back to memory, so it can be read from memory by the requesting device.

- *Data arbitration signals.* Similar to the address arbitration signals, these signals arbitrate for the data bus.

- *Data transfer signals.* These signals, which consist of the data bus, data parity, and data parity error signals, transfer the data and ensure the integrity (parity) of the transfer.

- *Data transfer termination signals.* These signals acknowledge the end of a data beat or an entire data tenure and indicate when a data tenure should be repeated.

- *System status and control signals.* These signals are not directly involved in address and data transfers. The external interrupt, soft-, and hard-reset signals are used to signal asynchronous exception conditions. Other signals are used to indicate to other processors that a processor has entered the checkstop state.

- *Clock signals.* These signals determine the system clock frequency. These signals can also be used to synchronize multiprocessor systems.

- *Processor state signals.* These two signals are used to set the reservation coherency bit and set the size of the 601's output buffers.

- *Miscellaneous signals.* These signals provide information about the state of the reservation coherency bit.

- *Test interface signals.* The common on-chip processor (COP) unit is the master clock control unit and it provides a serial interface to the system for performing the built-in self-test (BIST). Additional test signals are used for production testing.

The data bus is designed to allow as many as 64 bits of data to be transferred in a single clock cycle. This is referred to as a single-beat transaction. Of course, there is considerable other activity that must occur before data can be transferred—the processor must request and be granted access to the address bus, the address must be successfully broadcast to external memory and acknowledged to the processor. This access to the address bus (or address bus tenure) is described in three stages—address arbitration, transfer, and termination. The data tenure, which also requires arbitration, transfer, and termination, can overlap the address tenure, as shown in Figure 16.4.

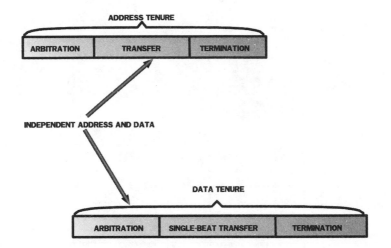

Figure 16.4
Pipelining of
Address and Data
Tenures.

Data transfers on the 601 allow 8, 16, 24, 32, 40, 48, 56, or 64 bits to be transferred in one bus clock cycle. These are called single-beat read and write operations and are generated by explicit load and store instructions. However,
the most prevalent type of bus activity is the transfer of entire cache blocks of
data (eight words per block) in a four-beat transaction (64 bits per beat). This
is called a burst transaction, and because the entire series of bus operations
necessary to generate a data transfer need not be repeated for each beat, data
is transmitted much more efficiently. Although the processor may not always
use all of the data or instructions that may be read into the cache, it does
most of the time.

Additionally, the 601 also supports address-only transactions used to affect
caches and TLBs on other devices that share memory. These can be generated
by explicit memory control instructions or as the side effect of other processor activity. For example, although a cache block of data in the write queue
snoops address transactions just like blocks in the cache, this does not occur
for single-beat write operations. So, when a single-beat write operation is
written to memory, it also broadcasts a cache-block "kill" address-only operation that invalidates the cache block in any other cache that holds this physical address.

Figure 16.5 shows the 601's logical pin configuration, and how the signals are
grouped.

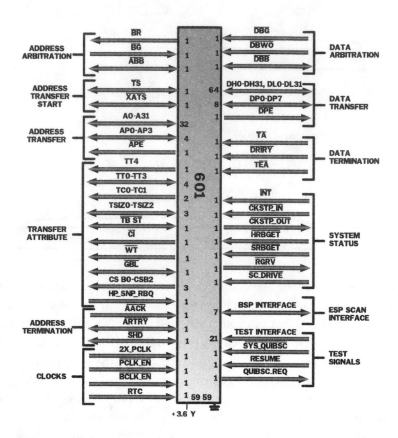

Figure 16.5
PowerPC 601
Microprocessor
Signal Groups.

Summary

This chapter has taken a closer look at the internal workings of the 601 processor, emphasizing its special features and the way in which it implements the PowerPC Architecture.

The next chpater examines more closely how the RISC nature of the 601 design provides for efficient instruction execution.

Chapter 17

PowerPC 601 RISC Processor Instruction Timing

A simple statistic, such as the latency of an instruction or the number of instructions that can execute per second, or even a more elaborate benchmark based on coding examples, can be misleading unless those statistics are provided with the appropriate context. This chapter looks at instruction timing in the 601 processor. It is important to keep in mind, however, that the 601 is but one realization of the PowerPC Architecture. And even though other processors are likely to take advantage of many of the same techniques as the 601, implementations can vary drastically from one to the next, adopting instruction-processing techniques that are most appropriate for the price/performance issues that determine each design.

This chapter provides a general description of how the 601 processor fetches, dispatches, decodes, executes, and writes back the results of certain PowerPC instructions. This description demonstrates the implementation techniques, such as pipelining and superscalar dispatch, for which the PowerPC Architecture has been designed to support.

It is important to bear in mind that the instruction timing model presented here is a conceptual model that characterizes the behavior of a very complex device.

In examining instruction timing, it is useful to understand a few key concepts and terms. Instructions progress through a pipeline in stages that are typically associated with a task that takes a certain amount of time—typically a

This chapter focuses on the following instructions that are processed in the PowerPC 603 processor:

- The pipeline structure of the PowerPC 601

- The common stages through which all instructions must pass before they can be dispatched to individual instruction pipelines

- The integer pipeline

- The branch pipeline

- The floating-point pipeline

single cycle. For example, an integer instruction typically requires one clock cycle to decode, one clock cycle to execute, and one clock cycle to write back its results. These events are referred to as the integer decode, execute, and write-back stages. The term clock cycle in the context of instruction timing refers to one tick of the processor clock. In this chapter, the term boundary is used in conjunction with the pipeline drawings to indicate when a clock cycle elapses between stages. The number of clock cycles required to perform a particular task is referred to as latency. This may be used to refer to the amount of time required to traverse a particular execution pipeline. For example, it is said that most floating-point instructions have a three-cycle latency. This is referred to as instruction latency, or the amount of time required to access a cache or external memory (generally referred to as memory latency). The number of instructions that can complete per cycle is referred to as throughput.

An instruction is said to be stalled when it is forced to remain in a particular stage because of another instruction or because of a register dependency. A register dependency occurs when the read-and-write operations to a register must be kept in order to ensure that data remains valid. When the stall is caused because a source operand requires data that has yet to be provided by another instruction, this is referred to as a data dependency. Subsequent instructions in the pipeline also are said to be stalled. The 601 provides several mechanisms to avoid stalls due to data dependencies. For example, an integer instruction can specify the same GPR as a source operand that the previous instruction specifies as a target operand. At the end of the execute stage, the results are sent to the target GPR and to the dependent instruction as it enters the execute stage via a feed-forwarding path so the dependent instruction does not stall.

In a superscalar implementation, such as the 601, instructions are said to be dispatched when they are issued to the various execution units to be decoded and executed. The 601 has three execution units and three pipelines that correspond with those units—the branch pipeline, the integer pipeline, and the floating-point pipeline.

With respect to the integer pipeline, if no instruction is available to be dispatched, a *bubble* is propagated through the integer pipeline instead of an instruction. A bubble can be viewed as a missed opportunity to dispatch an instruction, and the bubble reduces by one the number of instructions that can be executed per clock cycle.

Bubble

A missed opportunity to dispatch an instruction. Propagates through the pipeline, but may disappear if the previous instruction in the pipeline stalls and the subsequent instruction catches up. Sometimes a bubble carries tags through the integer pipeline, cannot be eliminated, and must pass entirely through the pipeline.

601 Instruction Timing—An Overview

The 601 instruction timing is characterized by the following:

- The use of a unified cache, which is shared by multiple processor resources, determines to a great extent the nature of the instruction fetching mechanism.

- The branch processing unit (BPU) is closely coupled with the instruction unit and checks for dependencies when branch instructions are dispatched in order to provide quick resolution of conditional branches.

- Resolved branches without data dependencies can be replaced in the program flow by the correctly predicted instruction. This is called branch folding.

- Instructions can be dispatched out of order to the branch and floating-point pipelines.

- Each execution pipeline is fully pipelined. The floating-point pipeline cannot get ahead of the integer pipeline and the branch pipeline will always necessarily be ahead of the integer pipeline.

- The integer unit pipeline executes all integer instructions, including load and store instructions. The integer unit also executes floating-point load and store instructions, taking advantage of the fact the integer arithmetic is required for calculating effective addresses. Floating-point store operations also must pass through the floating-point pipeline in order to ensure that the floating-point data in th e FPR is properly formatted before it is written to memory.

- Instructions are allowed to complete and record their results out of program order, although they appear to a user program to complete in strict order. In other words, instructions can record their results providing they do not corrupt how data would appear had the instructions been executed in strict program order; order among instructions that have data dependencies is still strictly maintained. These dependencies are synchronized by a tagging mechanism that records the order of such instructions.

- Additional resources are provided to reduce the occurrence of stalls and the effect of stalls when they do occur. For example, additional paths are provided so execution results and load store data can often be passed to the dependent unit at the same time that they are sent to the register files, preventing the unit from having to wait for the results to arrive in the register file to be accessed. This typically saves a clock, not only to the dependent instruction but to all of the instructions behind it in the pipeline. Buffering is provided in several places to allow instructions or data to be "posted" when a resource is busy. This also allows subsequent instructions to keep moving.

Pipeline Description

Figure 17.1 shows the 601 pipeline model, which incorporates additional pipelines associated with branch, integer, and floating-point execution units.

Figure 17.1
Master Instruction
Pipeline.

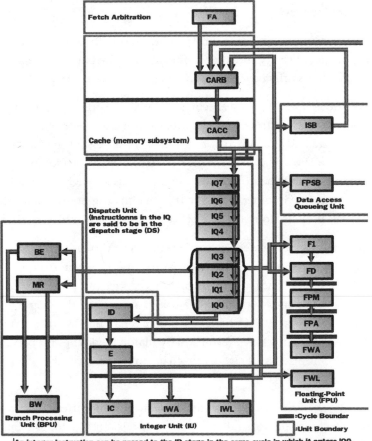

¹An integer instruction can be passed to the ID stage in the same cycle in which it enters IQ0.

All instructions must pass through all pipeline stages up to the dispatch stage (DS), at which point instructions are dispatched to one of three execution units—the integer unit (IU), the floating-point unit (FPU), and branch processing unit (BPU). Instructions are dispatched out-of-order, although order is maintained strictly within the integer and floating-point pipeline. Order is maintained among branch instructions that write back in the branch pipeline, but many branch instructions can be removed (folded) from the branch pipeline if no write back is required.

Instructions may write back results out of order in the 601—there are no common stages that follow those in the three execution pipelines to force results to be written back in-order (as is the case with the 603). It is useful to make a distinction here between writing back and completion. An instruction is allowed to write back (that is, record the results of a calculation or initiate a load or store) before it actually completes. However, an instruction also may have other dependencies that cannot be resolved early, such as those instructions that update the condition register. These actions are performed when the instruction completes, and instructions must complete in order.

As instructions are dispatched to the floating-point and branch pipelines, they are tagged to the integer pipeline. These tags provide an orderly way for branch instructions to write to the link and count registers to ensure orderly write-back. These tags are resolved in the IC stage. Additional dispatch logic maintains a precise exception model.

Consistent with the conceptual processor model to which the PowerPC instruction set was designed, the IU and the FPU each maintain dedicated register files (GPRs and FPRs, respectively).

Several operations must occur before an instruction can be executed, as follow:

- The program path must be determined.

- The effective address of the instruction must be determined and translated to a physical address.

- The physically addressed, unified cache must be arbitrated for.

- The instruction must be loaded into the instruction queue in the instruction unit.

- The instructions must be dispatched to the appropriate execution units.

The program path is determined according to the following priorities:

1. If an exception is taken, the instruction is fetched from the appropriate exception vector. The PowerPC Architecture defines a vector offset, which is appended to a string of hexadecimal F's or 0's to form the address. The choice is determined by the exception prefix (EP) bit in the MSR.

2. If a branch has been resolved and it is determined that the direction had been predicted incorrectly, the BPU provides a mispredict recovery address, which is the address of either the branch target instruction or the sequential instruction that was not predicted.

3. When a branch instruction is encountered that cannot be resolved, the direction is predicted by the encoding in the BO field. Instruction fetching continues at the predicted address (either the branch target address or the next sequential address, depending on the prediction).

4. The lowest priority in the instruction fetching scheme is the next sequential instruction. This address can be calculated because of the simplicity of the instruction queue and cache mechanism made possible by the implementation of uniform-length instructions. Because each instruction is a word long, the next address can be determined by adding the number of instructions loaded into the IQ on the previous cycle to the address of the previous access.

During fetch arbitration (FA), the next fetch address is generated (often in conjunction with the BPU) and sent to the memory subsystem (CARB). Stalls may occur when the fetch address cannot be accessed or translated.

When a branch instruction is dispatched to the BPU, its target EA is calculated and then sent to the MMU for translation. For conditional branches that depend on the CR, the CR is checked for coherency while the target EA is calculated.

The branch direction is resolved when no instructions below the branch can update the CR field to which the branch refers; otherwise, the branch is predicted. The address of the path that is not predicted is saved in the MR stage of the BPU pipeline to be made available to the FA stage if the prediction fails. Based on the direction of the branch prediction, either the target address or the next sequential address is sent to the memory subsystem.

This translated address is withheld if a previous branch prediction fails and the current branch instruction is removed as part of the mispredict recovery.

After branch prediction, the CR is checked on each cycle until it becomes coherent, at which point the branch is resolved. If the prediction is correct, fetching continues (either sequentially or from a target address from a subsequent branch that does not depend on the CR). If the prediction is incorrect, instructions are purged and fetching begins at the translated address in the MR stage.

Before an instruction can be fetched, the instruction unit must arbitrate and access the cache. The cache arbitration (CARB) and cache access (CACC) stages are required for fetching instructions and also for load and store accesses, and by the memory subsystem for cache reload operations and for some snoop operations.

Cache access is prioritized as follows:

- Cache maintenance accesses generated by the memory subsystem. These include the following (in order of priority):

    1. The reload access for reloading a cache line on a cache miss.

    2. The cast-out access for casting-out a modified adjacent sector.

    3. The snoop push required by a snoop operation.

    4. Load and store requests generated by the processor core. Note that loads precede stores with respect to the memory queues; however cache accesses occur in program order (assuming cache hits).

    5. Instruction fetch requests.

It is important to note that instruction fetching, because it is attempted continuously, has the lowest priority for cache access, because other resources (such as the memory unit, the MMU, and the integer unit, which access the cache to handle loads and stores) share access to the unified cache, additional hardware is provided (an eight-entry instruction queue that is fully multiplexed from the cache) to avoid a condition where the instruction queue could be empty. Likewise, having such a large instruction queue (and enough paths to fill it in one clock) reduces the frequency with which the cache must be accessed.

For most instructions, cache arbitration overlaps with one or more other stages (for example, FA and CARB occur in one cycle). Cache accesses (on cache hits) require only one cycle. The cache is nonblocking, so if an instruction fetch misses in the cache, the cache can be accessed by another instruction while the additional activity generated by the cache miss takes place.

During the CACC stage, instructions from the addressed cache block are loaded into the instruction queue (IQ). The number of instructions fetched depends on the following conditions:

- If the requested instruction is in the cache, as many as eight instructions can be fetched, depending on how much room is in the IQ. Instructions that do not fit into the IQ are refetched. Newly fetched instructions can replace instructions that are dispatched from the IQ in the same cycle.

- If the fetch misses in the cache, a cache reload is required.

- If the instruction fetch is from a page or block of memory that is non-cacheable, a maximum of two instructions can be fetched. This is the number of words that can be transferred in a single beat transaction.

- The alignment of the fetch address—if the address is not the lowest address in a cache block, only the instructions at the higher addresses in the block can be fetched. Instructions can be fetched only from one cache block at a time.

The dispatch stage (DS) includes the eight-entry instruction queue (IQ0-IQ7). As mentioned above, as many as eight instructions can be fetched, but no more than three can be dispatched per cycle; therefore, stalls in the fetch stage typically do not cause bubbles in the dispatch stage or in execution unit pipeline stages. As many as three instructions per clock can be dispatched from the bottom four positions, IQ0-IQ3. Integer instructions begin to decode in IQ0, branch instructions are decoded in IQ0 through IQ3, and floating-point instructions decode after they are dispatched to the floating-point pipeline.

To ensure orderly write back and a precise exception model, the dispatch stage follows these restrictions:

- Floating-point and branch instructions can be dispatched out-of-order.

- Floating-point and branch instructions are tagged to the immediately previous integer instruction in program order or to a bubble in the IU pipeline. Although floating-point and branch instructions are tagged to integer instructions (or bubbles) ahead of them in program order, those instructions may be dispatched ahead of the instruction or the bubble to which they are tagged.

- Floating-point instructions are dispatched in order with respect to other floating-point instructions, integer instructions are dispatched in order with respect to other integer instructions, and branch instructions are dispatched in order with respect to other branch instructions.

- Floating-point and branch instructions can be dispatched ahead of integer instructions.

- Floating-point and branch instructions can be dispatched out of order with respect to one another.

- Integer instructions dispatch cannot be dispatched until all instructions before it in program order have been dispatched.

- Branch and floating-point instructions can be dispatched from IQ0-IQ3. However, an integer instruction is dispatched only when it is the first instruction in the DS stage (typically IQ0).

- Branch and integer instructions are dispatched in zero cycles; floating-point instructions take one cycle to dispatch.

- Resource and data dependencies and instruction synchronization requirements of the precise exception model can cause stalls in the DS stage. Notice that GPR and FPR dependencies are not resolved when instructions are dispatched.

Integer Unit Synchronization Tags

Although the 601 allows instructions to write back their results out of order, instructions must appear to execute in order. In general, it is usually inconsequential that an integer instruction that follows a floating-point instruction in a program completes ahead of the floating-point instruction and reports its results to the GPRs. Floating-point and branch instructions are each tagged to instructions in the integer pipeline.

There are four types of tags:

- *Floating-point tags.* Each floating-point instruction generates a floating-point tag. These tags are resolved in the integer completion stage.

- *Branch to link register tags.* These tags ensure that branch to link register instructions update the link register in order. These tags are resolved in the integer completion stage.

- *Branch to count register tags.* These tags ensure that branch to count register instructions update the count register in order. These tags are resolved in the integer completion stage.

- *Branch mispredict recovery tags.* These tags are issued when a branch is predicted but is not resolved. Unlike the other tags, these tags are resolved in the integer execute stage.

These tags monitor program order. Although all floating-point instructions must be tagged, only those branch instructions that write back to either the LR or CTR or are unresolved require tags.

To ensure that the LR, CTR, and CR are updated in order, neither the BPU nor the FPU can write back their results until their tags complete the IC stage. Instructions in the IU cannot get ahead of instructions in the BPU, but may get ahead of instructions in the FPU by as many as three instructions if floating-point exceptions are disabled.

Because both integer and floating-point instructions may optionally update the condition register, indicated by appending a period to the instruction mnemonic, write back to the condition register must be done in strict order. Therefore, CR dependencies must be tracked so that data is not corrupted. This is handled by forcing the floating-point instructions to tag to bubbles in the integer pipeline. This does not increase the instruction execution time for integer instructions, but does affect overall throughput. Integer ALU instructions that have the RC bit set write the CR from IE and there is no additional latency.

When either a floating-point or branch instruction is dispatched, any instructions in higher slots in the IQ drop into the space left by the dispatched instructions in the IQ. This typically eliminates bubbles in the integer pipeline.

If a tag is taken and there is no intervening integer instruction to which an instruction may tag, instructions may be tagged to bubbles—place holders that serve only to carry tags through the integer pipeline. For example, when two floating-point instructions follow an integer instruction, the second instruction must tag to a bubble. All floating-point instructions that update the CR are tagged to a bubble. This also occurs when floating-point precise exception mode is enabled.

Multiple instructions can be tagged to a bubble in the same way—and with the same restrictions—in which multiple instructions can be tagged to an integer instruction (one branch to LR, one branch to CTR, and one floating-point instruction).

When the IC stage detects a tag, write-back is postponed until dependencies are resolved, ensuring that those operations that must occur in order are handled sequentially.

Because the tag typically reaches the IC stage before the associated floating-point instruction reaches floating-point write-back stage (FWA), the completion logic remembers that a floating-point instruction can complete when it arrives in the FWA stage. If floating-point precise mode is disabled, the completion logic can track as many as three floating-point tags for which no floating-point instruction has written back. In other words, the IU can complete instructions past three incomplete floating-point instructions without stalling. Link and count tags cause the LR and CTR to be updated in the BPU as the integer instruction clears the IC stage. The BPU is always ready to write back when its tags reach the IC stage, so it can always update these registers synchronously with the IC stage.

Branch and floating-point instructions are considered complete when their tags leave the IC stage (floating-point instructions may write back later, and branch instructions may get resolved later). Thus, the 601 supports in-order completion, but permits out-of-order write–back.

Integer Dispatch—an integer instruction is dispatched only after all previous instructions have been dispatched. To enforce this requirement, an integer instruction is only dispatched when it is the first instruction in the IQ stage (IQ0). Unless there are stalls in the IU pipeline, dispatch takes zero cycles. Although instructions can stall in the dispatch stage (for example if the instruction in IE stage has a dependency on the XER or CR), there are no conditions inherent to the dispatch stage that can cause an integer instruction to stall.

Branch Dispatch

A branch instruction enters the BE stage and the DS stage simultaneously. The BPU is the only execution unit for which dependency checking is done in the dispatch stage. This is another feature that was a consideration of the PowerPC Architecture, by allowing the BPU to check for dependencies before an instruction is dispatched it is possible to resolve a conditional branch instruction before it is dispatched.

A branch instruction may stall at the DS stage for the following reasons:

- A previous mtspr instruction that accessed the LR or CTR causes a register dependency.

- The link shadow registers are both full and the branch instruction that needs to be dispatched next has the link bit set.

- The next branch instruction that is to be dispatched depends on whether the CR and the MR stage is occupied.

- The branch is on a predicted path that is going to be purged.

Floating-Point Dispatch

Floating-point instructions take one cycle to dispatch. Floating-point instructions are dispatched from the DS stage into the floating-point decode (FD) stage or into the F1 stage if an instruction is stalled in the FD stage. If both the FD and F1 stages are full, floating-point instructions cannot be dispatched (even if the F1 stage is becoming available during this cycle). This is the only situation that can cause a floating-point instruction to stall in the dispatch stage.

Tagging Considerations at Dispatch

Some instructions require special treatment when they are dispatched:

- Floating-point instructions that update the CR complete write back (FWA) and the IC stage simultaneously. These instructions are always tagged to a bubble in the integer pipeline. This bubble waits at the IC stage until the instruction reaches the FWA stage.

- When precise floating-point exceptions mode is enabled (when MSR[FE0] and MSR [FE1] are both set), a floating-point instruction may cause an exception at the FWA stage. Its tag cannot leave the IC stage until the instruction is in the FWA stage. In precise mode, floating-point instructions must be tagged to bubbles in the IU pipeline. However, branch instructions can be tagged either to the integer instruction or to the bubble in the IU pipeline.

- Floating-point store instructions use the floating-point pipeline for fetching data and the integer pipeline for calculating the effective address. For these instructions, floating-point dispatch may occur before integer dispatch. A float tag is generated and placed on the floating-point store to be dispatched to the integer pipeline. If the store has not arrived at the FWA stage before the instruction clears the IC stage, the store address is buffered in the floating-point store buffer (FPSB) stage. If another floating-point (or integer) store reaches the IE stage before the first one leaves the FWA stage, it stays in the IE stage until the FPSB stage is available.

Branch Pipeline

The branch pipeline consists of three stages—branch execute (BE), mispredict recovery (MR), and branch write-back (BW).

All branch instructions pass through the branch execute (BE) stage during which the target address is calculated (the FA stage of the target instruction is simultaneous with the BE stage). If enough information about the condition register is available, the branch direction is determined (resolved); if information is not available, the branch is predicted.

Unresolved conditional branches simultaneously enter the BE and MR stages. When the branch is resolved and the prediction is incorrect, the MR stage provides the effective address that redirects the program flow to the path previously not taken (either the branch target instruction or the sequential instruction). This address is made available to the FA stage when the instruction enters the MR stage.

The branch write-back stage is used only by branch instructions that update the LR or CTR, and several branches can occupy the BW stage simultaneously. However, only one LR and one CTR update can occur per cycle.

Integer Pipeline

The integer pipeline handles execution for integer arithmetic and integer logical instructions, all integer and floating-point load instructions and store instructions, CR instructions, memory management instructions, and miscellaneous special purpose register instructions. The execution of some instructions is shared between the IU and other units. For example, for floating-point store instructions the IU generates the effective address and the FPU provides the store data (in the FPRs). Cache instructions (such as dcbz and dcbi) are decoded in the IU, and the instruction is passed into the IE stage and the CARB stage simultaneously. Subsequently, the instruction occupies the CACC (and ISB) stage where the appropriate actions are performed.

As described above, the integer pipeline also provides a tagging mechanism that ensures coherent write back of all three execution units. Not all integer instructions pass through every IU stage.

The IU pipeline is shown in figure 17.2.

Figure 17.2
IU Pipeline
Showing Data,
Instruction, and
Tag Flow.

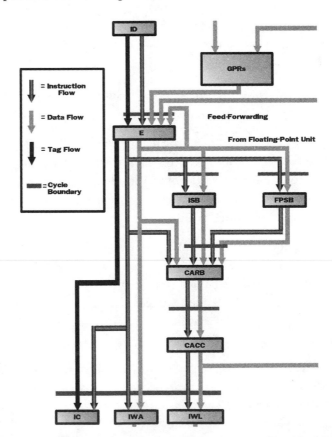

There are three different flows shown in the diagram—the instruction flow, the tag flow, and the data flow, with stages represented as rectangles. The gray bars represent boundaries; it requires a clock cycle to pass through one of these boundaries to the next stage.

Most arithmetic instructions require only one clock cycle in each stage, although division takes considerably longer. However, integer load and store instructions, which must access the memory subsystem, occupy the IE and the CARB stages (cache arbitration) simultaneously and exclusively. Also, instructions that are in write back can provide data to the ID/IE boundary and to the GPRs in the same cycle. The operations performed in each stage vary among instructions.

Instructions are decoded and operands are fetched from the GPRs in the decode stage (ID). Unless there is a stall, an instruction enters the ID stage and the IQ0 position simultaneously. If the integer pipeline is stalled, IQ0 acts as a buffer, so a subsequent integer instruction can enter the IQ0 slot even though the ID stage remains occupied.

Instructions may stall in the ID stage if a previous instruction (such as a divide instruction) requires multiple cycles in the execute stage (IE) or if the instruction in ID depends on CR or XER results that have not yet been provided by an instruction in the IE stage.

Integer Execute Stage (IE)

The IE stage receives the instruction and its associated register data from the ID stage. The following major functions are performed in the IE stage.

- All arithmetic, logical, CR logical, shift, and rotate manipulations are performed for all ALU instructions.

- Move to/from SPR instructions are executed.

- The MMU simultaneously performs any required address translation. If translations are in the TLBs, this does not affect timing. However, if the translation is not in the TLB, the pipeline stalls for at least 25 cycles while the translation is loaded into the TLB from memory. The MMU is described in Chapter 13, "PowerPC Memory Management Model."

- Unless they are stalled in the IE stage, all load and store instructions occupy the CARB stage prior to and including the last cycle of the IE stage. If the instruction is stalled in IE, it does not enter the CARB stage.

Stalls in the IE stage also cause instructions to stall in the ID stage. Instructions may stall in IE for a number of reasons, including the following:

- A load or store instruction needs cache access and the cache is busy.

- The previous instruction stalls in IWA.

- A predicted branch tag is in the IE stage and the branch has not been resolved.

- The IE instruction has a GPR dependency with an outstanding load.

Although the exact operations that occur in the IE stage depend on the instruction, integer instructions can be generally categorized into two groups—those that perform arithmetic or logical operations (ALU instructions) and those that use the IE stage primarily to calculate an effective address for a load, store, or other operation that accesses memory.

Integer Pipeline—ALU Instructions

The nominal function of the integer unit is to perform arithmetic and logical operations on values provided by the GPRs or specified as immediate values in the instruction. These include the following types of instruction:

- Integer arithmetic instructions, which perform addition, subtraction, multiplication, and division.

- Integer compare instructions, which perform algebraic comparisons on signed values and logical comparisons on unsigned values.

- Integer logical instructions, which perform logical operations, such as AND, OR, XOR, and NAND.

- Condition register logical instructions.

- Integer rotate and shift instructions, which manipulate bits in specified values.

Although instructions that move data to and from registers (SPRs, CR, SR, and MSR) do not perform arithmetic or logical operations, they are grouped with the ALU instructions because they do not generate effective addresses.

Most ALU instructions can execute in one cycle. During the IE stage, data is manipulated as required by the instruction and results are passed both to the IWA stage and to the latch between the ID and IE stages. This feed-forwarding loop eliminates stalls if the next instruction is data-dependent. In other words, there is no penalty if an instruction specifies a GPR as the source operand and that same GPR was the target operand of the previous instruction.

Multiply and divide instructions take multiple cycles in IE. Divide instructions take 36 cycles to execute. The mulli instruction always takes 5 cycles, as do mul, mullw, mulhw, and mulhwu as long as the data specified in rB does not exceed 16 bits (not counting sign bits), in which case the instruction takes 9 cycles. And if the most significant bit of rB is a 1, the mulhwu may take as many as 10 cycles.

If required, the CR or XER is updated as the instruction leaves the IE stage.

The IU write-back stage is different for ALU operations (IWA) than for load operations (IWL). ALU instructions have a write-back stage (IWA) on the cycle immediately after the IE stage. The IWA stage has a dedicated port into the GPRs. The IWA and IWL stages may have different instructions on the same cycle, and both write ports can be used simultaneously as long as they don't require access to the same register.

Some mtspr instructions spend two cycles in IE and multiple cycles in write back. (N varies from 1 to 20 cycles depending on the instruction.)

All integer ALU instructions pass through the IWA stage, even though some of these instructions (such as cmp and store instructions) do not write to the GPRs.

Integer ALU Instructions—Integer Completion Stage

The integer completion stage is provided to ensure that results—both of the integer instructions themselves and of those associated with the tags—are recorded in a coherent manner. So all integer instructions and all bubbles that carry tags through the integer pipeline must pass through the integer completion stage. When an instruction completes the integer completion (IC) stage, results are made available unless synchronous exceptions are detected. Tags flowing through the IC stage represent instruction completion for instructions that are executed in the BPU or the FPU.

An instruction (or bubble) enters the IC stage in the cycle after an instruction leaves the IE stage. When an instruction moves into IC, it indicates that the instruction is committed to recording its results even though that instruction's results may not have been written back to the appropriate register (or cache) yet. There's no stopping it at this point.

Integer Arithmetic Instruction Timings

This section provides timings for representative integer arithmetic instructions.

The timing of the add and subtract instructions is described in Figure 17.3.

Figure 17.3
Integer Add and Subtract Instruction Timings.

Number of Cycles	1	1	1
Pipeline stages	D		
		IE	
			IC
			IWA
Resources required nonexclusively		rA, rB, CA	
Resources required exclusively		CA, SO, OV, CR0, rD	

This timing is appropriate for the following instructions: addi, addis, add, addic, addic., subfic, subf, addc, subfc, adde, subfe, addme, subfme, addze, subfze, neg, abs, nabs, doz, and dozi.

The instruction spends one cycle in IE. The status bits (XER[CA], XER[OVSO], and CR0) are all written from the IE stage.

The timing for integer multiply instructions is shown in Figure 17.4 (mul, mullw, mulhw, and mulhwu) and Figure 17.5 (mulli).

Number of Cycles	1	5/9/0[a]	1
Pipeline stages	D		
		IE	
			IC
			IWA
Resources required nonexclusively		rA, rB	
Resources required exclusively		rD, MQ, CRO, SO, OV[b]	

a. Number of cycles is data dependent.

b. Update CRO if (RC 1), updates SO and OV if (OE 1).

Figure 17.4
mul, mullw, mulhw, and mulhwu Instruction Timings.

Number of Cycles	1	b	1
Pipeline stages	D		
		IE	
			IC
			IWA
Resources required nonexclusively		rA	
Resources required exclusively		rD, MQ	

Figure 17.5
mulli Instruction Timing.

Integer multiplication takes 5, 9, or 10 cycles in IE.

Figure 17.6 shows the timing for integer divide instructions (div, divs, divw, and divwu).

Number of Cycles	1	36	1
Pipeline stages	D		
		IE	
			IC
			IWA
Resources required nonexclusively		rA, rB, MQ,	
Resources required exclusively		rD, MQ, CRO, SO OV	

Figure 17.6
Integer Divide Instruction Timing.

Each divide instruction takes 36 cycles in the IE stage.

The timings of other integer ALU are described as follows:

- *Compare instructions.* Compare instructions spend one cycle each in the ID and IE stages, but essentially have no IWA stage. The compare results are written to the CR and forwarded to the BPU (for conditional branch evaluation) in the middle of the IE cycle.

- *Boolean logic instructions.* Boolean logic instructions include the standard Boolean logic functions, sign extension of a byte within a register, sign extension of a half word within the register, and a count leading zeros in a register instruction. These instructions each flow through the integer pipeline in the same manner, spending a single cycle in ID and IE and completing in IWA.

- *Rotate, Shift, and Mask instructions.* The 601 supports rotate, shift, and mask instructions of both the POWER and PowerPC architectures. These instructions each spend one cycle in each of the ID, IE, and IWA stages. However, there is a wide variation in the resources that these instructions access.

- *Condition register instructions.* Each of the eight CR logical instructions (crand, cror, crxor, crnand, crnor, crandc, creqv, and crorc) requires a single clock in the ID, IE, and IWA stages.

- *System Call (sc) and Return from Interrupt (rfi) instructions.* These instructions are context-synchronizing, and support the PowerPC Architecture's precise exception model. The sc instruction is used to generate a system call exception and the rfi instruction is used to indicate the end of exception processing. These instructions occupy the ID stage until all preceding instructions have completed. The sc instruction takes 16 cycles and the rfi instruction takes 13 cycles in IWA.

Integer Pipeline—Memory Access Instructions

Because both integer and floating-point load and store instructions (as well as certain cache control and memory synchronization instructions) must generate effective addresses, the unit that executes these instructions must provide an integer adder. In the 601, such instructions are executed in the IU. The effective addresses, are in turn translated to physical addresses by the MMU.

These instructions include the following:

- Integer load and store instructions (both single and multiple register).

- Floating-point load and store instructions.

- The load/store with reservation instructions (memory synchronization instructions).

- Cache control instructions (instructions that generate effective addresses for address-only bus transactions or for speculative loads).

This discussion is limited to integer and floating-point load and store instructions, although much of it can be generalized to include the other memory access instructions.

The translated address and additional information that identifies the type of instruction, the size of the operand, and the target register (for loads) are passed to the CARB stage in the same cycle that the instruction enters the IE stage.

Although floating-point load and store instructions execute in the IU, accesses must be made to the FPRs. Floating-point load instructions generate a cache or external memory access that updates the FPR; these instructions are dispatched only to the IU.

Floating-point store instructions are dispatched both to the floating-point and integer pipelines. The FPU provides the store data; however, it may not be available until after the memory request is made by the IU. The address and control information can be "posted" to the floating-point store buffer (FPSB) until the floating-point store data is available.

From the perspective of the integer pipeline, load and store instructions execute in one cycle as long as operands do not cross a double-word addressing boundary, in which case two cycles are required. This of course does not account for latency that may be encountered because of cache contention, memory bus activity because of cache misses, or exceptions that may be caused if the physical address translation cannot be located.

Memory Access Instructions—CARB Stage

Load and store instructions enter the IE and CARB stages at the same time. The cache can be accessed on the next cycle after arbitration completes. If arbitration fails, the request is held in one of the store buffers (ISB or FPSB), until it becomes the highest priority request. Load and store requests receive next-to-lowest priority for access to the cache—ahead of instruction fetches but behind operations required to maintain cache coherency.

The instruction can continue from the IE stage to the IC stage either when cache access is granted access or when it is queued by the cache arbiter. However, if an IU request is in the ISB stage, the instruction in IE cannot arbitrate for cache access and stalls until the ISB stage is cleared.

Only one request is granted per cycle and that request is forwarded to the CACC stage in the next cycle. If a cache miss occurs, no data is returned from the CACC stage and an instruction may stall in the ISB or FPSB stages. The instruction continually reenters the CARB state until it can successfully access the cache. The data is available during the CACC stage of the cache reload; thus in this case, a request can be satisfied even if it is not arbitrated into the cache (the CARB stage).

Memory Access Instructions—Cache Access (CACC) Stage

The CACC stage follows the successful completion of the CARB stage. Here, store data is written to the cache and load data is read from the cache. On a cache miss, the request is sent to the bus interface unit. On a cache hit, load data from the cache is also fed forward to the latches above the IE stage.

The byte-reversal instructions use this stage to perform those manipulations, and any sign and zero extension is also done here. On the next cycle, the data is available for the instruction in the IE stage and the data is written into the GPRs in the IWL stage.

> **Note**
>
> If consecutive load instructions and store instructions hit in the cache, the throughput is one per cycle. If the cache cannot be accessed on a given cycle, the instruction stalls in the ISB of FPSB stage. Subsequent load instructions stall in the IE stage until the ISB stage is vacant. Subsequent stores stall in the IE stage until both the ISB and FPSB are vacant.

Memory Access Instructions— Buffering Stages (ISB and FPSB)

Instructions simultaneously enter the CACC stage and either the integer or floating-point store buffer (ISB or FPSB) in case a cache retry is necessary, in which case arbitration must be repeated. The instruction remains in the buffer until the cache access completes.

Floating-point store instructions also use the FPSB to hold the store request and address while the FPU produces the data to be stored. As mentioned above, floating-point instructions are dispatched to both pipelines. For single-precision floating-point instructions, this is necessary to format the data properly. Because the contents of FPRs are always formatted as double-precision values, they must be converted to the appropriate single- or double-precision format before the data can be forwarded to memory.

When the data is available, the instruction in the FPSB participates in the arbitration and remains there until the cache access completes successfully.

Memory Access Instructions—Load Write-back Stages (IWL)

Load instructions have a write-back stage (IWL) on the cycle after the CACC stage. The IWL stage has a dedicated write port into the register file. As noted above, the IWA and IWL stages may have different instructions on the same cycle—both write ports can be used simultaneously—with the exception that they cannot both write the same register on the same cycle.

Update-form load instructions and store instructions write the EA into the addressing register (rA) during the IWA stage in parallel with the cache access.

Load and Store Instructions—Integer Completion Stage (IC)

The integer completion stage serves the same function for memory access instructions as for integer ALU instructions. Whereas ALU instructions complete and record their results in the same cycle in which they complete the IC stage, memory access instructions are generally permitted to complete the IC stage as soon as it is determined that neither this nor any previous instructions can cause an exception.

Single-Register Load Instruction Timing

The timing for load instructions depends on whether an operand crosses a double-word boundary, whether the instruction is a single-register or a multiple register load or store, and whether the GPR specified with the rA operand is updated with the effective address.

All single-register load instructions spend one cycle in IE. Timing for these instructions is shown in Figure 17.7.

Figure 17.7
Load Instruction
Timings.

Number of Cycles	1	1	1	1
Pipeline stages	ID			
		E		
		CARB		
			CACC	
			IC	
				IWL or FWL
Resources required nonexclusively		rA, rB		
Resources required exclusively		rD	rD	

The timing in Figure 17.7 applies to the lbz, lbzx, lhz, lhzx, lha, lhax, lhbrx, lhrx, lwz, lwzx, lwarx, lfs, lfsx, lfd, and lfdx instructions. The FWL stage is used by the floating-point load instructions to access the FPRs.

If an operand crosses a double-word boundary, an additional cycle is required in the IE and CARB stages. The CACC and IC stages still begin in the third clock cycle as before, but an additional cycle of CACC is required. These additional cycles are required because two cache accesses are required. The timing for this situation is shown in Figure 17.8.

Number of Cycles	1	1	1	1	1
Pipeline stages	ID				
		F	F		
		CARB	CARB		
			CACC	CACC	
			IC		
					IWL or FWL
Resources required nonexclusively		rA, rB			
Resources required exclusively		rD	rD	rD	

Figure 17.8
Load Instruction Timings—Operand Crosses a Double Word.

Load instructions that also update the addressing register, rA, with the EA are similar to conventional load instructions except that rA is required exclusively when the instruction is in IE. When these instructions have operands that cross a double-word addressing boundary, they must spend an extra cycle in IE and CACC.

Single-Register Integer Store Instruction Timings

Like load instructions, the timing for integer store instructions depends on whether an operand crosses a double-word boundary, whether the instruction is a single- or multiple-register store, and whether the instruction updates the register specified by rA with the effective address.

Although floating-point instructions are dispatched to the integer pipeline, which generates the EA and performs cache arbitration and access, they also must be processed through the floating-point pipeline, so those instructions are discussed later.

Like load instructions, store instructions calculate the EA in the IE stage and arbitrate (CARB) for cache access in parallel with the IE stage. However, they do not require a write back stage unless the update option is chosen.

Timings for aligned single-register store instructions that do not update are shown in Figure 17.9.

Figure 17.9
Store Instruction
Timings.

Number of Cycles	1	1	1	1
Pipeline stages	ID			
		E	IE	
		CARB	CARB	
			CACC	CACC
			IC	
Resources required nonexclusively		rA, rB, rS		
Resources required exclusively				

As with load instructions, if an operand crosses a double-word boundary, additional cycles are required in the CARB and CACC stages, for a total latency of four cycles.

Store instructions that update with the EA are identical to regular load operations, but they require a write-back stage (IWA), which in both cases occurs in the third clock cycle.

Floating-Point Pipeline

The FPU executes all floating-point arithmetic instructions and operand conversion for instructions such as floating-point store and floating-point conversion instructions. The FPU conforms to IEEE/ANSI standards for both single- and double-precision arithmetic. Operands are held in the thirty-two 64-bit floating-point registers (FPRs).

Figure 17.10 shows the floating-point pipeline.

The F1 stage is a buffer that allows floating-point instructions to dispatch from the IQ if the previous instruction stalls in FD; otherwise, it is not used. Except for F1, floating-point instructions must pass through all floating-point stages.

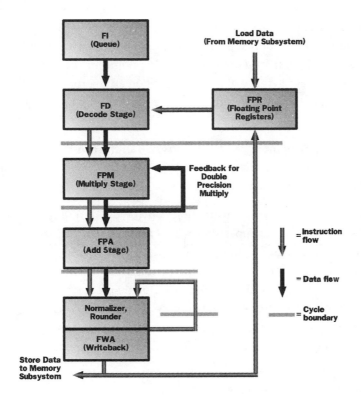

Figure 17.10
Floating-Point Data and Instruction Flow.

Single-precision instructions typically require one cycle and double-precision instructions require two cycles per stage. Many instructions may occupy multiple stages simultaneously. Special-case numbers, such as denormalized numbers, NaNs, and infinity, are handled in hardware and may repeat the path through the floating-point pipeline.

Floating-Point Decode Stage (FD)

The floating-point decode stage (FD) is like the integer decode stage—instructions are decoded and operands are fetched from the FPRs. Some instructions require multiple cycles to be decoded. Divide instructions occupy the FD stage until the final cycle in the write-back stage (FWA). Double-precision multiply instructions spend two cycles in the FD stage—as well as in each of the FPM and FPA stages. Instructions can occupy these stages simultaneously. Special-case numbers require many cycles.

Instructions may stall in FD because of true data dependencies (read-after-write, or RAW, dependencies) between the source operands of the instruction in the FD stage and the target registers required by instructions in the FPM, FPA, or FWA stages, or between the source operands of the instructions in the

FD stage and the target register of an outstanding load instruction. All dependency checking is performed at FD regardless of the stage at which the operand is first required. In other words, a floating-point move instruction may stall in the FD stage because of a dependency on an instruction in the FPA stage even though the register move instruction does not need its operand until the FWA stage.

However, floating-point store instructions stall in the FD stage not because of a dependency on an instruction in the FPM stage, but rather because of a dependency on an instruction in the FPA or FPW stage.

Multiple-cycle floating-point instructions—two types of multiple-cycle instructions in the 601 can appear in the FPU pipeline. Divide instructions, which require repeated iterations through the FD, FPM, and FPA stages and therefore must hold all three stages during execution, limiting the degree to which these instructions can be pipelined. Double-precision Multiply add and multiply instructions require two successive cycles in each of the FD, FPM, and FPA stages, but these stages are allowed to overlap in such a way that they can be pipelined with a one-instruction-per-two-clock-cycle throughput.

During execution, intermediate and final values may not be representable in the double-precision form required to be recognized as operands and to be stored in the FPRs. The process of making numbers conform to operand conventions is called normalization, and most typically this is performed in the write-back stage (FWA) to prepare the data for storage in the FPRs. because the logic for normalization is in the FWA stage. If it is determined that operands in the FD stage require prenormalization, they must pass through the pipeline to be normalized in the FWA stage before the actual calculation can begin. Denormalized operands for multiply and divide instructions require prenormalization in the 601.

Normalization is described in Chapter 12, "PowerPC Memory Conventions."

If the FPU predicts that execution will generate denormalized results, those results must also pass through the pipeline to be normalized in the FWA stage. This causes the instruction to retain control of the FD and FPM stages until normalization completes.

The execute stages in the floating-point pipeline closely match the design criteria of the PowerPC instruction set—in particular, it consists of three stages that can perform one single-precision floating-point multiply-add operation per clock cycle.

Floating-Point Multiply Stage (FPM)

The FPM stage can perform 27- by 53-bit multiplication in a single clock cycle. Because double-precision multiplication requires 53- by 53-bit multiplication, these operations take two cycles in this stage. Instructions can stall in the FPM stage only because of an instruction ahead of it in the pipeline.

Floating-Point Add Stage (FPA)

The FPA stage performs addition for add instructions and completes multiply or accumulate instructions.

The FPA stage shifts the results of the two halves of the double-precision multiply/accumulate instructions to correctly calculate double-precision sum. There are no stalls inherent to this stage.

Floating-Point Write-Back Stages (FWA and FWL)

The floating-point arithmetic write-back (FWA) stage performs any normalization or rounding necessary to make the results conform to the conventions for double-precision format required to be stored in the 64-bit FPRs. Results are stored to the FPRs and bits are set in the FPSCR.

Additionally, as shown in Figure 17.10, a feed-forwarding loop is provided so results can be sent to the FPRs and made available to an instruction in the FD stage in the following cycle.

If normalization is required, the instruction may stall in the FWA stage for as many as seven cycles.

The floating-point load write-back (FWL) stage is required only by floating-point load instructions. These instructions are dispatched only to the IU and behave like the integer load instructions except that they access FPRs instead of GPRs. During the FWL stage, load data is written into the FPRs and simultaneously made available to the FD stage.

Floating-Point Instruction Timings

Most single-precision instructions take one cycle and double-precision instructions take two cycles in each stage.

As mentioned above, the floating-point stages can perform the operations required to perform a floating-point multiply-add instruction with a throughput of one single-precision instruction per clock cycle and one double-precision every other clock cycle. This can be represented by the following equation:

$$A = BX + C$$

Most other floating-point instructions use a subset of those multiply and add instructions, as shown in the following:

- Add instructions can be calculated by setting the B operand to 1 ($A = 1*X + C$).

  This group of instructions includes add, subtract, round-to-single-precision, and floating-point compare instructions.

- Multiply instructions can be calculated by setting the C operand to zero ($A = B*X + 0$).

- Divide instructions use the base equation, but require multiple iterations through the pipeline.

- Other instructions that use the floating-point pipeline include move, convert-to-integer, and floating-point store instructions, which are dispatched to both the floating-point and integer pipelines (where the effective address is calculated).

- Floating-point load instructions are handled entirely in the IU although they access the FPRs.

Floating-Point Store Instruction Timing

Floating-point store instructions are dispatched to both the IU and to the FPU, which formats the data. The instruction need not be dispatched in the IU pipeline at the same time that the floating-point instruction is dispatched to the FPU pipeline. Because the integer pipeline typically takes fewer clock cycles to traverse, the "portion" of the instruction dispatched to the integer pipeline may complete in the IC stage and be buffered in the FPSB stage for the data to be available before it can arbitrate for the cache. This frees the integer unit for other operations.

Like other load and store instructions, the timing can be affected by whether an operand is double-word aligned or whether the address update option is chosen.

Like other load and store instructions, floating-point store accesses that cross a double-word boundary require an additional cycle in each of the CARB and CACC stages.

However, because the FPSB stage is only one-element deep, the instruction remains in the FPSB stage until the data is made available from the FPU, delaying arbitration for the second cache access for three cycles.

The timings for floating-point store instructions that update are similar to other update loads and stores in that they require an additional write-back stage on the third clock cycle and otherwise have the same latency as their nonupdating counterparts.

Single-Precision Instruction Timings

As described, the FPM, FPA, and FWA stages form a three-stage execution pipeline that can perform floating-point multiply-add instructions with a throughput of one per clock cycle (after all three stages have been occupied). The timing for these instructions (assuming no normalization is required) is shown in Figure 17.11.

Number of Cycles	1	1	1	1
Pipeline stages				
	FD			
		FPM		
			FPA	
				FWA
Resources required nonexclusively	frA, frB, frC			
Resources required exclusively				frD
Cache access				

Figure 17.11
Single-Precision
Floating-Point
Multiply-Add
Instruction
Timing.

The same figure describes timing for single-precision add and single-precision multiply instructions, with the slight exception that these instructions access only two source operands in the FD stage (frA and frB) instead of three (frA, frB, and frC required for the multiply-add instructions).

Single-precision floating-point divide instructions, like their integer counterparts, require considerably longer to complete, and because they loop through the pipeline iteratively, these instructions cannot relinquish the FD until the operation is complete. Timing for a single-precision divide instruction is shown in Figure 17.12.

Figure 17.12
Single-Precision
Floating-Point
Divide Instruction
Timing.

Number of Cycles	1	1	1	28	1
Pipeline stages					
	FD	FD	FD	FD	
		FPM	FPM	FPM	
			FPA	FPA	
				FWA	FWA
Resources required nonexclusively	frA, frB				
Resources required exclusively					frD
Cache access					

Double-Precision Instruction Timing

This section shows the timings for the double-precision versions of the instructions described above. Typically, these operations require two successive stages in each of the execute stages; however, these stages are allowed to overlap, as can be seen in the timing examples in Figure 17.13 for the double-precision floating-point multiply-add instruction.

Figure 17.13
Double-Precision
Floating-Point
Multiply-Add
Instruction
Timing.

Number of Cycles	1	1	1	1	1
Pipeline stages	FD	FD			
		FPM	FPM		
			FPA	FPA	
					FWA
Resources required nonexclusively	frA, frB, frC	frA, frB, frC			
Resources required exclusively					frD
Cache access					

As seen in Figure 17.13, the instruction requires two cycles in each of the FD, FPM, and FPA stages, but these stages are allowed to overlap so that as the first portion of the instruction leaves the FD stage and enters the FPM stage, the second portion of the instruction then enters the FD stage. Likewise, as the first portion enters the FPA stage, the second portion enters the FPM stage. This resembles the behavior of two successive single-precision instructions in the floating-point pipeline.

As a result, the pipeline can be completed in five cycles, but a throughput of one instruction every other clock cycle can be attained. This timing can be generalized to describe floating-point multiply instructions.

Double-precision, floating-point add instructions do not require two cycles in each stage and exhibit the same timing as single-precision add instructions. This timing is the same for the fcmpu and fcmpo instructions, which write back to CR[BF] instead of frD.

The timing for a double-precision divide instruction is identical to that of its single-precision counterpart, except that it requires twice as many iterations (28 instead of 14) through the FD, FPM, and FPA stages.

Summary

This chapter has provided an in-depth look at how the PowerPC 601 processor handles instructions, showing in particular characteristics of the branch, integer, and floating-point pipelines. The chapter traced many of the PowerPC instructions through the pipelines to illustrate how the PowerPC 601 takes advantage of RISC architecture to provide efficient instruction processing.

The next chapter provides a detailed look at the PowerPC 603 processor, noting in particular how its design takes advantage of the flexibility of the PowerPC Architecture to provide a powerful and efficient processor for low-power systems such as notebook computers and hand-held computing devices.

Chapter 18

The PowerPC 603 RISC Processor

The 603 is the second 32-bit PowerPC processor and is important in that it is the first PowerPC chip to bring the type of floating-point functionality formerly associated with workstation systems to low-power applications, such as laptop, notebook, and hand-held systems. This ability to achieve such high performance in such a small chip figures heavily in designs that will stretch the definition of personal computing into entirely new types of computing devices.

The 603 uses an advanced, four-level, 0.5 micron, 3.3V CMOS process technology and maintains full compatibility with TTL devices. The 603 processor was initially made available with processor speeds of 80 MHz.

The 603 illustrates the flexibility of the PowerPC Architecture, not only because of the substantial differences between how the 601 and the 603 realize the PowerPC Architecture, but because of how the 603 design takes advantage of the architecture's latitude to meet the specific needs for a processor designed for a low-power environment.

The 603 Processor Optimization for Low-Power Environments

Because the 603 is intended for low-power implementations, some facilities that are implemented in hardware in the 601 are not in the 603. For example, in the 601 much of the address translation table search operation is performed in hardware rather than in software, as it is in the 603. Likewise, the 601 provides considerable hardware support for snooping—a separate port

In this chapter, you learn the following:

- Design goals for the first low-power PowerPC processor

- Details of how the 603 processor implements the PowerPC Architecture

- Comparisons to design details of the 601 processor

- Information about the power-saving features of the 603 processor

- Information about other characteristics unique to the 603 processor

into the cache tags so snooping is done without affecting bus activity. On the 603, the snooping is performed as a separate bus activity.

Reducing the amount of hardware is important for several reasons:

- Less hardware means a smaller chip—a design goal that is common to all computers, but is especially important for very small computing devices. (The 603 has an 85 mm die size while the 601 is 120 mm.)

- Less hardware requires less power consumption, the benefits of which are an important factor in very small computers.

- Less hardware and less power consumption usually correspond to lower heat dissipation, which is another critical factor in portable system designs.

Like the 601 processor, the 603 is a superscalar, fully pipelined processor, but with several basic differences:

- The 603 dispatches instructions and writes back instruction results in order—the 601 allows out-of-order dispatch and write back. The instruction unit can dispatch as many as three instructions per clock cycle, and execution occurs in parallel.

- In addition to the branch-processor unit, floating-point unit, and integer unit, the 603 implements a separate load/store unit for both integer and floating-point load and store instructions, and a system resource unit (SRU), which executes instructions for accessing registers besides the GPRs and FPRs.

- The 603 implements additional features such as reservation stations and rename buffers to reduce the effect of resource contention and data dependencies. Reservation stations provide a buffer at the front end of an execution unit so instructions can be dispatched even though there may be a stall in an execution unit. Rename buffers reduce latency due to contention for the FPRs and GPRs.

- The 603 implements separate instruction and data caches; the 601 has a unified cache.

- To support the separate instruction and data caches, the 603 implements separate and identical memory-management units (MMUs).

- The 603 implements additional registers, instructions, and exceptions for providing several levels of power.

This section describes details of the 603's implementation of the PowerPC Architecture. Major features of the 603 are shown in Figure 18.1.

The block diagram in Figure 18.1 shows the 603's five execution units—the integer unit (IU), Floating-point unit (FPU), branch processing unit (BPU), load store unit (LSU), and SRU—which operate independently and in parallel.

Instruction Unit and Branch Processing Unit

The instruction fetch unit, with help from logic within the BPU and the completion unit, determines the address of the next instruction to be fetched from the instruction cache. Two instructions at a time can be fetched into the six-entry instruction queue. Typically, these accesses are from the instruction cache, but if the requested instruction is not in the instruction cache (that is, an instruction cache miss occurs), the request is passed to system memory. Although the instruction cache is updated on a per-cache-block basis, the double word containing the requested data is fed forward to the instruction unit at the same time that it is written into the instruction cache. This is referred to as a *critical-double-word-first cache interface*. The ability to access two instructions per clock (interrupted only when there is not room in the instruction unit or a cache miss occurs) ensures that instructions are almost always available for decoding and dispatching. The dispatch unit issues instructions, usually in pairs, to the five execution units.

Critical-double-word-first cache interface Passed to the requesting unit so that it can be used without having to wait for the entire cache block to be updated.

The instruction unit incorporates the BPU, which uses static branch prediction for conditional branch instructions to determine whether to begin speculatively fetching from the branch target address or to continue processing instructions sequentially. Instructions are fetched from the predicted path and can speculatively execute while a conditional branch is being evaluated. Typically, because branch instructions do not execute in the sense that floating-point, integer, or load/store instructions do, they can be removed from the instruction stream and replaced by the target instruction or by the next sequential instruction if the branch is predicted, not taken. This removal of the branch instruction is called *branch instruction folding*. Folding can occur here when unconditional and conditional branches are not affected by instructions that are currently executing.

Branch instruction folding Branch instructions resolved early can be removed (folded) from the instruction stream.

Figure 18.1
603 Block Diagram
Showing the Major
Features and
Functional Units.

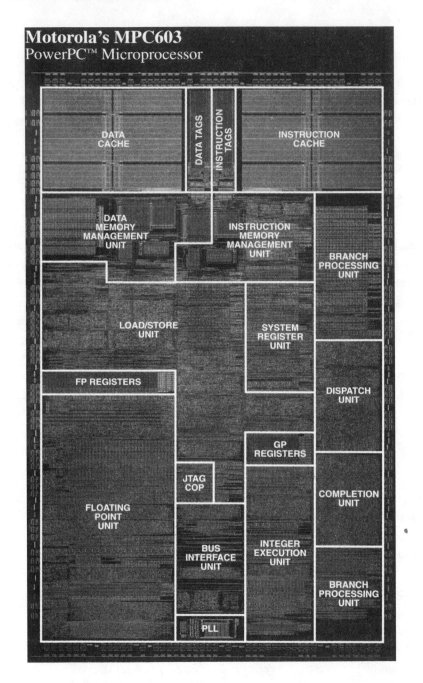

Motorola's MPC603
PowerPC™ Microprocessor

DATA CACHE

DATA TAGS

INSTRUCTION TAGS

INSTRUCTION CACHE

DATA MEMORY MANAGEMENT UNIT

INSTRUCTION MEMORY MANAGEMENT UNIT

BRANCH PROCESSING UNIT

LOAD/STORE UNIT

SYSTEM REGISTER UNIT

FP REGISTERS

DISPATCH UNIT

GP REGISTERS

JTAG COP

FLOATING POINT UNIT

BUS INTERFACE UNIT

INTEGER EXECUTION UNIT

COMPLETION UNIT

BRANCH PROCESSING UNIT

PLL

However, instructions issued beyond a predicted branch cannot write-back until the branch is resolved. Subsequent branch instructions are decoded, but not issued. When a branch is predicted incorrectly, the instruction unit flushes all incorrectly predicted instructions, and begins fetching instructions from the correct path.

The instruction queue (IQ) holds as many as six instructions and loads up to two instructions from the instruction unit per cycle. The instruction fetch unit continuously loads as many instructions as space in the IQ allows. As many as two instructions per cycle can be dispatched either to the execution unit or to the reservation station that buffers instructions when the execute stage is busy. The dispatch unit checks the FPRs and GPRs for data dependencies and determines the dispatch order.

When a branch instruction reaches the BPU, it can look ahead to determine how the condition register will be affected by unexecuted instructions. If enough information is available, the branch can be resolved immediately without the need for a prediction. The BPU decodes the BO field in branch conditional instructions to predict the direction of those conditional branch instructions that cannot be resolved. The 603 speculatively fetches instructions from the predicted instruction stream until the branch can be resolved. If the prediction was correct, instructions from the predicted path are allowed to write back their results. Otherwise, those instructions are flushed from the processor and instruction fetching resumes along the correct path.

The BPU contains an adder for computing effective addresses and the three registers used for branching instructions—the link register (LR), the count register (CTR), and the CR, used for testing branch conditions. The use of dedicated registers (instead of FPRs or GPRs) to hold branch target address reduces implementation complexity and resource conflicts between branch instructions and integer and floating-point instructions.

Instructions are dispatched, two at a time, to any of the 603's five independent execution pipelines. The parallel nature of the execution allows different kinds of instructions to execute without interfering with one another; for example, an integer instruction and a floating point instruction can execute without interfering with one another, and they use separate independent registers (the GPRs and FPRs) for source and destination operands. Pipelining allows each unit to process more than one instruction at a time. For example, the floating-point pipeline can have a different instruction in each stage.

The 603 Integer Unit

The IU executes all integer arithmetic and logical instructions, performing computations with its arithmetic logic unit (ALU), multiplier, divider, integer exception register (XER), and the GPRs, which provide register space for source and destination registers. Instructions from the dispatch unit are sent to the reservation station at the head of the integer unit pipeline. This reservation station is multiplexed in such a way that operand data can be provided from the GPRs, the rename buffers, or from other stages further down the instruction pipeline.

Most integer instructions require only one cycle to complete execution, and series of integer instructions can generally provide a throughput of one instruction per cycle, regardless of whether there is a data dependency or if there is contention for a GPR.

Effects due to contention for GPRs are often eliminated by the automatic allocation of rename registers. The 603 writes the contents of the rename registers to the appropriate GPR when integer instructions are retired by the completion unit. Simultaneously these result operands can be made available to dependent instructions.

The 603 Floating-Point Unit

The FPU contains a single-precision multiply-add array, the floating-point status and control register (FPSCR), and thirty-two 64-bit FPRs. The multiply-add array allows the 603 to efficiently implement multiplication, addition, subtraction, and division, and multiply-add operations.

As with the integer unit, a reservation station is provided at the head of the floating-point pipeline to which operand data can be accessed though the FPRs, the rename buffers associated with the FPRs, and from other stages down the instruction pipeline.

The FPU is pipelined so single-precision instructions and double-precision instructions can immediately follow one another. As with the integer units, rename registers are allocated automatically to minimize stalls due to contention for FPRs. The contents of the rename registers are written to the appropriate FPR when floating-point instructions are retired by the completion unit.

The 603 supports all IEEE 754 floating-point data types (normalized, denormalized, NaN, zero, and infinity) in hardware, eliminating the latency incurred by software exception routines.

The 603 Load/Store Unit (LSU)

The load/store unit (LSU) executes all load and store instructions and provides a way to transfer data between the cache/memory subsystem and the GPRs and FPRs. The LSU has a dedicated adder for calculating effective addresses. The LSU also aligns data, and orders load/store multiple and move string instructions.

Notice that the LSU is not defined by the PowerPC Architecture. The 601 processor, for example, uses the adder in the integer unit to calculate effective addresses.

The LSU also uses a reservation station. Load and store instructions are issued and translated in program order; however, the actual memory accesses can occur out-of-order. Synchronizing instructions are provided to enforce strict ordering.

Cacheable load instructions without data dependencies can execute speculatively. These instructions have a latency of two cycles but a throughput of one per cycle. Data returned from the cache is held in a rename register until the completion logic commits the value to a GPR or FPR. Store instructions cannot be executed speculatively; they remain in the store queue until completion logic signals that the store operation is to be completed to memory. The latency of load or store operations depends on whether the operation involves the cache, system memory, or an I/O device.

Load/store unit (LSU)
An execution unit that handles instructions that transfer data between memory, GPRs, and FPRs; and contains a dedicated adder for calculating effective addresses.

The 603 System Register Unit (SRU)

The SRU executes instructions that explicitly read, write, or manipulate bits in registers, such as the condition register and the SPRs. For context synchronization, instruction execution is delayed until all previous instructions complete.

The 603 Completion Unit

As instructions are dispatched, instruction state and other information required for completion is kept in a five-entry first-in-first-out (FIFO) buffer. An instruction cannot be dispatched unless an element is available in the completion buffer—if no room is available in the completion buffer, instructions cannot be dispatched. A maximum of two instructions per cycle are completed in order from the queue.

The completion unit tracks instructions from dispatch through execution, and then completes them in program order. In-order completion ensures a precise exception model and accurate recovery from a mispredicted branch.

The 603 Memory Management Units (MMUs)

The 603 implements two MMUs, one for instructions and one for data. These MMUs adhere to the PowerPC Architectural definition for 32-bit processors.

The MMUs provide 4GB of logical address space accessible to supervisor- and user-level programs with a 4KB page size and 256MB segment size. Block sizes range from 128KB to 256MB and are software-programmable. As defined by the architecture, the 603 uses the intermediate 52-bit virtual address and hashed page tables, defined by the architecture for generating 32-bit physical addresses. The hashed page table is a variable-sized data structure that defines the mapping between virtual page numbers and physical page numbers. The page table size is a power of 2, and its starting address is a multiple of its size.

The MMUs perform the logical-to-physical address translation for effective addresses generated by the LSU (for load, store, and other operations) and by the instruction unit and BPU for instruction fetching. Unless translation is disabled (by clearing MSR[IT] for instruction addresses or MSR[DT] for data accesses), these addresses must be translated by the MMU in order to access the appropriate locations in physical memory, including the on-chip caches.

Each MMU contains a 64-entry, two-way set-associative, translation look-aside buffer (DTLB and ITLB), which is defined, but is not required by the PowerPC Architecture. TLBs are special-purpose caches that hold the most recently used translations for page and block addresses. The operating system can invalidate TLB entries selectively. In addition, TLB control instructions defined by the architecture can optionally be broadcast on the external interface for remote invalidations and synchronization. The 603 defines two additional TLB access instructions (tlbli and tlbld), that the operating system can use to load an address translation into the instruction or data TLBs.

The MMU looks up an address in both the 64 entries of the appropriate TLB and in the BAT array. The BAT array translation is given priority if hits occur in both places. For when the translation is not present, hardware assistance is provided for software to perform a table search of the translation tables in memory. Notice that processors have the option of performing this operation entirely in hardware. In the 603 it is implemented partially in software to reduce the size and power requirements of the chip. Any effective addresses that are not found in the TLBs are saved in the IMISS and DMISS registers. These registers are not defined by the PowerPC Architecture. These addresses are used to generate the primary and secondary hashed real addresses of the page table entry group (PTEG), which are written to the HASH1 and HASH2 registers, which also are specific to the 603. A PTEG contains eight page table entries (PTEs) of eight bytes each; therefore each PTEG is 64 bytes long. PTEG addresses are entry points for table search operations.

> **Note**
>
> The 603 also provides shadow registers for GPR0-GPR3 to allow table search software to execute without affecting the GPRs.

The 603 Cache Units

The 603 provides two independent 8KB, two-way set-associative instruction and data caches. The cache block (or line) is 32 bytes long (eight contiguous words from memory), so each cache is configured as two sets of 128 cache blocks. The caches adhere to a write-back policy, but the 603 allows control of cacheability, write policy, and memory coherency at the page and block levels. The caches use a least recently used (LRU) replacement policy, meaning that when the cache is updated, the block is written to the least recently used of the two potential locations associated with the block's address.

The caches provide a 64-bit bus to the instruction fetch unit and to the load/store unit. Accessing is most efficient when aligned within an eight-word boundary. Accesses that cross a page boundary may incur a performance penalty. Write operations to the cache can be performed on a byte, half-word, word, or double-word basis. The 603 can perform a complete read-modify-write operation in one cycle.

The load/store and instruction fetch units provide effective (logical) addresses for the load and store operations, instruction fetches, and special cache control operations. The caches are physically addressed, and the instruction and data MMUs are required for the logical-to-physical address translation. In the case of a cache hit for a read (or fetch), the cache returns two words to the requesting unit. This allows the instruction unit to be updated with as many as two instructions per clock cycle.

Because the 603 data bus can be configured as 32 or 64 bits wide, a four-beat burst fills the cache block when the bus is configured as 64 bits wide and an eight-beat burst fills the cache block when the bus is configured as 32 bits wide.

When a block of data is burst into the cache, the first double word contains the requested data that missed in the cache and generated the bus transaction. A feed-forwarding path passes this double word to the requesting unit at the same time it is written to the cache.

The cache implementation is optimized for single-processor instead of multiple-processor systems. However, since other caching devices may have access to system memory, coherency must be maintained. Because the 603 is not optimized for multi-processor systems, the data cache is not dual-ported to the address bus as is done in the 601. Instead, the 603 generates a separate access to the address bus for snooping. Snooping is given highest priority access to the bus, and the load or store operation that generated the snooping occurs on the following bus clock cycle, unless there is a snoop hit. Note that because instructions should not be self-modifying, the instruction cache is not snooped.

Each data cache block has an address tag and two state bits, which are used to implement a subset of the MESI protocol. To optimize the 603 for single-processor implementations, the 603 coherency logic does not enforce the shared state. The data cache can be updated by burst read operations that completely fill cache blocks from memory and by explicit load instructions. The instruction cache is updated only by burst read bus operations.

The 603 Power Management System

The 603 provides four power modes selectable by setting bits in the machine state register (MSR) and hardware implementation register 0 (HID0) registers. The four power modes are as follows:

- *Full-power*. This is the default power state of the 603. The 603 is fully powered and the internal functional units are operating at the full processor clock speed. If the dynamic power management mode is enabled, functional units that are idle will automatically enter a low-power state without affecting performance, software execution or external hardware.

- *Doze*. All the functional units of the 603 are disabled except the time base/decrementer registers and bus-snooping logic. When the processor is in doze mode, an external asynchronous interrupt, a system management exception, a decrementer exception, a hard or soft reset or machine check brings the 603 into the full-power state. A 603 in doze mode maintains the PLL in a fully powered state and locked to the system external clock input (SYSCLK), so a transition to the full-power state takes only a few processor clock cycles.

- *Nap*. The nap mode further reduces power consumption by disabling bus snooping, leaving only the time base register and the PLL in a powered state. The 603 returns to the full-power state upon receipt of an external asynchronous interrupt, a system management exception, a decrementer exception, a hard or soft reset, or the assertion of the machine check input signal (MCP_). A return to full-power state from a nap state takes only a few processor clock cycles.

- *Sleep*. Sleep mode reduces power consumption to a minimum by disabling all internal functional units, after which external system logic may disable the PLL and SYSCLK. Returning the 603 to the full-power state requires the enabling of the PLL and SYSCLK, followed by the assertion of an external asynchronous interrupt, a system management exception, a hard or soft reset, or a machine check input (MCP) signal after the time required to relock the PLL.

The 603 Register Set

The 603 implements the basic set of SPRs defined for the 32-bit subset of the PowerPC Architecture. In addition, the 603 implements the following additional supervisor-level registers:

- The external access register (EAR) is defined as optional by the PowerPC Architecture.

- The Data TLB Miss Address (DMISS) and Instruction TLB Miss Address (IMISS) registers are read-only registers that are loaded automatically upon an instruction or data TLB miss.

- The Primary and Secondary Hash Address registers (HASH1 and HASH2) contain the physical addresses of the primary and secondary page table entry groups (PTEGs).

- The Instruction and Data PTE Compare registers (ICMP and DCMP) contain a duplicate of the first word in the page table entry (PTE) for which the table search is looking.

- The physical page address register (PPA) is loaded by the processor with the second word of the correct PTE during a page table search.

- The hardware implementation (HID0) register provides means for enabling the 603's checkstops and features.

- The instruction address breakpoint register (IABR) is loaded with an instruction address that is compared to instruction addresses in the dispatch queue. When an address match occurs, an instruction address breakpoint exception is generated.

The time base and decrementer registers in the 603 are updated once every four bus clock cycles; external control of the time base is provided through the time base enable (TBEN) signal. The decrementer is a 32-bit register that generates a decrementer exception after a programmable delay. The contents of the decrementer register are decremented once every four bus clock cycles, and the decrementer exception is generated as the count passes through zero.

The 603 Instruction Set

The 603 implements the instructions defined for the 32-bit subset of the PowerPC instruction set, as well as the following instructions defined as optional by the PowerPC Architecture:

- External Control Input Word Indexed (eciwx)

- External Control Output Word Indexed (ecowx)

- Floating-point Select (fsel)

- Floating-point Reciprocal Estimate Single-precision (fres)

- Floating-point Reciprocal Square Root Estimate (frsqrte)

- Store Floating-point as Integer Word (stfiwx)

The 603 Exception Model

The 603 implements the basic set of exceptions defined by the PowerPC Architecture. In addition, the 603 implements the exceptions described in Table 18.1.

Table 18.1 603-Specific Exceptions	
Exception	**Description**
Instruction translation miss	An instruction translation miss exception is caused when an effective address for an instruction fetch cannot be translated by the ITLB (01000).
Data load translation miss	A data load translation miss exception is caused when an effective address for a data load operation cannot be translated by the DTLB (01100).
Data store translation miss	A data store translation miss exception is caused when an effective address for a data store operation cannot be translated by the DTLB (01200).
Instruction address breakpoint	An instruction address breakpoint exception occurs when the address (bits 0-29) in the IABR matches the next instruction to complete in the completion unit, and the IABR enable bit (bit 30) is set (01300).

(continues)

Table 18.1 Continued	
Exception	**Description**
System management exception	A system management exception is caused when MSR[EE] is set and the SMI input signal is asserted (01400).

The 603 does not implement any exceptions defined as optional by the PowerPC Architecture.

The 603 Processor Bus Interface

The 603 bus interface is similar to that of the 601 processor, with most of the same signals and using a very similar bus protocol. The major differences lie in the fact that the address bus is not dual-ported to allow simultaneous bus snooping as is done on the 601 processor. This is one of the ways in which the 603 is simplified for a smaller and lower-power chip implementation. Additional signals are provided to support the 603's more elaborate power management scheme.

Like the 601 bus, the signal configuration is optimized for cache read and write operations. In the 603, the most common bus transactions are burst-read operations, followed by burst-write operations to memory. The next most common transfers are single-beat (noncacheable or write-through) memory read and write operations. The 603 also supports accesses to I/O controller interface operations, although memory-mapped I/O operations are more efficient. As with the 601, the 603 supports address-only operations.

Memory accesses can occur in single-beat (up to 8 bytes) and four-beat burst (32 bytes) data transfers when the data bus is configured as a 64-bit bus, and in single-beat (up to 4 bytes), two-beat (8 bytes), and eight-beat (32 bytes) data transfers when the bus is configured as a 32-bit bus. The address and data busses operate independently to support pipelining and split transactions during memory accesses. The 603 supports one level of pipelining—that is, a second address tenure can begin before the first data tenure must begin.

Typically, memory accesses are weakly ordered—sequences of operations, including load/store string and multiple instructions, do not necessarily complete in the order they begin—maximizing the efficiency of the bus without sacrificing coherency of the data. The 603 allows read operations to precede store operations (except when a dependency exists). Because the processor can dynamically optimize run-time ordering of load/store traffic, overall performance is improved.

System Interface

The system interface is specific for each PowerPC microprocessor implementation.

The 603's data bus is configured at power-up to either a 32- or 64-bit width.

When the 603 is configured with a 64-bit data bus, memory accesses can transfer from one to eight bytes in one bus clock cycle, or beat. Data transfers occur in either single-beat transactions or four-beat burst transactions, which are the most common bus transactions. Single-beat transactions are the result of load and store operations either when caching is disabled or memory is configured as cache-inhibited or write-through, or data is transferred to or from a portion of memory configured for a memory-mapped I/O device. Four-beat burst transactions, which transfer an entire cache line (assuming a 64-bit data bus), are initiated when a line is read from or written to memory.

When the 603 is configured with a 32-bit data bus, memory accesses allow transfer sizes of 8, 16, 24 or 32 bits in one bus clock cycle. Data transfers occur in either single beat transactions that transfer as much as one word, or two- or eight-beat burst transactions. Because the bus is 32-bits wide and floating-point operands are 64-bits wide, a two-beat burst is required to transfer a double-word operand. To transfer an entire eight-word cache block, an eight-beat burst transaction is required.

The system interface allows for address-only transactions as well as address and data transactions. The 603 control and information signals include the address arbitration, address start, address transfer, transfer attribute, address termination, data arbitration, data transfer, data termination, and processor state signals (see fig. 18.2). Test and control signals provide diagnostics for selected internal circuits.

The system interface supports bus pipelining, the extent of which depends on external arbitration and control circuitry. Similarly, the 603 supports split-bus transactions for systems with multiple potential bus masters.

Figure 18.2
603 System
Interface Showing
Basic Signal
Groupings.

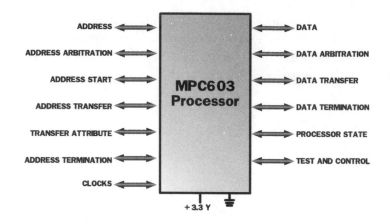

The 603 supports multiple masters through a bus arbitration scheme that allows various devices to compete for the shared bus resource. The arbitration logic can implement priority protocols, such as fairness, and can park masters to avoid arbitration overhead. The EMI protocol ensures coherency among multiple devices and system memory. The on-chip caches, TLBs, and optional second-level (L2) caches can be controlled externally.

The 603's clocking structure allows the bus to operate at integer multiples of the processor cycle time.

The following sections describe the 603 bus support for memory and I/O controller interface operations. Note that some signals perform different functions depending upon the addressing protocol used.

603 Signals

The 603 signals are grouped as follows:

- *Address arbitration signals.* These signals are used when the processor needs to be granted access to the address bus.

- *Address transfer start signals.* After address bus mastership has been granted, these signals indicate that the address bus transaction has begun.

- *Address transfer signals.* These signals, which consist of the address bus, address parity, and address parity error signals, transfer the address over the address bus and ensure the integrity (parity) of the transfer.

■ *Transfer attribute signals.* These signals indicate the type of data transaction (whether it is a four-beat burst transaction and how much data is to be transferred if it is a single-beat transfer). The transfer is also characterized by whether it is write-through, coherency enforced, or cache-inhibited. The global signal indicates whether the access is to a portion of memory that should permit snooping.

■ *Address transfer termination signals.* These signals acknowledge (address acknowledge, AACK-) the end of the address phase of the transaction. If the address tenure needs to be repeated (such as when the address is snooped and hit by another caching device), a new address tenure must be initiated to allow the modified data to be written back to memory, so it can be read from memory by the requesting device.

■ *Data arbitration signals.* Similar to the address arbitration signals, these signals arbitrate for the data bus.

■ *Data transfer signals.* These signals, which consist of the data bus, data parity, and data parity error signals, transfer the data and ensure the integrity (parity) of the transfer.

■ *Data transfer termination signals.* These signals acknowledge the end of a data beat or an entire data tenure and indicate when a data tenure should be repeated.

■ *System status and control signals.* These signals are not directly involved in address and data transfers. The external interrupt, soft-, and hard-reset signals are used to signal asynchronous exception conditions. Other signals are used to indicate to other processors that a processor has entered the checkstop state.

■ *Clock signals.* These signals determine the system clock frequency. These signals can also be used to synchronize multiprocessor systems.

■ *Processor state signals.* These two signals are used to set the reservation coherency bit.

■ *Miscellaneous signals.* These signals provide information about the state of the reservation coherency bit.

■ *Test interface signals.* The common on-chip processor (COP) unit is the master clock control unit and it provides a serial interface to the system for performing built-in self test (BIST). These signals are used for internal testing.

■ *IEEE 1149.1(JTAG)/COP interface signals.* The IEEE 1149.1 test unit and the common on-chip processor (COP) unit are accessed through a shared set of input, output, and clocking signals. The IEEE 1149.1/COP interface provides a means for boundary scan testing and internal debugging of the 603.

■ *Test interface signals.* These signals are used for production testing.

■ *Clock signals.* These signals determine the bus clock frequency and to synchronize multiprocessor systems. The internal clocking of the 603 is generated from and synchronized to the external clock signal, SYSCLK, by means of a voltage-controlled, oscillator-based PLL. The PLL provides programmable internal processor clock rates of 1x, 2x, 3x, and 4x multiples of the externally supplied clock frequency. The bus clock is the same frequency and is synchronous with SYSCLK.

Figure 18.3 illustrates the 603 microprocessor's logical pin configuration, showing how the signals are grouped.

Figure 18.3
603 Signal Groups.

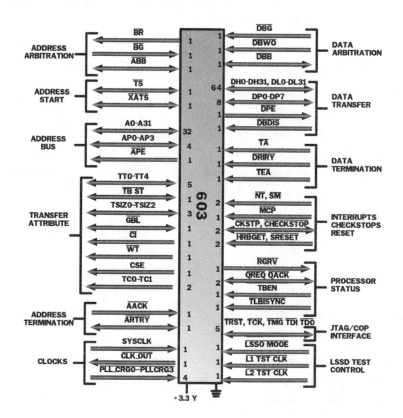

Summary

This chapter has looked closely at design details of the PowerPC 603 processor, the first PowerPC processor to bring the efficiency and power of RISC computing to battery-operated systems. The 603 represents a step into the future of personal computing, not just for giving birth to a new generation of super-portables, but for wedding the computer industry with high-tech communications, personal-entertainment systems, and new types of computing devices never seen before.

The next PowerPC processors, the 604 and the 620, will further stretch the frontiers of processor design, and the PowerPC Architecture provides a flexible platform to propel computing into the next century.

Index

Symbols

GO AHEAD. PLUG YOURSELF INTO
PRENTICE HALL COMPUTER PUBLISHING.
Introducing the PHCP Forum on CompuServe®

Yes, it's true. Now, you can have CompuServe access to the same professional, friendly folks who have made computers easier for years. On the PHCP Forum, you'll find additional information on the topics covered by every PHCP imprint—including Que, Sams Publishing, New Riders Publishing, Alpha Books, Brady Books, Hayden Books, and Adobe Press. In addition, you'll be able to receive technical support and disk updates for the software produced by Que Software and Paramount Interactive, a division of the Paramount Technology Group. It's a great way to supplement the best information in the business.

WHAT CAN YOU DO ON THE PHCP FORUM?

Play an important role in the publishing process—and make our books better while you make your work easier:

- Leave messages and ask questions about PHCP books and software—you're guaranteed a response within 24 hours
- Download helpful tips and software to help you get the most out of your computer
- Contact authors of your favorite PHCP books through electronic mail
- Present your own book ideas
- Keep up to date on all the latest books available from each of PHCP's exciting imprints

JOIN NOW AND GET A FREE COMPUSERVE STARTER KIT!

To receive your free CompuServe Introductory Membership, call toll-free, **1-800-848-8199** and ask for representative **#597**. The Starter Kit Includes:

- Personal ID number and password
- $15 credit on the system
- Subscription to CompuServe Magazine

HERE'S HOW TO PLUG INTO PHCP:

Once on the CompuServe System, type any of these phrases to access the PHCP Forum:

GO PHCP   **GO BRADY**
GO QUEBOOKS   **GO HAYDEN**
GO SAMS   **GO QUESOFT**
GO NEWRIDERS   **GO PARAMOUNTINTER**
GO ALPHA

Once you're on the CompuServe Information Service, be sure to take advantage of all of CompuServe's resources. CompuServe is home to more than 1,700 products and services—plus it has over 1.5 million members worldwide. You'll find valuable online reference materials, travel and investor services, electronic mail, weather updates, leisure-time games and hassle-free shopping (no jam-packed parking lots or crowded stores).

Seek out the hundreds of other forums that populate CompuServe. Covering diverse topics such as pet care, rock music, cooking, and political issues, you're sure to find others with the sames concerns as you—and expand your knowledge at the same time.

Complete Computer Coverage